Telephone: MOUntview 3343.

HIGHGATE LITERARY & SCIENTIFIC INSTITUTION

920
SHE

11, SOUTH GROVE, N.6.

10194

Time allowed FOURTEEN Days

Date Issued	Date Issued	Date Issued
JUN 1959		
9 JUL 1959		

2000-5-58

FLIGHT OF THE SKYLARK

THE DEVELOPMENT OF
SHELLEY'S REPUTATION

FLIGHT OF THE SKYLARK

THE DEVELOPMENT OF
SHELLEY'S REPUTATION

by

SYLVA NORMAN

FIRST PUBLISHED IN 1954 BY
THE UNIVERSITY OF OKLAHOMA PRESS
IN THE UNITED STATES
AND BY
MAX REINHARDT LTD, LONDON
IN GREAT BRITAIN

*The publication of this volume
has been aided by a grant from the
Carl and Lily Pforzheimer Foundation, Inc.*

MADE AND PRINTED BY OFFSET IN GREAT BRITAIN
BY WILLIAM CLOWES AND SONS LTD
LONDON AND BECCLES

FOR

Edmund and his Claire

in

lasting friendship

Preface

I~N OFFERING ANOTHER BOOK~ on a much belauded and belabored poet, I believe I may claim that its angle is a new one; and this although it is built on no controversial or speculative basis, but relies on historical fact. In brief, it is a chronicle, and might have been termed a biography but that it begins at its subject's death instead of his birth, and goes straight on for some eighty years to the end of the nineteenth century. Yet, if it had been anything less than a life story, it would not have been presented: the attempt to write it must have failed. The experiment of depicting a Romantic poet's "after-life" on earth has not, so far as I am aware, been tried before; and apart from Shelley there is only Byron whose character and circumstance lend themselves to it. For this is not an academic study of the growth of a literary reputation; that has been frequently done in part and parcel, and even, by the late Newman Ivey White, reduced to a tabulated analysis of references to the poet in print. The use of figures has its merits—safe within limits, dry and unemotional—in assessing reputations. But it makes small contact with the personal story; and this, in Shelley's case, is necessary for an all-round view. Others, choosing the personal side, have written the life stories of those who were for a few years Shelley's associates. Some, again, have tried to hack their way through the dead wood of forged and spurious correspondence, to be caught up unavoidably in the niceties and technicalities of their task. Or they have set out to prove the truth or falsehood of a rumored baby, an attack in a farmhouse or a post office, a phantom visitant or a deserted wife. Some have studied Shelley as a metaphysician, as an unbeliever, as a revolutionary, or as a Platonist.

I have attempted here a synthesis of the situation as it has presented itself and altered since the poet's death. I have traced out the activities of friends and relatives, especially where these were conditioned by

Shelley; I have watched his own status moving from disrepute to popularity, looked at the myths that have sprung up like weeds or wild flowers, noticed his widow struggling with a complex temperament and his son grow up as a genial country squire. I have shown his fanatical daughter-in-law attempting, with a team of picked biographers, to impose her idealized vision on the cultured world; noted the reactions and the rivalries among those who studied Shelley; observed the rogueries that have warped his progress, the embittered attacks of bigoted moralists, and the mystical worship accorded to his small material relics. My aim has been serious but not solemn; inevitably there is a cool shaft of amusement directed alike at those who worship and at those who growl. But the history is as true and unbiased as research could make it, and—unless my pattern has quite failed to impress itself—the outcome is a Shelley who, however differently judged by rivals and successors, continues to live with an increasing amplitude.

In such a general and progressive survey no attempt at exhaustive reference to books and journals has been made in either text or notes. This applies also to the lives of Shelley's survivors, shown only when they abut on our main purpose; though Mary, in her unique position of widow, mother, editor, and society lover, has been more closely followed. Salient features and prevailing tendencies have been picked on; in the later years especially it has been impossible, and luckily inadvisable, to try to gather in all that has been written, spoken, or performed in Shelley's name. After the turn of the century, where the record properly ends, an excursion in the final chapter skims the last fifty years in a freer, more speculative way, indicating rather than recording. Here I have allowed myself an opinion or two, resigning, to some degree, the office of detached historian.

The book was planned and worked on many years ago, but, from one and another reason due to war's unsettlement, it was laid aside, again for many years. During that time other Shelleyan students had written on some of the subjects belonging to its general scheme. Chief among these are the Major Byron forgeries, examined, with biographical details of the perpetrator, by Theodore G. Ehrsam; and the social activities of the Shelley heirs at Boscombe, told in their essentials by Miss R. Glynn Grylls. I have in consequence curtailed my account of such features, thus lightening the book considerably, perhaps to its advantage. Again, if some apparent modern references are unacknowledged, the reason is that my material had already been gathered from older sources before these works appeared. For example, letters and documents drawn direct from *Shelley and Mary* have since been published by Frederick L. Jones, R. Glynn Grylls, and others.

Grateful acknowledgments are owing to many for their help. It is accurate to say that without Mr. Edmund Blunden, C.B.E., M.C., the ever dependable all-round authority on Shelley, the project would never have been followed up at all. His genius in deducing references and authorities, in digging out passages from forgotten memoirs, letters, or periodicals, and giving me the clue to dig for more, has been an ever lively encouragement; besides which I am truly appreciative of his vivid perception of the unity that underlay this motley patchwork, of the sense behind the words, and the balance between prejudice and prejudice. It is equally accurate to say that without the active and generous patronage of Mr. Carl H. Pforzheimer the book would have had no chance of publication in these meager and cautious postwar years. I owe to him and to Mrs. Pforzheimer a big debt of gratitude for trusting it on the strength of a brief specimen, and so giving me that confidence and encouragement that the writers of the first Elizabethan Age enjoyed.

My thanks are due also to Miss Rosalie Glynn Grylls (Lady Mander) for giving me several piquant products of her own energetic researches and much friendly help besides; to Mr. Frederick L. Jones for some notes on the letters of Mary Shelley before his edition of these was published; to Mr. Neville Rogers, who sent me extracts from the Bodleian microfilms of letters in Lord Abinger's collection; to Sir John Murray, K.C.V.O., D.S.O., for kindly allowing me to reproduce the portrait of Washington Irving by Gilbert Stuart Newton; to Mr. John Woodward of the Ashmolean Museum, Oxford, for helpful advice with the illustrations; to the Master of University College, Oxford, for permission to use correspondence relating to the Shelley Memorial; to Hilaire Belloc (then living) and his son-in-law, Mr. Reginald Jebb, for answering my questions on the attitude of Mr. Belloc and of his mother (Bessie Rayner Parkes) to Shelley; to Sir Shane Leslie for information connected with Mrs. Leigh Hunt's bust of Shelley; to the editor of the *Times Literary Supplement,* who has allowed me to reprint passages from an article on this bust; to Mr. C.

Day Lewis and Harper and Brothers, New York, for permission to quote from *An Italian Visit*.

For some helpful remarks on Shelley's present-day status in countries outside England I am indebted to Signora Vera Cacciatore, curator of the Keats-Shelley Museum in Rome; to Herr Fritz Schneider, English professor at Holzminden, Germany; to Professor Louis Bonnerot of Caen University; to Mr. Shōgorō Ogita for the use of his manuscript thesis on "Shelley in Japan"; and to Mrs. R. P. Boas, of Massachusetts, for untiring and stimulating help and suggestions, arising largely from her own Shelleyan researches on both sides of the Atlantic. Thanks are due also to Miss Aki Hayashi, who transcribed several items for me at the British Museum; to Miss Hilary Hughes, who pursued researches in Bournemouth and Boscombe; and to my mother for much general help and encouragement. Not least, I am indebted to Miss Mary Eugenia Stith, associate editor of the University of Oklahoma Press, for her care and industry in compiling the index.

Owing to the many years I have been at this work, several to whom I should have liked to make acknowledgments are no longer with us. Newman Ivey White sent me several notes and transcripts while working on his biography; Lady Butterworth elicited for me some first-hand comments on the Boscombe Manor society; Fred Edgcumbe, late curator of Keats House, Hampstead, supplied several items; Wilfrid Meynell gave me his personal recollections of Sir Percy and Lady Shelley; and George Bernard Shaw replied at generous length on one of his typical post cards to a query of mine about his part in the meetings of the Shelley Society.

SYLVA NORMAN

London
February 14, 1954

Contents

Illustrations

FLIGHT OF THE SKYLARK

THE DEVELOPMENT OF
SHELLEY'S REPUTATION

Epilogue as Prologue

"SHELLEY, the writer of some infidel poetry, has been drowned; *now* he knows whether there is a God or no." So ran a comment in the British press when Shelley died in Italy.

The tragic story has been told, retold, and told again. It has been told by the actors and the sufferers: by Mary Shelley, whose intimate "Notes" were the nearest approach to a memoir she was allowed or willing to make; by Trelawny, who deemed his own part in the funeral rites handsome enough to justify repeated and varying accounts throughout his long career. So-called disinterested biographers have told it—some with urgency and detail, some with apologies for its familiarity. There is hardly a storm in meteorological records so famous as this typical Mediterranean squall that blew up on the afternoon of July 8, 1822. No case of drowning returns so often to the mind. Nor is any picture of racked womanhood, unless it be in the Brontë parsonage, so moving as this of the two anxious wives comforting each other with hollow hopes at San Terenzo, posting in an agony to Pisa, to Leghorn, and back again, at last to be told that their monstrous fears were true.

Each time the catastrophe is repeated, it comes with a fitting sense of climax and completion. The boating accident seems magnified into the one inevitable end to a swift, tameless spirit. After it the rest—except for a movement or two of minor characters—is silence. For a man's death ends his career on earth, unless his influence and his reputation enjoy a posthumous one. In the career of a religious leader death is only a beginning. It is, in fact, a necessary prelude to the spreading of his doctrine, the persecution of his followers, and the deification of his memory. Aside from the Biblical prophet this still applies. A man of uncommon quality needs only to have preached and acted contentiously enough for echo and argument to carry his name forward until it becomes the subject of a myth. Shelley was of this caliber. In spite of the "full close" of the biographers, the silence of his drowning was not prolonged. The first act had closed impressively, but the performance went on, less concentrated, less dramatic, far less imperative and vivid—yet a play. From a romantic tragedy it turned into something like a *comédie de moeurs,* the characters betraying all kinds of human inconsistencies and petty foibles. They allowed the spirit of irony to creep in amongst them, so that their most tragical sighs now reach the audience accompanied partly by a titter. But between them also moves the ghost of their former leader; or, rather, it is tugged and pulled from one to another of them, stamped down with ineffective finality, raised proudly aloft by faithful followers, to be pelted with rude missiles by their opponents.

The present biography, then, contrary to the usual custom, begins with its hero's death instead of his birth. Instead of dealing with the thirty restless years of a poet's life, it covers a period of some eighty years or more beyond it. Even here the posthumous life of Shelley does not cease; but a view of the arguments, personalities, and busy penmanship that marked this period, while the satellites shone further from their luminary and the detractors growled on secondhand evidence, is enough to show the Shelley myth arising, and to show, too, what particular human agencies were at work creating it. Here it may be as well to define my meaning of this word "myth." Far from synonymous with "invention," it indicates a popular conception encircling a fair nucleus of truth. The nucleus becomes hidden by the wrappings, so that arguments may arise about the observed phenomena of the surface, having little or no reference to its core. The personality handed, as Shelley's has been, to the multitude for open debate is in this quandary; fame obscures him, and the most honest inquirer can never see him plain. I have not attempted to do so, but have set out rather to be a plain historian of the growth of the outer layers.

In speaking thus of myth, I am not suggesting that Shelley was a religious leader. There is, though, nothing new to be suggested about Shelley: on this particular point H. Buxton Forman ventured that if the poet *was* not, yet he might have been, the Savior of the World. That was among the bolder heresies of the eighties, and naturally evoked its corresponding snarl (in two thick volumes), while between them, but drooping a little towards the snarler's side, loomed Matthew Arnold's "ineffectual angel." Shelley was a "spirit," coming and going inexplicably, to his intimate friends while he still lived; but his own choice of a spirit was Ariel rather than Raphael or even Abdiel. Present judgment and controversy are not in any case the business of this chronicle, which will be amply occupied with the report of past ones. After examining so many of these, the only apt comment I can hazard is that Shelley has been all things to all men, not forgetting that he has appeared to the shocked sensibilities of one of Aldous Huxley's characters in the mixed shape of fairy and white slug.

Whatever the proportion of Shelley's divinity, it could not immediately shine through the death of his mortal part. Despair came in successive pulses, like the moment of totality in a solar eclipse. From Leghorn harbor, Trelawny had watched a boat move out; the abating storm showed not a trace of it. At the Casa Magni, Mary Shelley and Jane Williams had hoped obstinately that their husbands were still safe in Pisa with Leigh Hunt; a letter from Hunt to Shelley dispelled the hope. Trelawny recognized a punt, a water keg, and some bottles as having been in the missing *Don Juan*. Their corpses were washed up near Viareggio and some three miles distant—widely separated, mutilated beyond easy recognition, but identifiable. The approaching shadow at last covered the sky; and when the blaze of anguish from Trelawny's funeral pyre had guttered down, earth appeared dark and silent with the unmitigable finality of death.

That abrupt cessation stood out the more dramatically in contrast to the turmoil that preceded it. There was always activity where Shelley was, usually trouble and discomfort. He was too bent on reforming evils and playing the knight-errant to unhappy souls for his life to take the quiet course of a conformer's. Whenever there is action, criticism follows, for no absolute canons of good and evil can be laid down where personalities are involved. The man with the "highest" motives usually manages only to pay Paul by robbing Peter, and who is to determine whether Paul or Peter is the more deserving? So it comes about that almost every point in Shelley's career is capable of two interpretations. Both have been harped on down the years. They were harped on already in his lifetime; or, rather, Shelley's own clear note (outgrowing its early shrillness) was clashed into discord by the booming of Eldons, Westbrooks, Southeys, and Timothys, while even Mary's sweeter melody could go badly out of tune. Little wonder that the poet at last sang, from his happiest abode among Italian pine woods by the Mediterranean,

> *Less oft is peace in Shelley's mind*
> *Than calm in waters seen.*

The facts of his life are well enough known. If I recall some of them here in order, it is because they are the spikes on which the later controversialists were to scratch themselves; and they introduce some characters of our comedy.

⸪{ II }⸪

Percy Bysshe Shelley was born at Field Place, Horsham, Sussex, on August 4, 1792, into a family of Whig aristocrats. His grandfather, Sir Bysshe Shelley, had been marked by eccentricity, but passed on to his son Timothy, besides a solid fortune, no richer traits than an orthodox moral sense and a rigid mind. To do him justice, these traits need never have appeared other than admirable but for his misfortune in begetting so uncompromising a rebel as Percy Bysshe. Sir Timothy has been damned for an ogre because he was called on to make extraordinary concessions. Any normal son of such a father, sent, as his own son was, to go through the mills of Eton and Oxford, would have emerged as good a country gentleman as his ancestors and as law abiding as Percy's younger brother John. But Shelley was impossible from the outset. The pranks and irregularities of a small boy, as reported by his sisters, may have no importance; the behavior of a public schoolboy—above all an Eton boy—is a test that counts. How many children, who are later to acquire some independence of outlook, have a shrinking horror of being *different* in their school days! Even the wrong sort of underwear may cause anguish and produce furtiveness. To be alike is comfort; to be popular by adding an individual flourish to conformity is the grandest distinction. Such boys develop into statesmen, diplomats, cricketers, or bishops. Success is written on them.

Shelley was outside these standards of success and failure, as he remained outside them all his life. He was different, without glorifying or regretting his difference. Alone, lacking sympathy or support for his ideas, he had the audacity to rebel against the hated system by refusing to do as the others. By Eton standards he was a mug and a laughingstock. Even his little experiments with a burning-glass were lunacy to the majority. Besides playing with chemistry and electricity, he had begun to write verse and fiction; and he pursued both these activities at University College, Oxford, whither he followed—outwardly only—in his father's footsteps in 1810. At this point Thomas Jefferson Hogg, who will be much heard of later, enters the story as a fellow undergraduate. Hogg, the future lawyer and classicist, was to prove anything but a rebel or a poet; yet the two were drawn together, perhaps by their mutual inability to mix with other youths. They became partners in walks, in talks, in literature. But where Shelley strove earnestly, the rougher-minded Hogg preferred to clown, and saw to it that the *Posthumous Fragments of Margaret Nicholson* obtained a "sale" by their burlesque quality. (In this he harmed no masterpiece.) The notorious *Necessity of Atheism* followed. Hogg was supposed to have written the preface. In any case he performed the bravest action of his life when he insisted on sharing the glory and the blame. (It has been suggested that he only made a virtue of expediency, in that his share was known already.) The two were sent down in March, 1811, to the deep grief of their respectable parents, and took lodgings together in London. There was even a plan to unite Jefferson to Shelley's sister Elizabeth, but it was hard enough to smuggle him into Field Place at all.

Shelley, on his side, entered, that same summer, into the marriage with Harriet Westbrook which has been a leading controversial subject ever since. According to the moralist Southey, he seduced a schoolgirl. In his own view he rescued Harriet from intolerable tyranny, although the weightiest tyrant, her sister Eliza, remained as duenna to the grateful girl. What must be admitted is that Shelley renounced his eager theories against marriage in order to take Harriet to Edinburgh. If he had lost one heresy, he clung fast to another which he had not been called upon to test in action. The "philosophical" poem *Queen Mab,* attacking Christian practices and hailing Necessity as the only god, was finished and printed for private circulation when he was eighteen. Later he publicly deplored an attempt to republish it. This fact has frequently been urged and as often ignored. In this

7

immature and repudiated poem lies Shelley's main claim to the title of "Atheist," which will be heard echoing and reverberating through the years that follow. Despite his early death, he lived on long enough to outgrow these first mistaken championships; but they glow on, brightly colored, attracting the hasty eye. And from the time of his drowning onwards it will be found that the main causes of argument over Shelley are these two wild oats—his early atheism and the results of his early marriage.

At this time his ardor stretched to other matters. He was a keen vegetarian, a would-be reformer of the wrongs of Ireland, and an admirer and disciple of William Godwin, whose *Inquiry Concerning Political Justice* had already influenced him. He had been disappointed by that minor apostle, Miss Elizabeth Hitchener, schoolteacher, enthusiast, and, alas, Brown Demon, as hard to abolish as the ogreish Westbrook sister. He had been disappointed in Jefferson Hogg, who could not be trusted alone with the charms of Harriet. A more discreet admirer, and later a champion, of Harriet was Thomas Love Peacock, for whom Shelley developed a friendship in these years. They shared, along with Jefferson, a pure enough passion for the ancient Greeks. But the Godwin connection was to prove a fateful one. Correspondence led to a meeting (the Sage of Skinner Street was susceptible to young men's flattery) and to a meeting, too, with Mary, the daughter of Godwin and the feminist Mary Wollstonecraft, who had died after giving her birth.

❧ III ❧

The relationships in the Godwin household might have puzzled a casual caller. Fanny, a lovable but unhappy creature, was the daughter of Mary Wollstonecraft and the negligent American Gilbert Imlay, although she was usually called Godwin. The sage himself had, in the words of a popular song, "got married to the widow next door," the raucous Mrs. Clairmont, whose two children, Charles and Jane, came to swell the party. Mary, born in 1797, was to acquire a half-brother in William, the son of Godwin by his second wife. A delicate child, Mary was sent on long visits to her friends the Baxters in Scotland, so that, except for a glimpse when she was fifteen and still a "child," it was not until the summer of 1814 that she and Shelley met and immediately loved. A sharp point of controversy arises here: the marriage of Shelley and Harriet had proved a failure and for some months they had lived more apart than together. Was it the sudden witchery of Mary Godwin that led Shelley to run away with her from a wife who was merely uncongenial, or had Shelley received what he thought was conclusive evidence of Harriet's unfaithfulness to him?

Whatever the answer may be, Shelley and Mary eloped on June 28, 1814. It has been suggested that this was a second Seduction of the Innocents—that the daughter of such a pair of revolutionary philosophers as Mary Wollstonecraft and Godwin was brought up ignorant of the principles of both. The evidence shows only that Godwin dropped his principles to indulge in outrage, while his bustling wife pursued the fugitives. She was not after Mary, but her own daughter, Jane, who had forced her company on them. Jane, or Claire, Clairmont, as she preferred to call herself, was to prove a yet more persistent and mischief-making third than the Brown Demon and Eliza had been. From Switzerland, Shelley wrote the famous letter to Harriet inviting her to join them. It was the letter of an impractical idealist, as the world sees it, and was received by Harriet as another insult. Funds giving out, the trio came home again to a winter of poverty and unrest for Shelley and Mary. In 1816 the three were abroad again, sailing on the Lake of Geneva with Lord Byron. At this point the prying biographer asks again if they went there by Claire's instigation, knowing of the intrigue with Byron which had taken place. It was here that the proposed competition over tales of horror spurred Mary to conceive the story of *Frankenstein,* and begin to write it.

Back in England in the fall of the same year, they heard with dismay the news of Fanny Imlay's suicide, then of Harriet's drowning. Was Shelley responsible for the latter? How far was he responsible? Could he have averted it? The questions go ringing out again. On December 30 he married Mary and went to live and write at Great Marlow. The case of the custody of his and Harriet's two children— Ianthe and Charles—was Shelley's next ordeal, when Lord Eldon gave judgment against him, not, as some alleged, merely on the strength of his heretical writings, but on consideration of his "improper" life. He was driven, in 1818, by dissatisfaction and poor health, to Italy, whence he never returned. The party included the inevitable Claire, her daughter Allegra (to be handed over to her father Byron), and Mary's two children, Clara and William. The next years saw a constant moving between Florence and Pisa, Rome and Venice, Leghorn and Naples, while Shelley contrived to write, amongst much else, *Prometheus Unbound, The Cenci, Hellas,* and, on hearing of Keats's death in Rome, the *Adonais.*

One may look on this period through Mary's eyes as a series of martyrdoms. Her daughter, Clara, died at Venice in 1818. Before another year was out, she had buried William in the Protestant Cemetery at Rome, and, not foreseeing the greater tragedy, it seemed to her that all her joy had died. She was worried by a scandalous report that Claire had had a child by Shelley, which had died in Naples at the Foundling Hospital. She was hurt by Shelley's obsession for the Italian girl Emilia Viviani, whom captivity had ennobled in his eyes. When Allegra died, the burden of Claire's grief was on the Shelleys. Another incident made Mary happy and unhappy. It was the arrival in 1821 of Captain Edward Williams and his pretty "wife," Jane, introduced by Shelley's kinsman Thomas Medwin (later of doubtful fame in this narrative). Jane, prevented by a former disastrous union from marrying her Williams, should have been, and was, a friend of Mary's. But Shelley idealized her, too. Both families lived at Pisa, in the Tre Palazzi, then shared for a few months the gaunt-arched Casa Magni by the sea at Lerici in the Gulf of Spezia. When Mary was irritable, unwell, and despondent, Shelley turned a little to the musical Jane. *Epipsychidion* had enshrined Emilia; now he wrote delicate lyrics in the pine woods to his newer friend. The phrase "Mary does not understand me" slipped into a letter, and has been construed into exaggerated meaning. In England, Godwin's financial affairs were in a tangled state, in spite of Shelley's overgenerous help. His letters had latterly to be kept from Mary, and this piece of innocent dissembling helped to foster strain and coldness between her and Shelley.

Yet these Italian years had held glad consolations, sunny hours, and cheering friendships. Mary's son Percy Florence was born in 1819 in the town he is named after—the only one of her children to survive. Byron was frequently to be met, with or without his lovely Contessa Guiccioli; the Gisbornes, John and Maria, with the latter's son, Henry Reveley, were at first in Leghorn, and later joined Hogg, Leigh Hunt, and Peacock at faithful English correspondents. Lady Mountcashell, that active proselyte of Mary's mother, now lived as plain "Mrs. Mason" in Pisa, united in happy freedom to her Mr. Tighe. Horace Smith of the *Rejected Addresses,* though never managing to visit Italy, proved himself a practical and helpful friend. Not least, if perhaps last, of these acquaintances was the dashing Cornishman Edward Trelawny—"Pirate Trelawny," as he liked to call himself. Years later, discussing this whole circle, Trelawny doubted if any, except himself and Hogg, were really Shelley's friends. We are not bound to follow his opinion, and may feel half-inclined to invert the doubt; but in watching some of their later activities, we shall find other views, conflicting, emphatic, or tentative; and, as we are posterity, the decision is ours.

In their lovely but lonely abode at Lerici, which they reached in April, 1822, the Shelleys made few contacts except with their housemates, the Williamses. The men's happiest hours were to be spent on board that "perfect plaything for the summer," the new yacht. There were trips along the coast in azure weather, forenoons writing in the buoyant dinghy, and much work, as Williams noted in his journal, in improving and refitting the *Don Juan.* The women, chained more securely than their husbands to the daily round, endured housekeeping troubles and domestic differences. More ominous were the strange hallucinations that began to visit them. Shelley saw the figure of dead Allegra rising from the sea. Jane—neither visionary nor highly imaginative—saw a ghost of the living Shelley on the terrace. The poet was terrified one night by a dream of Jane and Edward, dead and lacerated. Mary, herself ill after a miscarriage, was disturbed and frightened by his shrieks. . . . For a peaceful summer it was singularly restless.

In June, Leigh Hunt and his family succeeded at last in reaching Genoa. Hunt was to run the *Liberal,* a new periodical, for Byron; Shelley was to contribute. In high spirits, early in July, Williams and Shelley put to sea in their brave yacht to meet the new arrivals in Leghorn, the poet leaving a great unfinished composition in his workshop:

> *Then, what is life? I cried—*

it broke off. No answer but Shelley's death was to be given.

11

⊰{ IV }⊱

Through the darkness objects began to be detectable. Almost at once the poet's *heart* took on a separate life. Trelawny, seeing it unburnt, had plucked it out from the funeral pyre; Leigh Hunt and Mary, reduced to greedy relic-gatherers, quarreled over its possession. The friend would not part with it, the widow grew passionate; until sad Jane Williams, undisputed owner of her husband's ashes, calmed that teacup storm and secured the heart for Mary. Shrunken, half-burned, and falling into dust, the curious emblem was to take its independent course on earth, unburied for nearly seventy years. It was to attract interest and set up arguments about its location—arguments that crop out in the papers to this day, although there is no real doubt concerning its end. Its treatment has been slightly absurd, a trifle vulgar, wholly sentimental—which is not to be wondered at, since, after leaving Shelley's body, it was handled by no one free from fanaticism, exaltation, misery, or some such abnormality of feeling towards Shelley. Besides the heart, "the only portions that were not consumed," Trelawny tells us, "were some fragments of bones, the jaw, and the skull." We are to hear of these again in fifty years or so; for the present he stows them secretly away.

The poet's immediate remains included, then, the heart, his widow, those friends in Italy and England, that father who was not disposed to friendship, and three children—Harriet's Ianthe and Charles and Mary's Percy Florence. To these must be added his published and unpublished works, his notoriety as a rebel, and his incipient reputation as a poet.

With the dimmed stage so generously peopled we need only refocus our gaze and readjust our mood from their former intensity to be ready to follow the succeeding acts.

PART ONE

The Mourners

1822–1851

"The decision of the cause, whether or no I am a poet, is removed from the present time to the hour when our posterity shall assemble; but the court is a very severe one, and I fear that the verdict will be, 'Guilty—death!' "
—*P. B. Shelley to John and Maria Gisborne, July 19, 1821.*

CHAPTER I

The Infidel Is Drowned

NEARLY A MONTH had gone by since Shelley's drowning before the catastrophe was known generally in England. Thanks to Leigh Hunt, the first public announcement was as accurate, appreciative, and regretful a tribute as could well be worded in a newspaper column. His *Examiner* of August 4 contained the following notice:

> Those who know a great mind when they meet with it, and who have been delighted with the noble things in the works of MR. SHELLEY, will be shocked to hear that he has been cut off in the prime of his life, and genius. He perished at sea, in a storm, with his friend Captain WILLIAMS, of the Fusiliers, on the evening of the 8th ult., somewhere off Via Reggia, on the coast of Italy, between Leghorn and the gulf of Spezia. He had been to Pisa, to do a kind action, he was returning to his country abode at Lerici to do another.—Such was the whole course of his life. Let those who have known such hearts, and have lost them, judge of the grief of his friends. Both he and Captain WILLIAMS have left wives and children. Capt. W. was also in the prime of life, and a most amiable man, beloved like his friend. The greatest thing we can say in honour of his memory, (and we are sure he would think so), is, that he was worthy to live with his friend, and to die with him.

But it was not every journalist who knew a great mind on meeting with it. They knew, even without this reminder, that Shelley was of the Leigh Hunt Cockney School and something of a lawbreaker. With alacrity they grabbed the *Examiner's* theme and jigged out new accompaniments. On the following evening the *Courier*[1] wound up its editorial column with a paragraph beginning:

[1] The "witty sentence" that stands at the beginning of the Prologue was the *Courier's* first announcement.

Shelley, the writer of some infidel poetry, for the republication of which a man of the name of Clarke either has been, or is about to be, prosecuted, is dead. . . .

It was true that the Strand bookseller, W. Clark, for issuing (and selling not unsuccessfully) a pirated edition of *Queen Mab,* had been prosecuted in 1821 by a Society for the Suppression of Vice, described by the publisher as "self-constituted".[2] The unfortunate coincidence of Shelley's death inevitably fixed the poet's status in the minds of scandal lovers who had never read a line of his works. Clark was convicted, the bench being duly shocked by such immorality. How opportunely then came God's severer judgment that the vicious author should perpetrate no more of it! On the eleventh of the month—a Sabbath Day—*John Bull,* ever alert to expose wickedness, called out to virtue in no measured terms:

> Mr. Byshe Shelley, the author of that abominable and blasphemous book called *Queen Mab,* was lately drowned in a storm somewhere in the Mediterranean. His object in visiting that part of the world, it was stated, was to coalesce with some others of his own opinions to *write down* Christianity. The visitation is, therefore, striking; and the termination of his life (considering the creed) not more awful than *surprising.*

This paper had its own Whig antagonist, *The Real John Bull,* warranted to write down, on the following Sunday, any hyperbolical views its rival uttered. *The Real John Bull* of August 18 was shocked by the "religious bigotry and party spirit" that could lead the "infamous *John Bull*" to utter "a demoniac yell of joy at the Poet's drowning."

The *Morning Chronicle* of July 25 having published a long letter from Leigh Hunt to Horace Smith about the "dreadful calamity," there followed a ding-dong journalistic battle with Shelley used largely as a weather vane to register the prevailing political winds. *John Bull* railed at the *Chronicle* at huge length, the *Chronicle* cen-

[2] At the end of the volume, Clark advertised as preparing for the press "an Answer to the Principles contained in Mr. Shelley's *Queen Mab* . . . written by a Gentleman of first rate literary talents who has challenged the Publisher of *Queen Mab* to publish a refutation of it." This work might have expected an extra welcome in 1822, but there are no signs of its appearing.

sured the *Courier,* the *British Luminary* parodied *John Bull,* the *Republican* reprinted the *Luminary,* and finally the Leigh Hunt letter reappeared in the Paris *Monthly Review* for August, attached to a long article written probably by Horace Smith. In September the *Gentleman's Magazine* added to its formal obituary, "Mr. Shelley is unfortunately too well known for his infamous novels and poems. He openly professed himself an atheist." And a laudable attempt to enumerate his works begins with the title *Prometheus Chained.*[3]

Already, then, Shelley is a rallying point for rival pressmen. On August 10 the *Country Literary Chronicle* had made some slight effort to be fair, describing him as "a man of extraordinary but perverted talents, and the author of the *Cenci, Queen Mab,* and some less censurable productions." What so much rankles, as we read the comments, is the complacency of these journalists, all of whom, on the strength of their chance to write for sponsored periodicals, set themselves up as ethical and theological judges. Of publishers, the only one to take immediate advantage of Shelley's death was Stockdale, who reissued his 1811 production of the boyish novel *St. Irvine, or the Rosicrucian,* with a new date on the title page. The public was not interested.

❦{ 11 }❦

To turn from the press to more personal susceptibilities, it chanced that by a curious oversight neither of the two anxious fathers—Shelley's and Mary's—had been directly informed. The news must have reached them almost simultaneously, and on August 6 each of these affected gentlemen sat down to write a letter—Sir Timothy Shelley from Field Place to his solicitor Whitton, and William Godwin from his new premises in the Strand (he had just been ejected from Skinner Street) to Mary. Sir Timothy's loss being, on the face of it, the more intimate, his letter deserves first place:

> My dear Sir,—The Sting of Death has its effects. God's will be done! Tho' we have it from the Public Papers only at present, such catastrophes are apt to be too true.

[3] For the full text of these notices and other obituaries, see Newman Ivey White, *The Unextinguished Hearth* (Durham, N. C., 1938).

In regard to the enquiries you mention, I leave to you. John at present requires a steady young man as his Tutor, where, if He could be found to form a Friendship with Instruction, and masters for employment.

I was most perfectly satisfied with Mr. Warnford, but the Clergyman of the Parish form'd a Friendship for John and I fear has not been that Friend that could be wished, His prospects being held up to him that do not accord with my wishes. Could I beg of you to write to me that John might see the letter that this unforeseen event has chang'd the face of circumstances in my family, that he must think of something in order to better his condition in life.

It is wonderful what artful men there are in the world, and those whom you may consider Friends confidentially are grounding the mischief of youth.

May I once more request to hear from you upon the above subject, it wd. be of Service at this period of Time. Lady Shelley and my Family offer their best Compts.

> Believe me, my dear Sir,
> Yrs most faithfully
> T. Shelley.

I open'd the letter that I omitted to mention I had formed the intention of sending John to a Gentleman at Sutton Coldfield, Mr. Birmingham, and was abt. to take him. He takes 4 only, but we see Private Tutors cannot keep youth in order where there are others. I must find some person if possible, whatever I do about this Gentleman. He is highly spoken of by a friend of mine.[4]

Without doubt Sir Timothy felt his position keenly—although his erratic syntax is habitual and not due to sudden emotion. Since the rebel, already lost to law and society, had gone under, it was the more imperative to provide wisely for the education of his uninfected son. "Never read a book, Johnnie," he is said to have counseled, "and you will become a rich man." It is even asserted that John never did read one, nor his son, nor his grandchildren. Sir Timothy might learn his lesson, but he was not one to bewail past errors. Still, he modified his tone to Whitton in a day or two.

Dear Sir [he wrote]—I have given up my intention of going to London at present, not having any mourning, and the etiquette

[4] Roger Ingpen, *Shelley in England: New Facts and Letters from the Shelley-Whitton Papers* (London, 1917).

18

Imaginary Picture of Shelley's Cremation

From W. Howitt's *Homes and Haunts of the British Poets* (1846)

The spot where Shelley's body was found on the beach near Viareggio,
Italy, July, 1822. Engraved from a photograph of the painting
by Dwight Benton.

From *The Graphic,* May 5, 1883

here not to appear in Public, except in case of necessity until we have been to Church: and under the peculiar circumstances the general acceptation of the world may be set at rest in regard to the Family....

To lose an eldest son in his life time and the unfortunate manner of his losing that life, is truely melancholy to think of, but as it has pleas'd the Great Author of our Being so to dispose of him I must make up my mind with resignation....

That should have been the dignified end of the matter. But the old squire's troubles had just begun. To his infinite distaste, he read a request for payment of one hundred pounds owing by Mr. Shelley to a woman referred to as "the late Miss Hitchener." Her executor, with some cunning, reported having obtained no answer from Mr. Shelley himself at Pisa, and affected to know nothing of his death. For Sir Timothy the incident was a prelude to the dogged siege his unwelcome daughter-in-law was to maintain on his possessions. Henceforward this unfortunate country squire's long life was to be darkened by unending financial conferences, negotiations, payments, and annuities that could hardly cure his gout or sweeten his existence. There were reverberations even from an earlier episode. John Slatter, plumber and glazier of High Street, Oxford, had, or thought he had, an outstanding account against young Shelley, who had borrowed money in his undergraduate days. "Tolerably impudent" was Sir Timothy's comment on Slatter's letter of January 1823. He himself had lodged with the Slatter family at Oxford; he had asked John's son, Henry Slatter, to indulge Percy in his printing freaks, but, as he now insisted, had desired the family to warn his son against irregularities—especially debt "for which there was no occasion as he had an ample allowance." Whitton, in conveying this negative answer, added a hearty rider: "The officious interference of you and of others did a most serious injury to the Gent that is now no more—it led him into expenses and a Society and conduct the very reverse of what Sir Tim wished."[5]

---

[5] Among the creditors who sent in accounts to Sir Timothy were Shelley's coachmaker in Edinburgh and a Welsh surgeon, William Roberts, who had lent him six pounds to save him from imprisonment for debt. These and other demands, ignored by Sir Timothy, had swollen inordinately by the time the baronet died in 1844, when Peacock received the bulk of the applications. See Ingpen, *Shelley in England*.

Godwin's troubles were precisely opposite. How to *get* money was his perpetual problem. The philosopher late of Skinner Street was arrogant, temperamental, touchy when a personal slight could be imagined. Three months before Shelley's death he had bitten the very dust in his hurt pride, declining, from his position of sordid bankruptcy, to write any more to Mary on her prosperous heights. At the same time his hopes were firmly centered on her husband's promise of assistance. Suddenly that husband and his financial help were gone. Godwin had not even been considered worth informing. But his daughter's downfall (as he saw it) appealed at once to his dramatic sense, and there is some egoism in his affectionate proposal for mutual consolation:

No 195, Strand, August 6, 1822.

Dear Mary,

I heard only two days ago the most afflicting intelligence to you, and, in some measure, to all of us, that can well be imagined— the death of Shelley, on the 8th ultimo. I have had no direct information; the news only comes in a letter from Leigh Hunt to Miss Kent, and, therefore, were it not for the consideration of the writer, I should be authorized to disbelieve it. That you should be so overcome as not to be able to write is, perhaps, but too natural, but that Jane[6] could not write one line I could never have believed; and the behaviour of the lady at Pisa towards us on the occasion is peculiarly cruel.

Leigh Hunt says you bear up under the shock better than could have been imagined; but appearances are not to be relied on. It would have been a great relief to me to have had a few lines from yourself. In a case like this, one lets one's imagination loose among the possibilities of things, and one is apt to rest upon what is most distressing and intolerable. I learned the news on Sunday. I was in hope to have had my doubts and fears removed by a letter from yourself on Monday. I again entertained the same hope to-day, and am again disappointed. I shall hang in hope and fear on every post, knowing that you cannot neglect me for ever.

All that I expressed to you about silence and not writing to you again is now put an end to in the most melancholy way. I looked on you as one of the daughters of prosperity, elevated in rank and fortune, and I thought it was criminal to intrude on you for ever the

[6] "Jane" is Claire Clairmont; Godwin had yet to meet Jane Williams.

sorrows of an unfortunate old man and a beggar. You are now fallen to my own level; you are surrounded with adversity and with difficulty; and I no longer hold it sacrilege to trouble you with my adversities. We shall now truly sympathise with each other; and whatever misfortune or ruin falls upon me, I shall not now scruple to lay it fully before you.

This sorrowful event is, perhaps, calculated to draw us nearer to each other. I am the father of a family, but without children; I and my wife are falling fast into infirmity and helplessness; and, in addition to all our other calamities, we seem destined to be left without connections and without aid. Perhaps now we and you shall mutually derive consolation from each other.

Poor Jane is, I am afraid, left still more helpless than you are. Common misfortune, I hope, will excite between you the most friendly feelings.

Shelley lived, I know, in constant anticipation of the uncertainty of his life, though not in this way, and was anxious, in that event, to make the most effectual provision for you. I am impatient to hear in what way that has been done; and perhaps you will make me your lawyer in England, if any steps are necessary. I am desirous to call on Longdill, but I should call with more effect if I had authority and instructions from you.

Mamma desires me to say how truly and deeply she sympathises in your affliction; and, I trust, you know enough of her to feel that this is the language of her heart. I suppose you will hardly stay in Italy. In that case we shall be near to, and support, each other.

> Ever and ever affectionately yours,
> William Godwin.

If Mary was to be a burden on Sir Timothy, she for her part was to bear that of her father, who had already been promised the royalty on her novel *Castruccio*,[7] assuming he could find a publisher for it. Despite his expectations, she was in no immediate hurry to return to England and share those extra sorrows. As for "Mamma's" language of the heart, it could hardly have been a mother-tongue to Mary. The former Mrs. Clairmont, with her coarse and vulgar attractions, her lavish incapability and obtuseness, was a figure to be avoided by the fastidious. Charles Lamb, who had borne gallantly enough with Godwin's foibles, almost gave up visiting the house in the Polygon when she took possession.

[7] Published as *Valperga*.

The mention of Lamb brings us to the most deplorable, perhaps the one truly deplorable, comment on Shelley's tragedy. After all, the journalistic gibes were dictated by policy and ignorance in men whose duty was to follow the fashion and supply entertainment. So fair-minded and warm a spirit as Lamb's seemed made for subtler appreciations, tenderer sympathies. But Lamb had his perverse facet, and it seemed always to be uppermost when Shelley was in question. The latter's own regret was "that the calumny of an enemy" had set Lamb against him. Prejudice had been strengthened, too, by a mere surface detail: "Shelly [*sic*] I saw once," Lamb wrote to his moral Quaker friend Bernard Barton; "His voice was the most obnoxious squeak I ever was tormented with." In the summer of 1822, Lamb had escaped from his office desk at the India House to visit the Continent. Returning full of vigor and remembered excitement, he dashed off a hurried and gay letter on September 22 to Barron Field. "My dear F.," he charged into it, "I scribble hastily at office. Frank wants my letter presently. I and sister are just returned from Paris!! We have eaten frogs. It has been such a treat! You know our monotonous general tenor. Frogs are the nicest little delicate things—rabbity-flavoured. Imagine a Lilliputian rabbit! They fricassee them; but in my mind, drest seethed, plain, with parsley and butter, would have been the decision of Apicius. Shelley the great Atheist has gone down by water to eternal fire! Hunt and his young fry are left stranded at Pisa, to be adopted by the remaining duumvir, Lord Byron—his wife and 6 children and their maid. What a cargo of Jonases, if they had foundered too! The only use I can find of friends, is that they do to borrow money of you. Henceforth I will consort with none but rich rogues."

He goes on, darting to one subject after another—to Paris, to London, to portraits of Shakespeare—and winding up his breathless dance at last with: "The letter is wanted, and I am wanted. Imagine the blank filled up with all kind things." Those kind things are not for Shelley, we suspect. The Atheist has played his part in the bright pattern of composition. For once there is not a scrap of humanity in this most humane of writers. Frogs, Shelley, the half-dozen Hunt children—all serve their purpose as excellent topics for his sprightly scribbling. He had, indeed, already written to Shelley's publisher Ollier at the end of August:

The Infidel Is Drowned

I have been in France
I have eaten frogs.
* Poor Percy Bishe!!*

The two subjects seemed inseparably linked for him.

In October the poet's name and notoriety had again been tossed about the literary press. The revival was occasioned by a young admirer, John Chalk Claris of Canterbury, who owned and edited the *Kent Herald,* and wrote under the name of Arthur Brooke. He had never met Shelley, but the tragic news had moved him, within a few days of his learning it, to compose an *Elegy on the Death of Percy Bysshe Shelley.* The work appeared as a pamphlet of seventeen pages dedicated to Leigh Hunt. It was no *Adonais,* but a painstaking laudatory effort to commemorate "the talents and virtues of that highly-gifted individual." Here is the final stanza:

> *For me,—alike unknowing and unknown,—*
> *To deck the cenotaph of honouring thought*
> *Where richer flowers shall soon be fitly strewn,*
> *These fresh-culled buds,—such as I could,—I*
> *   brought.*
> *Glory protect his tomb! and if my own*
> *Be left neglected or be sometimes sought,*
> *May those who scorn be such as would not sigh*
> *For him, and those who seek love half so well as I.*

If Brooke had dared to hope that his tomb would be sought by virtue of these verses, he was not to be gratified. The *Monthly Magazine* was quick to fall in with the author's suggestion that Shelley's more talented friends might raise a fitter monument. We may honor Arthur Brooke now as one of the first of an unending stream of versifiers to be inspired by Shelley after his death.[8] At the

---

[8] That is to say, the first to publish his verse. A worthier tribute, belonging to this year, is contained in the lines written at Oxford, by T. L. Beddoes on a blank leaf of his *Prometheus Unbound:*

> *Write it in gold—a Spirit of the sun,*
> *An Intellect ablaze with heavenly thoughts,*
> *A Soul with all the dews of pathos shining,*

time he succeeded only in raising a new storm of volleying, some of it directed against his verses, but the main barrage roaring away at the Atheist himself. The *Literary Chronicle* acknowledged that Mr. Shelley had "sacrificed a fine genius at the shrine of infidelity," being "consequently dangerous in the proportion that his talents were splendid." Its comments were mild, compared with the galloping insults in the *Gentleman's Magazine,* more often quoted than the writer, with his mouthfuls of opprobrious terms, deserves. Regretfully, we must give it again, since it touches a low level of spleen and ignorance:

> Concerning the talents of Mr. Shelley, we know no more than that he published certain convulsive caperings of Pegasus labouring under cholic pains; namely, some purely fantastic verses, in the hubble bubble, toil and trouble style; and as to Mr. Shelley's virtues, if he belonged (as we understand he did,) to a junta, whose writings tend to make our sons profligates, and our daughters strumpets, we ought as justly to regret the decease of the Devil (if that were possible), as of one of his coadjutors. Seriously speaking, however, we feel no pleasure in the untimely death of this Tyro of the Juan school, that pre-eminent academy of Infidels, Blasphemers, Seducers, and Wantons. We had much rather have heard, that he and the rest of the fraternity had been consigned to a Monastery of La Trappe, for correction of their dangerous principles, and expurgation of their corrupt minds. Percy Bysshe Shelley is a fitter subject for a penitentiary dying speech, than a lauding elegy; for the muse of the rope, rather than that of the cypress; the muse that advises us "warning to take by others' harm, and we shall do full well."

> *Odorous with love, and sweet to silent woe*
> *With the dark glories of concentrate song,*
> *Was sphered in mortal earth. Angelic sounds*
> *Alive with panting thoughts sunned the dim world.*
> *The bright creations of an human heart*
> *Wrought magic in the bosoms of mankind.*
> *A flooding summer burst on Poetry;*
> *Of which the crowning sun, the night of beauty,*
> *The dancing showers, the birds whose anthems wild*
> *Note after note unbind the enchanted leaves*
> *Of breaking buds, eve, and the flow of dawn,*
> *Were centered and condensed in his one name*
> *As in a providence—and that was SHELLEY.*

See *The Works of T. L. Beddoes,* ed. by H. W. Donner (Oxford and London, 1935). It is interesting to compare Beddoes' "Spirit of the sun" with the later, and evidently independent, "Sun-treader" of Browning.

Brooke, or Claris, was altogether an unfortunate agent: he had released yet another valve by sending an early copy of his *Elegy* to the Quaker poet and moralist Bernard Barton. Barton, who had long been shaking a sad head over the heretical Shelley, was goaded by Brooke's hyperbole into counteraction. When he read of Shelley as "a most distinguished philosopher and philanthropist," whose voice was "a living stream of love and wisdom" and his person "the last defence of the bewildered world," then Barton sat down to pen his corrective *Verses on the Death of Percy Bysshe Shelley* and lead deluded followers back to righteousness. The verses are indeed self-righteous, priggish, and intolerable with their Christian exhortation, or, as Barton expresses it, "one brief alarm":

> *You DOUBT the Gospel:—keep in view,*
> *What CAN BE DOUBTED—MAY BE TRUE!*

The *Verses* would have small claim on our attention but that Charles Lamb has appeared again. His letter on frogs was a bare fortnight old when he received a copy of the tract and wrote to Barton:

> Dear Sir—I am asham'd not sooner to have acknowledged your letter and poem. I think the latter very temperate, very serious and very seasonable. I do not think it will convert the club at Pisa, neither do I think it will satisfy the bigots on our side the water. Something like a parody on the song of Ariel would please them better.
> > *Full fathom five the Atheist lies,*
> > *Of his bones are hell-dice made—*
> I want time, or fancy, to fill up the rest. . . .[9]

Lamb's personal antipathy to Shelley must remain a mystery. It is not much easier to explain his friendship with Bernard Barton. He was probably concerned less with the pious poet's Quakerism than with his latent geniality; for a friend described the author of the *Verses on Shelley* as "more fat than bard beseems," comfortably relishing his good dinner, his pinch of snuff, and his bottle of old port.

---

[9] As we know, Trelawny was to fill it up, without the parody, as an epitaph. We can hardly claim that he caught the tip from Lamb.

CHAPTER II

Break-up

IN ITALY, the so-called "Pisan Circle" at once fell out of shape. There was an effort at friendship between Hunt and Byron, which could only be strained and unnatural on the latter's part. Shelley's death, the necessity of carrying through the projected *Liberal,* the boisterous presence of Hunt's (undrowned) family, and the obligation that seemed forced on everyone to help Mary, all combined to irritate Byron to a supreme degree. Trelawny, who preferred any form of cataclysm to a calm existence, went on plucking some satisfaction from the dire event. Nor was his satisfaction entirely selfish. The whole business of the cremation had been so abnormal that the pirate's dramatic sense and slightly aberrant outlook were almost essential to its completion. His funereal labors were not ended until the following spring. Meanwhile, the ashes, in a walnut case covered in black silk velvet, had gone in Byron's yacht, the *Bolivar,* to Leghorn and thence to Rome to be deposited, pending their interment in the Protestant Cemetery, with the acting British consul, John Freeborn, who was also a wine merchant.[1] Here in the cellar they dallied (a privilege wasted on Shelley, who was never a connoisseur of vintages), for there were hitches. The papal authorities had forbidden further burials in the Old Cemetery, and rumor says, too, that they were not partial to burying ashes.

Trelawny left them and arranged an expedition with Captain Daniel Roberts to drag for the foundered boat. She was brought to the surface; to this act we owe the recovery of Williams's *Journal* with its last entry, more ominous than he intended: "The gods are angry, or nature is too powerful." Two memorandum books of Shelley's were also salvaged. Some of the other relics were homelier: articles of clothing and a hamper of wine spoiled by the cork's being forced up.

[1] See H. Nelson Gay, in *Bulletin* of the Keats-Shelley Memorial, Rome, No. II (1913).

But relics were important now. The incredible Battle of the Heart was only the first episode in a series of proud and pathetic acquisitions. Fragments of skull and jawbone, locks or half-locks of poetic hair, were—as we shall notice later—presented in lockets, displayed in glass showcases, or sealed in small opaque blue jars.

Nothing of him that doth fade . . .

though this was not quite what Trelawny meant (for all that he was the arch preserver) when he had those lines carved on the tombstone.

For Mary, grief stricken, helpless, still weak from a recent miscarriage and already in a state of chronic depression before Shelley's death, there was no hope of spiritual consolation. Her thoughts floundered in a cruel abyss of despairing misery, partly because (in spite of harsher judgments) she loved Shelley, and partly because she had leaned on him in all matters and had no idea how to conduct herself mentally and practically without him. She was only twenty-five, and her intellect was more developed than her understanding. When she reached out to grasp comfort, she, too, grabbed at relics and fetishes. Naturally she must have a portrait of her lost one. The only portrait that might be available was the girlish head (all too responsive to the future "ineffectual angel" theory) painted by the amateurish Amelia Curran. Mary wrote to Rome for it at once. On July 26 she wrote again; on August 14 a third time. On October 6, Miss Curran at last wrote back, from Paris. The picture, coming under her critical eye, had barely avoided the fate of Shelley's body, it was "so ill done. I luckily saved it just as the fire was scorching it, and it is packed up with my other pictures at Rome." Poor Mary was as far as ever from getting it. And there was another, more curious petition to Miss Curran at the same time—a request that she herself felt was a little childish. She wanted "from one of those shops in the Piazza di Spagna two mosaic stones, about as large as a half-crown piece." On one a heartsease was to be depicted; on the other a view of the tomb of Cestius. "In a little poem of his," she wrote, "are these words: 'Pansies let my flowers be.' Pansies are heartsease; and in another he says, that pansies mean memory. So I would make myself a locket to wear in eternal memory, with the representation of his flower, and with his hair; such things must now do instead of words of love, and the dear habit of seeing him daily. Pity me, then, and indulge me."

Affairs more pressing and practical than these whimsies had to be attended to. Mary at once saw that Shelley's manuscripts must be assembled. She wrote to Peacock, who, as co-executor with Byron of the poet's will, replied promptly from the India House with a promise to have all papers collected for her. She was for long anxious about a desk containing Shelley's letters that had been left in England. When at last the desk arrived, its lock had been broken, and this fact has since been suspected as the origin of the inaccurate and forged letters that were to appear later. If so, we must credit one shady character with a fairly prompt appreciation of Shelley's future value, if not to literature, at least to the publishing trade and the autograph market. His actual value in terms of cash was negative, and Mary had now to consider her own maintenance. With magnanimous sympathy Godwin begged, "Come home," but only that she might comfort and support her fellow-sufferer. Her own inclination, strengthened by the advice of Byron who offered the help of his solicitors, was to stay in Italy. Sir Timothy Shelley had to be approached, and again her agent in England was T. L. Peacock.

It was almost a repetition of history for Peacock, who, with Sir Timothy's solicitor Whitton, had figured in similar negotiations six years ago, when Shelley's first wife was the petitioner. Harriet, dissatisfied with her annual allowance of two hundred pounds, had applied for an additional sum. It was pointed out then that Mr. Westbrook of the coffeehouse was supplying her with another two hundred—and indeed he had the means to do so.[2] Mary's case was harder. Not only was publishing a bankrupt trade for philosophical fathers; she herself had none of the self-righteous claims of the abandoned wife, figuring rather as seducer and shatterer of domestic harmony. It was an outrage on such a man as Sir Timothy to be asked now to support her. But for her child, who was after all his grandson, it is probable that the Baronet would have closed down at once. As it was, Mary's attempt to secure provision for herself and Percy Florence dragged on drearily for months, and hardly brightened

[2] An adroit American inquirer, Mrs. R. P. Boas, has questioned whether John Westbrook did in fact contribute this annual £200; it may have seemed enough that she was under his protecting roof. If so, this would greatly diminish Harriet's freedom and increase her unhappiness. But that, at the moment, is another story.

an existence that was gray and cold enough. In her misfortune, something of Godwin's egotism came out in Mary; she began complaining of her unsympathetic friends. "Is not Peacock very lukewarm and insensible in this affair?" she wrote on September 17 to Mrs. Gisborne. The dry, practical nature of his letters seemed harsh to Mary, who could hardly look beyond her sorrow to remember that her present helper had always stood by Harriet, believing her innocent and wronged.

Besides Peacock, the ever kind and helpful Mrs. Mason (*alias* Lady Mountcashell) was failing to satisfy Mary's hunger for sympathy. "Her coldness has stung me; yet she felt his loss keenly, and would be very glad to serve me; but it is not cold offers of sympathy one wants; one's wounded spirit demands a number of nameless slight but dear attentions that are a balm, and wanting these, one feels a bitterness which is a painful addition to one's sufferings." This complaint also went to Mrs. Gisborne; but by the end of the year her matured bitterness had driven her into the shelter of that journal which was at once an outlet for her feelings and a temptation to indulge the ecstacy of sorrowing utterance. "It is better to grieve than not to grieve," she had confided to it. "Grief at least tells me that I was not always what I am now." On the last day of the fatal year she wrote there, as though addressing Shelley: "Last year, having you, I sought for the affections of others, and loved them even when unjust and cold; but now my heart is truly iced. . . . I am a lonely unloved thing, serious and absorbed. None care to read my sorrow." The tone is a familiar one amongst introspective diarists. In Mary's case it calls out pity, not for its statements, but for their very aberration that declares the helpless and bewildered mind. No one wished to be harsh to Shelley's widow; her friends knew and understood her loss. It was only later that the talk arose of her having failed him as companion. For the moment she was defeated by her inconsistency—crying out for the love that only a husband could have given, while rejecting any help and friendship that might diminish the isolation of her grief.

After the tragedy she had gone with Jane to Pisa, then to Genoa— "this busy hateful Genoa, where nothing speaks to me of him, except the sea, which is his murderer." Despite her hatred, she decided to settle there for the winter, taking a house for herself and the Hunts to share, at Albaro, outside the gates. (It was to cost eighty francs, of

which Mary's share was thirty.) Here she made a point of seeing only
those who had known Shelley: the Hunts, Lord Byron, and Trelawny.
Of these, Hunt, not having known the later Shelley well, was unsatisfactory—as indeed Mary was to Hunt in the course of some trying
months together. The voice of "Albè" aroused the unheard echoes of
Shelley's voice in argumentative answer. With Trelawny she could
talk, and did, "for hours unreservedly of him." These were her only
present comforters. Claire and her solace (for what it was worth) had
set out, on Mrs. Mason's advice, for Vienna to join her brother
Charles;[3] while the bereaved Jane took her sorrowful course to
England in September, together with her children, Meddy and Dinah,
and the ashes of Williams.

⊰{ III }⊱

Jane was a simpler character than Mary, lacking her friend's tortuous
mental facets. Her grief was to yield later, like all normal wounds, to
the healing of time. For the moment it spoke clearly and poignantly,
especially when she reached Geneva on her homeward journey,
stabbed by the sunlit memories it called up. From there she wrote a
pathetic letter to Mary:

> My arrival at the inn here has been one of the most painful scenes
> I have yet undergone. The landlady, who came to the door, did not
> recognise me immediately, and when she did, our mutual tears
> prevented both interrogation and answer for some minutes. I then
> bore my sorrowful burden up those stairs he had formerly passed
> in all the pride of youth, hope, and love. . . .

On her arrival in London, Jane, who appeared to Mrs. Gisborne woefully thin and haggard, was not to be left utterly alone. For one thing,
her talent, grace, and personal charm had made it the easier for Leigh
Hunt to write a warmhearted letter of introduction to his musical
friends the Novellos. The letter, besides praising Jane's abilities, hinted

---

[3] In an immensely long letter to Mary in September, Charles Clairmont discussed his own
and Claire's prospects in Vienna, while condoling with Mary on the death of her poet, who
"was not made for here below. . . . His whole life was a sigh and a pant after a more ethereal
existence." To Mary he says, "You have relations and friends who admire you, who respect your
talents, who (more than all) love you."

30

at something peculiar in her history which she would perhaps feel inclined to disclose to them herself when she became better acquainted. This is the first indication that besides grief for Edward she was also troubled by her false status as his widow in spirit but the wife, legally, of another man.

Postponing our glimpse of the Novello family, we may see Godwin reporting to Mary, on November 15, his first impressions of Jane:

> From Hogg I had, amongst other things, to learn Mrs. Williams' address, for, owing to your neglect, she had been a fortnight in London before I knew of her arrival. She appeared in better health and better spirits than I expected; she did not drop one tear; occasionally she smiled. She is a picturesque little woman, and, as far as I could judge from one interview, I like her.

"Hogg and Mrs. Williams." They had in fact been seen together by Godwin. The old college friend of Shelley who had remained, in some rough-and-ready way, a friend despite his appetite for Harriet, his place in Mary's affections, and his distance from the poet for the last four years, had contrived to meet the beautiful Jane Williams almost as soon as she arrived. He had been cleverer than Godwin at discovering her—unless, indeed, a line from Mary had secured the meeting. Mrs. Gisborne, writing to Mary in October, reports Hogg's feelings on the death of Shelley, with a kindly estimate of his character:

> The letter which he wrote to Mr. Gisborne to ask for a confirmation of that event of which he himself had already no doubt, having been written when sudden mental anguish had thrown him off his guard, manifested most clearly the existence of that fine sensibility which in his intercourse with the world he so studiously endeavors to conceal.

Here then was Hogg, who had known Jane a bare fortnight, in a position to detail her address to the father of her great friend. It was hardly the treatment Godwin expected from his daughter, for whose sake he was interviewing all and sundry, besides seeking a publisher for her novel. His whole letter was a catalogue of Mary's bad behavior and imperfect judgments. She had commissioned three people to recover her manuscripts from Ollier—Peacock, Mrs. Gisborne, and himself. He had heard of Peacock's applying only just in time to prevent him from looking like a fool. ("He appears to me," he adds, in reply to Mary's wail to Mrs. Gisborne, "not lukewarm, but assiduous.") Again, Mary had commissioned both Jane and himself to inquire into Miss Curran's whereabouts. These double and treble commissions were a mistake. Turning to her literary plans, he threw cold water on her proposed subject, *Manfred,* as uninteresting to the public, and would have proposed a book about Italy but that Mary must be ignorant of the present race of Italians. He proceeded to a candid opinion of her novel *Castruccio,* as the eventual *Valperga* was then named. There were parts of genius, but he was not satisfied. "It appears, in reading, that the first rule you prescribed to yourself was, I will let it be long. It contains the quantity of four volumes of *Waverley*. No hard blow was ever hit with a woolsack!"

This last and essentially just blow must have been hard enough to Mary's vanity. Her later rambling novels show that she declined to learn by it, owing partly to the current necessity for filling three volumes, and partly perhaps because so scolding an epistle could only be read as the outpouring of a disgruntled father. The core of his carping was to be found in a further paragraph:

> As to my own affairs, nothing is determined. I expected something material to have happened this week, but as yet I have heard nothing. If the subscription fills, I shall, perhaps, be safe; if not, I shall be driven to sea on a plank.

A letter written to B. R. Haydon on October 9 by Charles Lamb (who still preferred Godwin to his son-in-law) told of the ruinous state of the philosopher's affairs and the effort to raise a subscription for him. "If he does not pay two years' arrears of rent, he will have the whole stock, furniture, &c, of his new house [in the Strand] seized when term begins." Poor Haydon, forever passing the hat round on his own behalf, can hardly have been the one to close the list. And indeed the subscription, which was still open in September of the following year, would probably never have been raised at all if Shelley had still lived to shoulder the impossible burden.

⟨ IV ⟩

To appreciate the manner of Mary's desolation, one must plunge into those long, long letters she wrote from Pisa and Genoa to Mrs. Gisborne. The first with its close account of all the incidents leading to the tragedy shows how engrossing a fascination the matter still had for her. Her literary and dramatic instinct never shone so clearly in her inventive work as now, in picking out the salient points of the fatal experience. Illness, visions, landscape, even a plan of the Casa Magni with a key to the numbering of its rooms—all are carefully and vividly sketched in. Compared with it, her stories, with their artificial characters and situations, are like imitations by another hand. In a sense they are so; for the vigor and independence Shelley had aroused in her were bound to fade when his influence was forgotten, even apart from the grief that dulled her energy. This first letter is all facts, down to the postscript saying that a fishing boat saw them sink and might have saved them. It is almost the only sustained piece of Mary's writing that is not overlong for its content. After that, the excitement of her misery faded out, the pain became a monotone. "I continue to exist— to see one day succeed the other; to dread night, but more to dread morning, and hail another cheerless day. My Boy, too, is alas! no consolation. When I think how he loved him, the plans he had for his education, his sweet and childish voice strikes me to the heart." About Shelley she sounded a note of prophecy more ardent than grammatical: "The world will surely one day feel what it has lost when this bright child of song deserted her." But for the most part she was driven inward, finding no subject now for her dramatic sense but that most piteous and monotonous one—herself. "The eight years I passed with him was spun out beyond the usual length of a man's life, and what I have suffered since will write years on my brow and intrench them in my heart. . . ."

Of the next letter she is again the tragic center. Claire has left; Jane has left. And although she is to live with the Hunts and close to Byron, she is painfully, almost exultantly, certain, while she sits before her sleeping baby, that none can fathom her suffering. "None are sufficiently interested in me to observe that though my lips smile, my eyes are blank, or to notice the desolate look that I cast up towards the sky." Before dismissing so theatrical an analysis, we may remember that the novel of Sensibility was in vogue. There are fashions even in feeling and the expression of it. To behave according to the fashion does not argue insincerity, for fashion indeed may influence feeling to a quite considerable depth, and if the novelists were imitated they, to begin with, took their models from life. Even when Mary proceeds, "Good-night. I will go look at the stars. They are eternal, so is he, so am I," we should suppress our sense of slight absurdity, and see it only as an elaboration of her anguished cry, "I am here alone in Genoa; quite, quite alone!"

Years ago, when Mary and Claire were children with a strict bedtime, Coleridge had called at the Polygon one evening to read *The Ancient Mariner* to the adults. But the two determined girls had sneaked under the sofa and heard it, too. Now, Mary's attitude seemed to echo the Mariner's lament:

> *Alone, alone, all all alone,*
> *Alone on a wide wide sea!*
> *And never a saint took pity on*
> *My soul in agony.*

As it happened, it was the other listener, Claire, who used the stanza that autumn, misquoting it generously to Mary and applying it to her own hard case.

❈{ v }❈

The weeks went on, and Mary helped Hunt produce his *Liberal*, contributing herself. Hogg, especially sought out by the Hunts to share from England in this verse and prose from the South, made use of his classical scholarship with alacrity. His chief contribution was an article on Longus, which shows that Hogg, like Trollope's arch-deacon, had a Rabelaisian curiosity in reading. Hunt's journalistic enemies were pained to find Byron in that monkey-house, but to Shelley, whose translation of Goethe's *Faust* appeared in it, they waved another typical farewell:

Goethe has puzzled us often, but Mr. Shelley has succeeded in making that, which was before dim, most profoundly obscure. To translate the extravagant German should be the task of a man less mad than himself; now Mr. Shelley, we take it, was more insane than he. But we have done, we cannot criticize inexplicable things.

Nor can we copy all the miscellaneous insults that the *Liberal* provoked.

A future admirer of Byron's, the Countess of Blessington, was listening to a kinder appreciation of the two poets during this same month of October. On her way to Italy she stopped at Geneva, where the boatman Maurice, once employed by Byron, rowed her (wrapped in warm shawls against the chill of autumn) on the lake. Maurice pointed out the Villa Diodati and the house in which Shelley had lived. "Poor Mr. Shelley," he sighed to her Ladyship,

"Ah! we were all sorry for him! . . . So gentle, so affectionate, so generous; he looked as if he loved the sky over his head, and the water on which his boat floated. He would not hurt a fly, nay, he would save everything that had life; so tender and merciful was his nature. He was too good for this world; and yet, lady, would you believe it, some of his countrymen, whom I have rowed in this very boat, have tried to make me think ill of him; but they never could succeed, for we plain people judge by what we *see*, and not by what we *hear*."

How far these boatman's sentiments were molded to shape by the Countess as she wrote, or revised, her journal, we are not compelled to guess.

The winter was a dismal one for Mary. It was distressing to know that Shelley's ashes, still awaiting permits and decisions from the authorities, were laid no deeper in the earth than John Freeborn's wine cellar. Joseph Severn, considered an authority on the Protestant Cemetery since he had buried Keats there, was asked by Hunt and Charles Brown to look into the delay. Permission to bury Shelley beside his son William being refused because the old ground was filled up, they now proposed to move William to the new enclosure. When this was at last attempted, William's grave was found to contain a full-sized skeleton instead of the child. Evidently someone had blundered. The search for William was given up. A memorial slab remains in the Old Cemetery, but it seems that no bones lie under it.

Trelawny, whose generosity Mary perceived under his eccentric shell, left Genoa to breathe the Maremman air with relief after the garlic breath of Genoese multitudes. (He was sailing with Captain Roberts in the refloated *Don Juan*.) At a safe distance he professed a tender friendship and offered himself for any and every service. How far this slave-like devotion was genuine can only be surmised. A blend of impulses and attitudes, he appears now as the blunt hero, now as the malicious scandalmonger; if a good part of him was rough-hewn honesty, there was also a grand façade of canvas and pasteboard that was only operative in limelight But he had earned Mary's gratitude in the days of suspense at Lerici, and was to earn it again yet. The Hunt family was a closer proposition, and one that almost drove Mary to distraction by proximity. The stove put up in her own room smoked too much to be lighted. Cold drove her for most of the day into Hunt's sitting room, where study and pleasure (besides indulgence in despair) were ruined. It was only after ten, when Hunt and Marianne had gone to bed, that she could be alone. Then her lamenting mood rose to the surface and she mediated on the mockery of her life. It must have been when the Hunts had gone to bed that she composed the long poem entitled *The Choice*. It was another excuse for retracing her life with Shelley and the loss of all her cherished ones in turn. Such writing raised her spirit towards exaltation even if it has no such effect now on the reader, but there were mundane intervals when her present unhappiness seemed to be centered on that smoking stove.

The truth was neither so grandiose nor so petty: she and Hunt were not at peace together. It is unnecessary to trace out all the argument and misunderstanding. Shelley was the cause of it; Hunt's jealous devotion to his memory was no less active than when he had tried to keep the heart. That controversy had been settled by Jane Williams; in this second instance Jane was herself accused by Hunt as mischief-maker. She had told stories that had set this Shelley-lover against Mary. But, protested Jane in a long defensive letter from England, was not Hunt an intimate? Could he not see as well as she did how unstable was the intercourse between Shelley and Mary? If Mary was repenting now of the trouble she had given Shelley, why was Hunt to feel guilty about his treatment of her, and why should he blame Jane?

So there was quarrel within quarrel, and who can say, amid the survivors' strained relationships, what truth, if any, was in this accusation—this self-accusation even—of Mary's being a thorn in Shelley's side? A passage in *The Choice* describes Mary's remorse for her

> *cold neglect, averted eyes,*
> *That blindly crushed thy soul's fond sacrifice.*

Did Hunt's criticism tend to awaken the remorse, or lead her to exaggerate her shortcomings? The argument that was afoot then has been taken up and settled a hundred times—settled to Mary's saint-hood and damnation—and still we shall have to please ourselves about it. There is no real evidence, except the evidence of Mary's wandering fancies at an earlier date as now supplied in her published letters to Hogg,[4] and this seems negligible when all is weighed. For the time being, Mary humbly took the blame and put an end to the alienation. Her young Percy, romping happily with the Hunt children, was scolded for his rowdiness in Italian (the poet's son having yet to learn his native tongue).

The new year found arrangements with Sir Timothy going badly. The stubborn baronet wrote to Lord Byron that as Mrs. Shelley was "the intimate friend of my son in the lifetime of his first wife and to the time of her death, and . . . estranged my son's mind from his family," he disputed her innocence and declined all interference. To the child he would afford suitable protection and place him with a person he should approve. Mary, who, for all her hatred of Sir Timothy, was hurt because he did not offer the child his home, indignantly rejected the proposal with a corroborative chorus from her friends.[5] To end the deadlock, she would be forced to go to England. Byron, who, with thoughts on his forthcoming Greek venture, was still chained by the Guiccioli in Albaro, promised financial help. In her perplexity Mary wrote, on February 28, an immense letter to Hogg,[6] appealing for advice from "Shelley's earliest friend" and one who, for all their early immature mistakes, might be

---

[4] *New Shelley Letters*, ed. by Walter S. Scott (London and New Haven, Conn., 1948).
[5] See Ingpen, *Shelley in England*, for a documentary account of these negotiations.
[6] *New Shelley Letters*.

trusted to understand her. "I believe you know my character sufficiently to be aware how deeply it is tinged with irresolution and an incapacity of action." Should she hug her solitude or go to England to protect the interests of the boy? "They will look on me indeed as a black, black sheep if I do not hasten to place myself beneath all the benefits of their clouded atmosphere and foggy virtue." Although she had appealed to him as "a true friend," Hogg answered, as even his admiring biographer surmises, from selfish motives.[7] Because both he and Jane Williams preferred to have Mary at a distance, he advised her to stay in Italy. Perhaps she guessed at his insincerity; she did not take his ruling.

Sir Tim's boredom with his grandson was probably increased by his having Harriet's son already on his hands. Appointed guardian to young Charles, he put him to school with Shelley's first teacher and left the Whittons to supply the child with clothes. Ianthe, Shelley's eldest and only surviving daughter, was placed under the guardianship of Mr. Westbrook and Mrs. Farthing Beauchamp—a name that now graces no other than Harriet's formidable sister Eliza. The "Beauchamp" was an addition—not invented, as we might have suspected, by Eliza herself to add value to the "Farthing." Value it did supply, for Mr. Farthing, a London bank clerk, had caught the love of an elderly lady called Beauchamp (but some say an aunt), who left him all her property, stipulating only a change of name. From Farthing to a fortune was no mean transfer, and Eliza benefited. If report speaks true, the change seems to have mellowed her into a most kindly guardian to Ianthe—perhaps kinder still when John Westbrook, dying in 1835, left her to inherit the property, his estate being sworn under £60,000. It certainly appears, then, that Mary's son will have a harder time than the children of Harriet, who, though dying so distressingly, has left behind so reputable an odor of legitimacy and family fortune.

❧{ VI }❧

The long-delayed burial of Shelley had at last taken place in Rome. On January 21, 1823, the Reverend Richard Burgess, English chaplain,

[7] *Jefferson Hogg,* by Winifred Scott (London, 1951).

called at the office of Mr. Freeborn, who conducted him to the wine cellar. There he was shown a square wooden box, painted chestnut color and engrained.

"I want you to bury that box," says Freeborn.

"What's in it?" Burgess asks.

"Mr. Shelley's ashes, sir," is the reply.

It was put in a coffin and buried in the New Enclosure of the Protestant Cemetery. General Cockburn was present, and Severn; also the chaplain and another English clergyman, who both knew vaguely that the victim was a great poet and a British subject.[8] It was to be said later, when Shelley's character was being polished up for the benefit of the country parsonage, that his funeral had been attended by many of the best families in Rome. It was attended, at least, by one eccentric in the person of Seymour Kirkup, who, living all his life in Italy and collecting the title of *Barone,* was to retain Trelawny's friendship and give him a sofa of Shelley's from the Casa Magni, acquired by Kirkup from Leigh Hunt *via* Charles Armitage Brown.

Trelawny, from his wanderings in the Maremman marshes, arrived in Rome in February and set to work landscape gardening in the Protestant Cemetery. Having found "the noble Shelley . . . confusedly mingled in a heap with five or six common vagabonds," he set about choosing and enclosing a "beautiful recess in a place peculiarly adapted for decoration." In this spot not far from the pyramid of Caius Cestius he planted six cypresses and four laurels, procured granite slabs, and fashioned everything in duplicate against the day when his own adventurous remains should need interment. "You may lay on the other side if you like," he offered generously to Mary. While in the mood and the surroundings, he drafted an epitaph for Keats's grave—which was not used—and desired Hunt to think of one for Trelawny's own. On Shelley's he had added the *Tempest* quotation to Hunt's misleading inscription of *Cor Cordium.* "Do not go to England to encounter poverty and bitter retrospections," he advised Mary; he himself was to return to Genoa. His friend Captain Roberts, who preceded him from Rome and had been sailing "that miserable boat," the refitted *Don Juan,* at eight knots an hour, brought with him a new verdict on the tragedy. *She was run down from*

---

[8] See *Shelley and His Friends in Italy,* by Helena Rossetti Angeli (London, 1911). She, however, gives the month as November.

behind was the opinion now; run down, Mary insisted to Maria Gisborne, "by that wretched fishing boat which owned that it had seen them."

By the time Trelawny reached Genoa, Mary had determined to forego the country of vines and olives for her boy's sake, but had exasperated Byron by her constant changes of mind. He himself had planned, quarreled with the Hunt family, vacillated, and now, bound at last for Greece and taking Trelawny with him, he felt no such generosity about parting with his funds. Provoked by his grudging and contemptuous attitude, Mary was driven to refuse his offer. Leigh Hunt agreed heartily with her decision. Over these last magnanimities the future Grecian martyr had made himself thoroughly unpopular and despised. Mrs. Mason (hardly justifying Mary's charge of coldness) had already done with Lord Byron forever on account of his neglect of Mary. "He may roll in riches or get drunk with fame, but he will never be happy." It was as well for Mary if she missed *John Bull's* acrid report of the situation that was to appear on August 31:

Byron has discarded Hunt, who exclaims bitterly against his Lordship.... The widow of the wretched Shelley is compassionated by her father-in-law, who, it is said, relieves Byron of the charge of keeping a whole family, and Hunt has withdrawn himself (at least, so the *Chronicle,* which knows the movements of such people, tells us) to Genoa, where, that paper says, The Poet—THE POET!!!—intends for the future to reside. One thing is certain, that Byron will write no more for the Liberal Magazine.

In fact, he had sailed for Greece with Trelawny, the one, as Mary put it feelingly to Jane, "escaping with all his crowns, and the other disbursing until he had hardly £10 left." She had been obliged, against her inclination, to draw on Trelawny's generosity, taking from the poor man that journey money which the rich would not provide.

She left at last on July 25, parting from Hunt in real affection, and writing him friendly, even sprightly, letters on her way. For the moment all her troubles seemed behind her or before, allowing her a sunny interval for prattle. At Susa she suggested a summer cottage where all should bustle with domestic duties to the music of Hunt's symphonies. From Dijon she reported an upsetting encounter with a "wretch" at Lyons, and sighed for her lost Italy. Between St. Jean de la Maurienne and Chambéry she "picked up" (the words are hers) two Frenchmen on a walking tour in the rain, and was told by the elder, who possessed six children, *"Madame, vous avez du caractère."* She passed the Montagne des Eschelles, "whose dark high precipices towering above, gave S. the idea of his Prometheus." In Paris she allowed herself to "run a little riot with my paper as well as my words," before crossing to England, where "I must think how to save tuppence postage by putting two thoughts instead of one into a sentence, and creep like Milton's devils, from 'gigantic paragraphs' into such full, overflowing, pressing down of the measure, that each word will be a three volumed novel." So she talks on, "clacking" as she terms it; advises Polly to throw a glass of water at Hunt when he is cross and silent ("only take care of the jacket"), to give the children a ducking, and not to be "offended at any of my nonsense. Absence seems to give one a right to be wilful. . . ."

It was more amusing, sometimes, to be wilful than to grieve.

Gray Skies after Sun

❧{ I }❧

"AND THEN," wrote the homeward traveler, "I enter the enchanted Island, or rather the Isle where all enchantments cease." We may look on Mary as being well launched, now, on her career of anticlimax. In 1818 she and Shelley had left England "for ever," loosening a hundred social ties and petty obligations. Five years later Shelley had fulfilled the curious destiny that demanded Keats's life in Rome and was soon to take Byron's at Missolonghi; and though Mary had spun out the aftermath, nothing in her nature or her circumstances was able to defy the eventual return to normal life. Such a return could not be happy to her analytical mind. At the same time it could not be faced with the flat rejection of a powerful revolutionary nature. There were conventionalities and social hankerings in Mary that earned her the later sneers of Trelawny, but acted as props and splints during her course. We may find these aids a little absurd when we come to look at them, but they have pathos. Mary, breathing a heartfelt prayer that her son Percy might be taught at school to think as others did, was not voicing a prim elegance so much as showing a fractured spirit tightly lashed in splints.

If Jane Williams, traveling from the blue to the gray skies, was not going towards an utter blankness, Mary, though she would have denied it, went home to stimulation. She was to fight out her maintenance with Sir Timothy—that was hardly the rosiest peak in her panorama. Her novel *Valperga,* with Godwin's ample alterations, had been published, four hundred pounds obtained on it (for Godwin!), and five hundred copies had been sold. A kind father thrust out offers of hospitality—with a warning to consider them temporary since the house was cramped. Like Jane, she had a letter from Hunt to the Novellos, who were already heartening her friend. There would be

Jane herself to meet, however encumbered she might be with Hogg's attentions. That she was encumbered, Mrs. Gisborne had reported vivaciously. To divert Mary from her evening groans in Albaro, she had selected the one figure of their circle who, for all his truculent self-importance, might be considered comic; and believing poor widowed Jane immune, she presented his courtship in a Falstaffian light. (Of Hogg's respect for Shelley we may say that appropriation is a form of flattery; he seems to have been incapable of choosing a quarry that lacked Shelley's stamp and authorization: first Elizabeth Shelley, then Harriet, Mary, and now Jane.) Of Hogg and Jane, then, Mrs. Gisborne wrote:

... They have made several appointments for the purpose of taking a long walk together, but the bad weather ... has constantly baffled the project till about ten days ago, when they contrived to reach the Regent's Park; but they were there caught in a tremendous shower of hail stones; and the poor gentleman was most famously pelted while sheltering his *cara donna* with a very indifferent umbrella, which he usually carries about with him, not so much for fear of rain as for fear of meeting Peacock and being scolded. Poor Hogg has endeavored to establish his calling in his way upon the lady in order to conduct her to our house, but of this display of gallantry she does not seem to approve, and has used various artifices to prevent his succeeding in his attempt. One evening she was just gone when he knocked at the door, and hastening his pace with the hope of overtaking her, he mistook another lady for her, and gently pulling her cloak, she looked round and cried out in an outrageous passion:—"You shocking monster!" Hogg did not stay to hear more abuse, or to make excuses, but laughed and ran on. He arrived in a terrible heat a few minutes after Mrs. Williams. ... Your poor friend took an affectionate leave of Mrs. Williams at our house last Friday week, and left town the following evening for his northern circuit; his tender heart, however, could not be satisfied with shaking (I do not mean pressing or squeezing) hands, and an anxious parting look; so he dispatched his diminutive messenger on Saturday morning with a note expressing his regret at being deprived of the pleasure of seeing her for six long weeks. ... (Here ends the *parte buffa* of my letter. I hope it may at least excite one smile on your dejected countenance.)

43

Before reaching England that "dejected countenance" was to be brightened by a taste of its literary and social news, to mingle with friends who were pursuing their interests and activities free from the overshadowing of a tragic death. The dramatist James Kenney and his family extended a welcome to Mary at Versailles, where the Horace Smiths were also of the party. A letter to Hunt shows how the widowed mind was adjusting itself to a general outlook and an appreciation of good gossip. There is news of the Lambs in France— Mary ill and Lamb imbibing the French wines; of Hazlitt becoming the "humble servant to all marriageable young ladies"; of Wordsworth looking old and Coleridge well. She had resolved to keep out of the "gulph of melancholy," but the work was done without her knowing it; consolation was awaiting her in England, for she arrived home famous. Under the title *Presumption: or the Fate of Frankenstein,* her novel was on the stage! Produced on July 26, it had drawn large audiences for twenty-two nights already, at the English Opera House in the Strand, and was to run yet longer. The very playbill was intriguing with its "—— by Mr. T. Cooke" in the list of actors. They had used this mode of "naming the unnameable."

Mary was thrilled. For playing the widow, there was time enough hereafter; meanwhile, it is not every theater lover who can celebrate a homecoming by watching her own piece on the boards. The family party was made up of Godwin and his son and Jane Williams, besides the authoress. They found the suspense at the end of the first act well managed, the story not so well; but "monster" Cooke played grandly and the audience sat in breathless eagerness throughout.

After that it was needless to pretend that life was over. She could hold her own, now, as a famous novelist, besides meeting friendly faces[1] and enjoying the conversation of Charles Lamb—"entertaining and amiable though a little deaf." He seems to have avoided mentioning frogs to Mary, contenting himself with criticism of Scott and Byron, to the advantage of Leigh Hunt. "Do they make puns in Italy?" he had asked immediately. "Yes," laughed Mary, "now Hunt is there." Economic prospects had improved as well. Godwin the businessman at once published a new edition of *Frankenstein*—"for

[1] Crabb Robinson notes in his diary on November 26, 1823: "Took tea and supped at Godwin's. The Lambs there, and some young men. We played whist, &c. Mrs. Shelley there. She is unaltered, yet I did not know her at first. She looks elegant and sickly and young. One would not suppose she was the author of 'Frankenstein.' "

my benefit," the author wrote meaningly. She had been scornful enough of her father's efforts in the disposing of her literary work; according to her, he had not made the slightest offer, and in fact, had "evidently *slinked* from the office." It was worth his while now to make a movement towards mutual support, especially as he put no faith in Timothy. But the bereaved wife doggedly pursued that glimmer, until she and her boy obtained an interview, not with the baronet, but with the baronet's solicitor. She came away from Whitton with one hundred pounds for her immediate expenses and a promise of the same sum annually for Percy, while time and patience might procure an allowance for herself. This relieved her "from a load of anxieties"; and "such, dear Hunt, is the outline of your poor exile's history." Who can help reflecting that the poor exile was somewhat fortunate—allowing, of course, for her supreme misfortune?

❦ 11 ❦

All that was wanting to increase her consolation was a ready sale for Shelley's poetry. She knew better than to expect it. Shelley had not written his poems, as Mary wrote her novels, to boil the pot, and while four hundred pounds could be wrenched out of a confident publisher for *Valperga,* the poet's works were usually to be entered as poor relations, on the debit side of his accounts. "I can only print my writings by stinting myself in food," he had once remarked. A quiet, gentlemanly firm of publishers had been found in Charles and James Ollier ("that pale bookseller," Shelley used to say of Charles), who were ready to publish on commission, and even at their own expense. We have only to read Shelley's letters from Italy to see that there was another side to the picture. The gentlemanly Charles and James were more than normally neglectful and appear to have made little attempt to carry out their author's wishes. It was the incredible number of misprints in *Prometheus Unbound* that impelled Shelley to have *Adonais* printed in Pisa, so as to make it difficult for the reviser to leave "such errors as *assist* the obscurity of the 'Prometheus.' " As early as 1817, Ollier's "terror," as Peacock expressed it, of being prosecuted for the publication of *Laon and Cythna* was the cause of Shelley's reluctant alterations to the poem and its title. In June, 1820, he remarked to Hunt on Ollier's heavy demerits, but he could rely on no one else to publish him—"and in fact they are all rogues." In the last months the Olliers consistently failed to answer Shelley's letters or send him news of his manuscripts and publications. These, indeed, made no profits, and from the bookseller's point of view had died with their author. The *succès de scandale* of Clark's edition of *Queen Mab* is characteristic of the so-called reading public which demands a subject for gossip, not for thought.[2]

In the autumn of Mary's return to England the firm went out of business and wound up its accounts. Shelley's widow received, in place of the check and royalty statement of more fortunate heirs, a report from Charles Ollier which is "all in order" but makes gloomy reading. "My dear Madam," he wrote on November 17,

> I have forwarded to Mr. J. Hunt, in compliance with your request, such copies of Mr. Shelley's works as remained in my possession. The unsold stock of those which were printed at our sole expense were disposed of in the general sale of our property; but, as I thought that, when you came to England, you might like to have a copy or two of each, I reserved some few for that purpose. We received from the printers only *a part* of the impressions of the "Revolt of Islam" and of the "Six Weeks' Tour"; of the latter, indeed, we were only joint publishers with Mr. Hookham.
>
> The sale in every instance of Mr. Shelley's works has been very confined. . . .
>
> On the other side is a list of the books forwarded to Mr. Hunt.
>
> As it was the wish of Mr. Shelley that the whole of the "Epipsychidion" should be suppressed, I would not, though it was printed at our expense, suffer the remainder to be disposed of. The whole of it is sent to Mr. Hunt.

The list follows:

160	"Epipsychidion"	(stitched)
12	"Hellas"	(Quires)
12	"Rosalind"	Do.
12	"Prometheus"	Do.
12	"Cenci"	Do.
3	Do.	Bds. Ist Edit.
4	"Hellas"	(Sewed)

[2] To this day it is the books of Shelley scandal that attract general attention rather than his own poetry and the work of serious critics.

15 "Revolt of Islam" . . . . . .   (Bds.)
41 "Adonais" . . . .   (Quires)
92 "Six Weeks' Tour" . . . . . .   Do.
18 "Proposal for Reform" . . . . .   (Stitched)

So Leigh Hunt's brother John now had the handling of Shelley's numerous works, and, like his predecessors, found little to handle.

III

When Leigh Hunt introduced Jane Williams and Mary Shelley successively into the household of his musical friend Vincent Novello, he was confident of their finding melody, companionship, and that easy gaiety both women now required. More tactful, wise, and sensitive introductions could hardly have been made: We have already seen his careful touch on Jane's perplexities; Mary's character was now drawn with equal delicacy:

> Do not [he warned Vincent] let anyone consider Mary S. in the light of a Blue, of which she has a great horror, but as an unaffected person with her faults and good qualities like the rest of us; the former extremely corrected by all she has seen and endured, the latter inclining her like a wise and kind being, to receive all the consolation which the good **and the** kind can give her. She will be grave with your gravities, and laugh as much as you please with your merriments. For the rest she is as quiet as a mouse, and will drink in as much Mozart and Paesiello as you choose to afford her, with an enjoyment you might take for a Quaker's, unless you could contrive some day to put her into a state of pain, when she will immediately grow as eloquent, and say as many fine things as she can discourse in a novel. . . .

And no doubt the musical ear of the recipient could detect the overtones in that cadence, advising him not to indulge (as Hunt had not indulged) her tendency to worship her own grief.

There was little fear of such indulgence. At the house on Shacklewell Green the musical gods were robust; Mozart, Haydn, and Handel being most regularly sung and played. The company at their supper parties was made up of the two Novellos and their daughter

47

Mary Victoria, Charles Cowden Clarke who was to marry her later, his friend Henry Robertson, a fine amateur tenor, Edward Holmes, the biographer of Mozart, and a number of further droppers-in. Amongst them were so many frank admirers, not to say almost lovers, of these romantic young widows in black, low-cut dresses, that their immediate danger was not desolation but excessive pride. The young Mary Victoria hero-worshiped Mrs. Shelley and was thrilled to have an autographed *Frankenstein*. "My father," she wrote long afterwards, "was her declared admirer, and she his, while Edward Holmes was equally unreserved in his bewitchment of her; and they both united in attributing to Charles Cowden Clarke a decided enthralment by the graces of Mrs. Williams." Playful and mutual gaiety was the result. Mary Shelley cooed her soft Italian, dwelling caressingly on the names "Vincenzo" and "Francesco" to the delight of their partly southern blood and displaying the singular flexibility of her hand and wrist to entrance her girlish admirer.

Nor were the children backward in their hardier demonstrations. The young Clara Novello remembered wars and passions that shook their miniature territory a year or two later. "Mrs. Shelley I adored," she writes, "also her six-year-old son, Percy, who was my tyrant, and I let him beat me, his abject slave, with his wooden cart, when the paper cannon-balls were insufficiently supplied by us little ones to the fighters of the Battle of Bunker's Hill—repeatedly fought on the top of a tiny mound by Percy, my brothers, and other boys."[3]

For the first time Mary was able fully to savor her unique position. To be so clever, so beautiful, so infinitely tragic in her precious loss, and yet to smile so bravely through her tears—here was a web of circumstance that could hardly fail to glitter, and to glitter the more in direct ratio to the number of admiring eyes. Warily, however, she confided to her dismal journal that no sparkle of society could deceive her. The English weather (as though arranged for her especial trial) was frightful; even to reach Shacklewell through the mud became almost more than womanhood (in party frocks) could endure. Her one occupation was to copy and prepare the unpublished poetry, for she had after all but "two sheet-anchors of hope" by which to live: her boy and Shelley's fame. And neither anchor was as yet in a con-

---

[3] For these and other pictures of the Novello household, see Charles and Mary Cowden Clarke, *Recollections of Writers* (London, 1878); Mary Cowden Clarke, *My Long Life* (1896); and Clara Novello, *Reminiscences*.

dition to hold her. She had nothing but a miserable hundred pounds per annum from Sir Timothy, now that he had defined his charity. Godwin, full of cares and debts, was doleful company and unenjoyable. Then there was Jane Williams; she loved Jane with a great basin of affection into which—to follow her metaphor—the less demonstrative widow contributed but a rill. She loved "some one or two more," with a discreeter measurement, but saw them seldom, while the reaction from excitement after meeting them pained her dreadfully. Thus in her journal she made the familiar mistake of blowing away her pleasures as mere froth, while she weighed and analyzed the flat liquid that remained. The art of *mingling* life could never be hers while she believed that her true self lived in her sorrows, instead of residing in a balance of spirits.

It was only her association with the hermit Shelley that made her fear to acknowledge her own preference. (He had been so sensible of the contrast, calling it "the living coupled with the dead," with himself in the latter role.) She needed town and company, admiration and judicious compliment; above all she craved that buoyed-up expectancy induced by contact with intelligent men of good appearance, not for their intellect alone, but for the human possibilities that lay in them. To attract, to be attracted, this was heaven, and the occasions of it were as "angels' visits."[4] She could not resist dwelling on them in her letters and journal. Before this year was out, the image of a new acquaintance, B. W. Procter ("Barry Cornwall") had assumed a romantic pose in Mary's mind.

She had certainly a plausible public reason for gratitude to this friend of Lamb's and Hunt's. He, with the poet T. L. Beddoes and Thomas Kelsall, had undertaken to pay for publication of the *Posthumous Poems* she was then editing. The Olliers, as we saw, had gone out of business, and John Hunt, who now owned the remaining Shelley stock, dared not risk the loss on these "last" gatherings from an unpopular poet—unpopular and generally unknown. Procter had himself once written to Ollier, asking, "Can you tell me where Shelley's *Epipsychidion* and *Adonais* are to be had? A friend of mine wants to get them, and indeed I should like to have a copy of the *Adonais* myself." Let us hope Ollier was able to provide these rarities.

---

[4] "Like angels' visits—few and far between." The quotation was from Campbell, who had himself, so Hazlitt asserts, adapted it from Blair's *Grave*.

Further, a bookseller being asked for *Prometheus Unbound* had replied that *Prometheus* was not to be had "in sheets"—an unintended joke which Theodore Hook worked up into a rhymed epigram.[5] Of those who had attempted to read Shelley, many no doubt agreed with the relentless Lamb that his poetry was "thin sewn with profit or delight." "For his theories and nostrums," Lamb went on,

> they are oracular enough, but I either comprehend 'em not, or there is miching malice and mischief in 'em. But for the most part ringing with their own emptiness. Hazlitt said well of 'em—Many are wiser and better for reading Shakespeare, but nobody was ever wiser or better for reading Shelley.

So the "three[6] poor honest admirers of Shelley's poetry," as Beddoes described them, came forward in February, 1824, with their modest means to guarantee 250 copies. As might be expected, their generosity was pressed to the uttermost. The usual publishers' sums and computations followed: Hunt, desiring double the number, declared that 250 was too few to pay for printing and advertisement, and that Mrs. Shelley ought to have a chance of making something. If only other professed admirers would contribute,[7] "nothing would be better," Beddoes wrote cynically to his fellow guarantor Kelsall, "than to print 500 or 750 copies (if it pleases the Gods of waste paper), for Mr. J. Hunt to sell at twopence a pound three or four years hence." Eventually Mr. J. Hunt published the other 250 copies at his own risk.

Mary had begun picture hunting again—this time for the adornment of the *Posthumous Poems.* Her plan was to secure that imperfect Curran portrait, touched up by the aid of one of Marianne Hunt's cleverly cut silhouettes. Again and again, in writing to the Hunts,

---

[5] *Sweepings of Parnassus* (1830). Epigram by "Steropes" *On Bysshe Shelley's "Prometheus Unbound."*

> Shelley styles his new poem, Prometheus Unbound,
> And 'tis like to remain so while time circles round;
> For surely an age would be spent in the finding
> A reader so weak as to pay for the binding.

[6] Procter's brother, Nicholas Waller, was possibly a fourth. See H. W. Donner, *T. L. Beddoes.*

[7] The elegist Arthur Brooke, rounded up by Kelsall as a probable subscriber, wrote a deplorably verbose letter from which it appeared that his wife's death had largely deflected his sympathy from the Shelleys to himself; but he spoke up for six copies. (Donner, *Beddoes.*)

she begged to have a profile sent to the artist. There is no record that Marianne ever sent one. The portrait itself hung fire. In April, 1824, Beddoes reported "the printing press moving slower than an eight-wheeled waggon . . . the portrait not arrived." It had still not arrived in June, by which month that restless wanderer was in Milan. "If I could be of any use in bringing the portrait &c," he wrote to Procter, "it would be a proud task, but most likely I only flash over Florence; entering in the flood of the stars, and departing with their ebb." This Shelleyan behavior came no nearer than the other attempts to capture the trophy; although at the end of July, when all hope of its appearing with the *Poems* had died, Mary was still confidently asserting that Mr. Beddoes was to get the portrait from Miss Curran, whom she fancied to be in Rome. It did at last reach Mary in September of 1826, four years after her first request. When it came, she apostrophized it lovingly, if a little hysterically: "Thine those speaking eyes, that mild yet animated look, unlike aught earthly wert thou ever and art now!" (The last words might have applied all too truly to the Curran effort.)

While she yet had no portrait to inspect, what could she do but examine the earthly countenances of those nearer, dazzled by at least one, and possibly two, of the three guarantors? On November 27, 1823, she wrote to Mrs. Hunt:

> I have seen also Procter with his beautifully formed head. . . . He is an enthusiastic admirer of Shelley, and . . . moreover, gentle and gentlemanly, and apparently endued with a true poetic feeling.— Besides, he is an invalid,—and some time ago I told you in a letter that I have always a sneaking (for sneaking, read open) kindness for men of literary and particularly poetic habits who have delicate health.

The kindness developed, until it was something of a bruise for Mary's "sneaking" regard when its object took a decisive step away from her by his marriage to Miss A. Skepper in the following autumn. Again her confidence was given to Marianne Hunt, who was not on the spot to laugh away her sentiments: "I was very much pleased with him, and I shall never see him again, which pains me." At the same period she was writing in her journal:

> I have only seen two persons from whom I have hoped or wished for friendly feeling. One, a Poet, who sought me first, whose voice,

laden with sentiment, passed as Shelley's, and who read with the same deep feeling as he; whose gentle manners were pleasing, and who seemed to a degree pleased; who once or twice listened to my sad plaints, and bent his dark blue eyes upon me. Association, gratitude, esteem, made me take interest in his long though rare visits.

The other was kind; sought me; was pleased with me. I could talk to him, that was much. He was attached to another, so that I felt at my ease with him. They have disappeared from my horizon. Jane alone remains. . . .

The second of these two was evidently Procter. It has been suggested that the first was Beddoes; but it has also been suggested that gentle and pleasing manners were not a characteristic of this poet. Besides, his eyes were brown. "The wisest and best have loved me," she goes on, "the beautiful, and glorious, and noble have looked on me with the divine expression of love, till Death, the reaper, carried to his overstocked barns my lamented harvest.[8] . . . But now I am not loved! Never, oh, never more shall I love."

⊰ IV ⊱

Before continuing the tale of Mary's attractions in a loveless age, we must return to Shelley's *Posthumous Poems.*

"The volume promises to repay something—at least the expenses," John Hunt, when it appeared in June, wrote to his brother in Italy. "Mrs. Shelley waited as long as possible for a notice from your pen—" (she had assured Hunt earlier that her heart would be broken should the book appear without one) "and not getting it, made a brief one herself; in which she alludes to the want of yours." The critics were less hostile than they had been, even those bugbears *Blackwood's* and the *Quarterly* allowing the poet some merit. Hazlitt wrote favorably in the *Edinburgh Review,*[9] which thus mentioned the name of Shelley for the first time. A writer in *Knight's Quarterly Magazine* found "the genuine mark of intellectual greatness" stamped on the work, and was so appreciative of the Shelley literary ménage as to sweep Mary's

[8] Who are all these noble corpses? Is Edward Williams referred to as her spiritual lover? Still more suspicious, has the martyred and purified Lord Byron been installed as such?

[9] Mary disliked the notice, but her anger faded into tears before the lean and melancholy appearance of its unhappy author.

Frankenstein and *Valperga* into his long article. The *Literary Gazette* of July 17 preached a sermon on the peace, pardon, and tenderness owing to the dead, found the poems a blend of beauty and blasphemy, and deplored the widow's "preface of panegyric." Shelley's declared enemy, *John Bull,* elected to review its books of the week in rhyme. The relevant stanzas run:

> *There's a "Loves of the Colours," not much to our* palate,
> *Composed by some bard, with a head like a mallet:*
> *And the Hunts—a bad spec., as we venture to tell ye,*
> *Have published some posthumous trash of Bysshe Shelly;*
>
> *In which you will find, as we found with much sadness,*
> *Some talent—obscured by much maundering madness;*
> *A good line, here and there, in an ocean of drivel,*
> *And a thought, once or twice, sunk in blasphemous snivel.*

The inspiration and the drivel had barely had time to reach their readers when both alike were snuffed out by the book's suppression. The dictator, this time, was no vice society, but that proud father who, as Mary put it, "writhes under the fame of his incomparable son, as if it were the most grievous injury done to him." Before the *Poems* appeared, a new arrangement had been proceeding between her and Sir Timothy—through Whitton and Peacock—by which Mary, heir to the estate by Shelley's will during the lives of Charles and Percy, was to buy an annuity of three hundred pounds, on a sum charged on the estate. That agreeable prospect suddenly became dependent on the suppression of the *Posthumous Poems.* Mary bowed tamely enough to this "indispensable preliminary." Between financial stability and poetic loyalty she was not long in making up her mind. She had even been "obliged to promise not to bring dear Shelley's name before the public again during Sir Timothy's life." As to that, she was not worrying overmuch; for death, which had played pranks with all her lovers, would not long neglect her aging persecutor. Sir Tim was over seventy; for some few years she was not inclined towards writing memoirs, nor was there much material to collect. All this she pleaded carefully to Hunt, lest he should be astonished at her mercenary attitude. To Trelawny she wrote that she would soon have an independent income, "and that with small sacrifice on my part." Her sensibility, like the *Poems,* had been suppressed.

53

⋙{ v }⋘

However, we have not written Mary's epitaph, even for the year 1824. Numbers of dark or gleaming facets gained her attention. Here was Hazlitt, newly remarried, with the first Mrs. Hazlitt paying the couple a wedding visit and declaring herself much taken with her successor. George Dyer, too, had married a woman who kept him clean—George Dyer who at midday had walked out of the Lambs' house at Islington straight into the New River, mistaking it for the road. Peacock the egoist had been actually heard to speak of his children with affection. Percy, a fine tall boy, was going to school and learning to read and write—or at least keeping himself busy and out of his mother's way. With Arthur Brooke, the elegist of the *Kentish Herald,* she was exchanging letters and souvenirs. Brooke sent his own poems, Mary presented the manuscript of Shelley's fragment of *Athanase,* Part I, and a lock of the poet's (seemingly inexhaustible) hair. She was living in Kentish Town and finding the country around her "really pretty; lawny uplands, wooded parks, green lanes, and gentle hills form agreeable and varying combinations." Besides, was not her indispensable Jane Williams living within a stone's throw, and were not the two of them contriving, at least throughout the winter months, to enjoy free theater and opera seats as often as they asked their influential friends for them? The most generous donors were John Hunt and John Howard Payne (of whom we shall hear more in a moment). The next year Harrison Ainsworth, meeting Mary at Lamb's house and finding her "very handsome" was to join her cavaliers of the playhouse.

This glamour of theater and tragedians (Kean in particular was her idol) led Mary to compose a tragedy on Manfred in defiance of her father's advice, and to put him in the awkward position of being forced to criticize it. Why not Procter? Why not Lamb? he demurred; but at least he would not—and certainly did not—mislead. Most of her scenes, he complained, were "neither good nor bad; they might be endured, in the character of cement, to fasten good things together. ... Your personages are mere abstractions." He was almost glad she had no dramatic talent on account of the heartaches concerning managers, players, and audience she would be spared. It was laziness that led her to attempt playwriting—the desire to write less and be equally rewarded. (Here Godwin may have been hardly just; there is no evidence that Mary did not enjoy the ease and luxury of writing at undisciplined length.) The paternal counsel seems at last to have weighed with her; she attempted no more tragedies, but continued at intervals to look upon herself as a dramatist *manqué,* and so add one more frustration to her list.

Apart from the drama invented for the stage, a curious comedy of mother-in-law and stepmother had been playing around the widows. It is remarkable how parallel their situations were. Of the two, Jane's was the more complicated. She had not only been married before meeting Williams, but it appears that Edward himself had (like Shelley for Mary) neglected a former wife for Jane. Unlike the West-brook family, who left Mary blessedly unnoticed, this unknown "Harriet's" mother persecuted Jane with feminine vigor and a slanderous tongue. All Jane's tact and secrecy were required even to guard the ashes of Williams from this jealous mother-in-law. The outraged lady called on Mrs. Godwin, warning that unnatural step-mother that Mary ought not to know such a hag as Jane. At the same time she knew and made capital of Mary's history, prattling to others that Jane's sins were magnified by her association with Mary.[10] All this can hardly have hurt Shelley's widow, whose situation had been so long in the sunlight as to have faded before the public's very gaze. But Jane had and desired no notoriety. She and Williams had left England together with as much relief, and perhaps as great a finality, as Shelley and Mary had done. If there was a scandal when they left, it was a private one, and all Jane longed for now was quietude and an orderly existence. Such a life might be provided by her faithful Hogg—"queer, unamiable and strange" as Mary now found him. Jane herself could not always fall in with his clumsy jesting, specimens of

---

10 See letter from Mary to Hunt, September 9, 1823. But I am not convinced as to the relationship of this truculent lady. Though in our day "mother-in-law" and "stepmother" are distinctive terms, they were used interchangeably in the eighteenth century. Gibbon referred to his father's second wife as either "mother-in-law" or "stepmother"; this usage is likely to have persisted into the next century, and the lady in question might have been, as Frederick L. Jones suggests, a stepmother of Edward's. His father, Captain John Williams, was married four times. Edward was the son of his second wife; the third died in 1803; the fourth, Mary Ann, had no children, but is likely to have been living at this date. (See Edmund Blunden, "The Family of Edward Williams," *Keats-Shelley Memorial Bulletin,* No. 4 (London, 1952). Surprisingly enough, this relentless woman, whatever her relationship, was by 1825 making Jane an allowance, and making it "without restriction or pretension." (Mary to Trelawny, February, 1825.)

which, and its effect on Jane, are exhibited in a letter he wrote to Mary. Applauding the news of the "young gentleman" Percy's being sent to school, he went on, hurling bricks too nobbly for their tender targets. Hogg was surely one "born out of time"; the boorish skepticism and rough pleasantries that shocked the Sensitive Age would have sat better on him as a Queen Anne coffeehouse wit or a latter-day Georgian.

> . . . Dina seems to be so well instructed by *Bonne* in the rudiments of modesty, that, when she is old enough to make an interesting catastrophe, she will no doubt show the same aversion, which I applaud and you condemn, to strip herself before sailors. Thank God! I have got Jane into a good humour again! I unfortunately said in a letter from York that all my friends were going to marry (which was true, for one is married since and another only waits until his wife's white satin is ready), and that I should probably follow their example, or some such thing; which foolish speech she took so ill, probably from being displeased that I should take such an important step without her advice, that she scolded me incessantly for six weeks. . . .[11]

Claire Clairmont, too, was writing sorrowful letters from the home of the trusting family who employed her as governess. Of the old Pisan circle she, the mother of lost Allegra, was the one who heard with least regret of Byron's death in April. She had schooled her impulses with all her might. Elsewhere sorrow reigned. Trelawny, who had wished so much to be unhampered by the noble poet in Greece and whose first instinct was to find—and not to find—the Truth about Lameness, set up lamentations. "I am sick at heart with losing my friend, for still I must call him so. You know with all his weakness, you know I loved him. I cannot live with men for years without feeling—it is weak, it is want of judgment, of philosophy—but this is my weakness. Dear Mary, if you love me, *write*—write—write, for my heart yearns after you. I certainly must have you and Jane out. I am serious." The pirate, "no more a nameless being," was now a chieftain, with his "boss" Odysseus, and would shelter and protect them. Following his procedure with Shelley, he sent home a long account of Byron's death. Mary, who had washed her hands of

[11] *Shelley and Mary.*

Byron less than a year ago, was once again prostrated. To make the matter more harrowing, his funeral procession passed by her house. "Albè, the dear, capricious, fascinating Albè—has left this desert world! God grant I may die young!"

The periodicals, too, that could only sneer at Shelley, indulged their copious sorrow for the noble lord, welcoming to their pages all that could conceivably be accommodated of the foam of elegies, memoirs, portraits, character studies, letters, and recollections that gushed over the crest of the popular wave. The *Literary Chronicle*, crowding out all notice of Shelley's *Posthumous Poems* with this flow of Byroniana, declared emotionally, "It will be long indeed before genuine anecdotes of this distinguished nobleman and poet will cloy the appetite." They never ceased deploring the destruction of his autobiography—and, no doubt, of the scandal liable to be contained in it. The incident is by now famous: Byron had given the life to Tom Moore in 1821 with liberty to sell it for the best price he could get, which the dapper little Irish poet took care to do, obtaining £2,000 from Murray. But instead of being published on Byron's death, the compromising memoirs were burned by Mrs. Augusta Leigh with the approval of John Hobhouse, and Moore had to refund the £2,000. "There was not much in them, I know," Mary wrote to Trelawny on July 28, "for I read them some years ago at Venice, but the world fancied it was to have a confession of the hidden feelings of one concerning whom they were always passionately curious. Moore was by no means pleased: he is now writing a life of him himself, but it is conjectured that, notwithstanding he had the MS so long in his possession, he never found time to read it. I breakfasted with him about a week ago, and he is anxious to get materials for his work."

In fact, the tiny, society-loving Irish bard who spent his days—after a few morning hours of literature—hurrying excitably from one titled family to another, and had been known to dine three times in one afternoon rather than lose a society invitation,[12] now found it worth while to honor the poverty-stricken widow of Shelley with his breakfast-time acquaintance; for Mary, besides having seen the memoirs, was bound to have anecdotes of Byron, and Tom Moore had his money to make again. He had himself introduced by Kenny on

12 "Oh, Tommy *loves* a Lord," Byron had said, commenting to Leigh Hunt on Moore's hobby of "tuft-hunting." (See Hunt's articles in *The Tatler*, January, 1831.)

July 17, found her "very gentle and feminine," and proceeded to pump her. Having pumped, he sang—and Mary was captivated. But for this susceptibility—and a snobbery less than Moore's, yet not inactive—it would be hard to account for her opacity during the several years while Moore was swotting up his facts. Every friendship had its purpose with this caroling bard: a title was its own justification, but a commoner had, a few years ago, to have known something useful about Sheridan; when that Life was done, the Byron circle defaced his visiting list. Yet he knew how to ingratiate himself, even with Mary, who was later to note in her journal, "He reminds me delightfully of the past, and I like him much. There is something warm and genuine in his feelings and manner, which is very attractive, and redeems him from the sin of worldliness with which he has been charged." Perhaps the glint of Irish roguery in Moore sent her thoughts back happily to Italian days.

⊸❧ VI ❧⊷

There was another link with the past and candidate for Byron gossip who earned no such grace of reception. Shelley's cousin Tom Medwin lost no time in seizing the journalistic chance, and wrote bombastically to Mary from Genoa about the piquant memoirs of Lord Byron he had been "urged to give the world" in place of the destroyed biography. He had made copious notes of his Pisan conversations, and Shelley was "a very prominent feature." He would like to consult Mary, who might be "of the greatest possible use" to him; he had been offered five hundred pounds and told the book was certain of success. Of course Lady Byron would not like it, and he would be assailed on all sides. He had heard that Moore was "manufacturing five or six volumes out of the *burnt* materials," so that Medwin must be prompt, and Mary must answer soon.

With those last words he set the seal, if seal was wanting, on the hostility of Mary, who was even then granting Moore her sanction. She replied that her own reminiscences of Lord Byron might have had more matter in them and defended Moore's dignified effort against Medwin's trash.[13] In October, Medwin answered with supreme

13 "Have you heard of Medwin's book?" she wrote to Hunt. "Notes of conversation which

clumsiness: his manuscript was already in London, and Mary's name did not occur in it. He bowed flatteringly to her superior knowledge of Byron, assured her that Moore's "serious" life would not be interfered with, asserted that Moore's songs were better sung by Grattan, and that Moore had littleness and jealousy in his character, having refused to give Byron as a toast at a public dinner "we gave him" in Paris.[14] So Medwin completed the ruin of his case with Mary without caring much. He was to care even less in a few years for her feelings. What's in a surname? Much, it may be; for while Tom Moore joined the ranks of heroes, Tom Medwin was cast as villain of the play for Mary, who was to die before Thomas J. Hogg had shown all he could do.

The *Conversations of Lord Byron* was in its second edition before the year was out; this despite the assurance of that zealous scandal-burner John Cam Hobhouse that "the Captain will never show his book again" and that his face might well be slapped by the relatives of those ladies he had belied.[15] As this is Shelley's first appearance in a gossiping chronicle—and one destined for popularity, thanks to its subject—we may as well glance at the Captain's treatment of him. It is not ponderous in the actual text, which is so diffuse that nothing has much weight. We are shown Shelley spotting two lines from Southey in Byron's *The Deformed Transformed*: quoting *Peter Bell* to Byron, whom he "dosed with Wordsworth physic even to nausea"; attracting the love of a Mrs. —— on account of his verses.

Byron's estimates of Shelley as given by Medwin are among the passages Mary was meant to enjoy:

> There's Shelley has more poetry in him than any man living; and if he were not so mystical, and would not write Utopias and set himself up as a Reformer, his right to rank as a poet, and very highly too, could not fail of being acknowledged. . . . The works he wrote

he had at Pisa with Lord Byron (when tipsy); every one is to be in it; every one will be angry. He wanted me to have a hand in it, but I declined. Years ago, when a man died, the worms ate him; now, a new set of worms feed on the carcase of the scandal he leaves behind him, and grow fat upon the world's love of tittle tattle. I will not be numbered among them."

14 Moore, in fact, confined himself to the toast of "Prosperity to England," which, in 1822, would possibly have been an awkward coupler with prosperity to the exiled Byron.

15 "It is, I think, the most infamous publication I ever read, and alike dishonourable to Ld Byron and Captain Medwin." *The Journal of Mrs. Arbuthnot, 1820–1832,* ed. by Francis Bamford and the Duke of Wellington (London, 1950).

at seventeen are much more extraordinary than Chatterton's at the same age.

In consequence of the infamous treatment of the *Quarterly,*

> everyone abuses Shelley,—his name is coupled with every thing that is opprobrious: but he is one of the most moral as well as amiable men I know. I have now been intimate with him for years, and every year has added to my regard for him.

These lordly praises might or might not have pleased those readers they were intended to placate; what specially offended was a lengthy memoir of Shelley printed as a "footnote" across sixteen pages— occupying all except two lines at the head of each—and excused, at the outset, as relating to Lord Byron. The memoir is inaccurate and in parts belittling ("blundering and disagreeable" is Mary's description), but Medwin seems to have meant it kindly. To Mary he refers as Shelley's "lovely and amiable wife." No doubt her revulsion from this patronage seemed to him unjust, and he treasured his grievance.

The reference to Southey, above, reminds us that the Laureate also had his complicated grievances: against Byron for calumny, Medwin for retailing Byron, and Shelley for refusing to toe the line. A number of his quarrelsome, defensive letters—of which the second, sent to the *Courier* in December, 1824, told the world how he admonished Shelley—were thought topical enough by this crowned head of poetry to be collected in a volume of his essays in 1832. Here they stand, with an extra word on Shelley in a footnote:

> I admired his talents, thought that he would outgrow his errors (perilous as they were,) and trusted that, meantime, a kind and generous heart would resist the effect of fatal opinions which he had taken up in ignorance and boyhood. Herein I was mistaken. But when I ceased to regard him with hope, he became to me an object for sorrow and awful commiseration, not of any injurious or unkind feeling.[16]

It is hard to feel much commiseration for Southey, who, beginning as an ardent revolutionary, had hardened into so prosaic and bigoted a Tory as to be violently opposed to free trade, Parliamentary reform, and others of the milder Shelleyan precepts that were to be endorsed

[16] Robert Southey, *Essays Moral and Political* (1832).

by a Whig government in the very year his *Essays Moral and Political* made their bleat.

The hail of Byron anecdotes brought falser and meaner prattle about Shelley than any the half-honest Medwin or the self-righteous Laureate could put forth. Some anonymous romancer managed to publish a *Narrative of Lord Byron's Voyage to Sicily, Corsica and Sardinia, in the year 1821; compiled from Minutes made during the Voyage of his Lordship's Yacht, Mazeppa, kept by Captain Benson, R.H., commander*. This yacht, with Byron and Percy S—— on board, being threatened with shipwreck, the infidel began calling on God to save him, and was soon at the valiant Byron's feet "in a state of insensibility." The vessel being spared, Percy S—— recovered on rum and water, "and in twenty-four hours, he was the same free-thinking, thankless dog as ever"; his Lordship "threatened to compose an elegy on the death and resurrection of Percy S——, and the Countess said she would set his 'dying speech' to music, and dedicate it to the spirit of the storm." We need only comment that Byron never sailed to Sicily, Corsica, and Sardinia in the year 1821, and record Leigh Hunt's assertion (1828) that the bold behavior of the one and the timidity of the other would have been reversed, had the voyage been anything but an impudent fiction.[17] (Hunt was of course indulging his resentment against Byron, who was no coward.)

Mary seems to have been spared this story in the year of its birth. Melancholy and poverty alike were driving her pen towards producing a three-decker novel on the strangely fashionable subject of *The Last Man*. To trace the origin and development of this notion would be a thesis in itself; something in the morbid picturing of one solitary survivor in an unpeopled world had a notable selling power amongst the living millions. To mention only a few begetters of "last men," Tom Campbell published his poem this year (1824) in the *New Monthly;* Beddoes began writing a tragedy, which he never completed; an anonymous writer contributed a sketch to *Blackwood's* in the same spring as Mary's publication; Thomas Hood characteristically borrowed the grim subject for a whimsical ballad.[18] Mary was

[17] Although Hobhouse at once published a contradiction, it is sad to find this absurd story making its way to the Continent and being presented in 1826, translated from the *French,* to a Germany that knew Shelley only by report as Byron's weaker friend. (See Solomon Liptzin, *Shelley in Germany* [New York, 1924].)

[18] Byron's *Darkness*, written when he was in Switzerland with the Shelleys in 1816, has

of course humorless. "The last man!" she commented; "yes, I may well describe that solitary being's feelings, feeling myself as the last relic of a beloved race, my companions extinct before me."

This fantasy of the future has its Shelley-puppet in the figure of Adrian, but in a pattern of events too lavishly fictitious to leave more than the merest breath of him for comparison. (Byron, as Lord Raymond, a politician, is at least identifiable by Greek wars.) Such as he is, though, Adrian directs the affairs of a nation for a while— a position that Shelley himself, in a Platonic community of philosophers, would not have found uncongenial.[19]

---

a similar theme. It may have influenced Mary. Campbell was accused of plagiarism from *Darkness*, both poems really being based on an anonymous romance: *The Last Man, or, Omegarus and Syderia* (1806).

[19] Since this was written, Elizabeth Nitchie has published a close examination of *The Last Man* and the partial portraits it contains, in her *Mary Shelley: Author of "Frankenstein"* (New Brunswick, N. J., 1953).

CHAPTER IV

Seeking New Centers

❧{ I }❧

STRUGGLING ON without their animating spirit, our survivors all show signs of strain and perplexity in adjusting themselves to a colder world. Even Byron, before his honorable end, had been infected. Having shuffled off his obligations to Hunt and Mary, he had been left politically entangled with the aftereffects of the "affair of the Dragoon"[1] and the banishment of Teresa's family, the Gambas. There is no doubt (despite all that was said in bitterness against him) that he was deeply disturbed by the death of his fellow writer, who, with Teresa, had pulled him out of a trough. Nor—since of the two characters his was the self-centered one—had he felt any of the burden that fell on Shelley when forced to fit in with Byron's inverted habits and tackle him on the treatment of his child. Shelley, as ever, had given something of his life-blood. Byron had taken it with egocentric negligence; but he was far from satisfied that it should all be given, and in a way that could benefit no one. If anything, it added to his impatience with an elaborate and purposeless existence. Although the Contessa set out to advise him on *Don Juan* (negatively, at that!) he could not seriously discuss English literature with his Italian mistress, nor could he love her with passion enough to swamp his intellect, his irony, and, alas his ever recurrent enemy, boredom. The Italian authorities, in exiling the Gambas, kept a vigilant eye on the English Milord as well, and this could only add annoyance to tedium. The Greek venture was a way of escape.

It has been hailed by the headier sort of admirer as a translation of poetry into action.[2] Though it may have touched these heights when imagination was not smothered, we shall not go far wrong to substi-

---

1 For new light on this incident, and especially the part played in it by Count Taaffe, see *Shelley, Byron, and Their Pisan Circle*, by C. L. Cline (London and Cambridge, Mass,. 1952).

2 See especially *Lord Byron: Christian Virtues*, by G. Wilson Knight (London, 1952).

tute "perplexity" for "poetry" in a general way. "Destined as he was to endless disenchantment," Tom Moore, who understood him a little, put this down to the duality of his nature, the very myths called up by his creative power being mocked in cold analysis as hollow delusions. Shelley, for all his hatred and despair of the immediate fabric, never lost faith in a Promethean triumph, such as Byron, parted from that almost occult influence, could not sustain. Given survival, the hero of Missolonghi, involved in the bickering affairs of Greek committees in England and rivalries among the patriots he led, would have turned in disgust from the phantom of independence—another discarded mistress. By losing his life on the heroic quest, he saved it. And at one blow, as we saw in the preceding chapter, he secured the fame that we are seeking over such long years for Shelley. The others of the circle were to rub along in their chains.

Our constant presentation of two Marys—the inconsolable recluse and the society widow—is an example of this maladjustment. One more must be added to her tale of contrasts: an incident that was ignored, perhaps unknown, by her first biographer, has since been overmagnified in brochures and articles, and pounced on by detractors as the key to her failure (if failure it is judged) to live an integrated and harmonious life. It has been unfairly singled out from her other emotional and social activities as a unique occurrence rather than a piece of typical behavior on her part. The "matter" in question is Mary's "love" for Washington Irving and her unfeeling use of the devoted John Howard Payne. She appears to have met the two Americans—or at least the second—during her visits to the Kenneys in Paris in 1823.

Payne, who was thirty-two, had begun his career as a boy actor in New York, then becoming a playwright in London. When Mary met him, he was forced to live in Paris to avoid arrest for debts incurred as an unsuccessful manager of Sadler's Wells Theatre. This failure may unconsciously have prejudiced her against his "eligibility"; it was too soon even for him to have acquired that halo due to his lyric "Home, Sweet Home" which had been sung with huge success some three months previously by Miss Tree at Covent Garden. Perhaps he never did acquire a full halo. Is it generally remembered now, in England, that such a piece of "typical British sentiment" was written by a young American, whose memorial monument, far from either home, is in Tunis, where he died as his country's consul?[3] But this is nearly thirty years ahead. In Paris he was the friend and correspondent of Charles Lamb and Coleridge. He was, too, the collaborator with Washington Irving in adapting French plays for the London stage. Irving, eight years older, was a fashionable writer in England, where his *Sketch Book* of 1820 had won fame. A friend of Scott, Tom Moore, and Campbell, and frequenter, by grace of his polished amiability, of the "highest literary circles," he was naturally a more glamorous figure to Mary. The notion of marrying a popular author in succession to a neglected poet must have flitted half-playfully through her mind. To be the brilliant wife and hostess beside an elegant and society-loving talent was a tempting prospect. As Mary's daydream, Irving was woven pleasantly amongst her solider experiences. Payne himself overestimated the seriousness of her feelings when his own prompted him to write a solemn and almost heartbroken letter to the innocent Irving. In the whole episode Payne was the only sufferer, for he had let himself cherish for Mary an affection on a deeper plane than the whims and preferences that stirred her.

Their acquaintanceship developed in 1825 because, in her eyes, he was the instrument to provide free passes to the theater, while in Payne's eyes the theater tickets were the instrument and excuse for an approach to Mary. He visited her in Kentish Town; he talked, and she talked too, in a manner to make him write, "Your yesterday's conversations filled my mind so full of yourself, that my poor pillow had but a small portion of its due." He began to worship the Mary he pictured, who combined intellect with purity of character, fervor, and simplicity. On her side she worked his bounty to the full in the matter of theater tickets, even becoming fussy over dates and seating. Then she would tantalize Payne by talking, one day in Lamb's garden, something that was nonsense, or half nonsense—"a veil, a make-believe, which means everything and nothing." One suspects her of enjoying her sense of power and superiority, since Payne, unlike Procter and some others, left her intact, without those "dreadfully painful reactions." And then, the dancing image of an almost imaginary Irving whom she had glimpsed again in company with Tom Moore, shone brighter and nearer when Payne was around.

While she half-jested, the lover's innate and humorless honesty

[3] *Home, Sweet Home* has gained a place on the inscription.

was shocked into an action of self-sacrifice worthy of a better cause. Irving was in Paris. Payne turned over to him the entire correspondence between himself and Mary, explaining his discovery that it was *he* she loved, and urging him not to "look on the affair in a ridiculous light." That it could be ridiculed Payne saw clearly, but nothing in his idol's conduct could diminish her for him, even while he found it unflattering to his pride and affections. Mary, singularly tactless, had told Payne that she would only form an alliance with "some one whose high character and mind should be worthy of him who had drawn her from obscurity, and that her selection must not dishonour his choice." (She was less specific later, to Trelawny, who might better have stood brutal treatment; then she had no reason for remaining a widow except that Shelley was a pretty name.) Payne wrote sadly: "I told you I knew my danger and could laugh at it. I am afraid now the laugh is not on my side. . . . I have given way to an absurdity, and have only myself to blame. . . . It is therefore better I should not meet you till this strange fever is over. . . . I am sure you will still allow me to be your friend in a corner." Indeed, he remained her friend in a *box* as long as theater tickets were obtainable; while Mary, aware of her own foolishness, could only beg him to shield her from the ridicule of Irving, whose attentions were so dilatory. The whole matter savors of a schoolgirl's "crush."

Mary and Irving never became intimates. Her father, in 1829, was to pour out his own tale of bankruptcy and misfortune, asking and obtaining Irving's help in securing an American publisher for his novel.[4] Mary's pain was probably eased a little when the ornament of literary circles betook himself as far off as Madrid; her theater-going privileges certainly suffered when Payne returned to New York in 1832 (where his benefit at the Park Theatre produced $4,200).

[4] Irving had his own preferences among women, though fortune never blessed him in his choice. His first beloved, Matilda Hoffman, had died of consumption in 1809. In 1823 he had been captivated while in Dresden by the very young Emily Foster, granddaughter of an English earl. She seems to have refused him, though the facts are uncertain. In any case there was real sadness and disappointment; Mary's kittenish game followed too closely on the heels of that richer episode to make any impression on the man she played for. See *Washington Irving Esq.*, by George S. Hellman (New York, 1925), and *The Life of Washington Irving*, by Stanley T. Williams (New York, 1935, 2 vols.).

Washington Irving

From an oil painting by Gilbert Stuart Newton, in the possession of
Sir John Murray, K.C.V.O., D.S.O.

Reproduced by kind permission of Sir John Murray

To return to Shelley's friends from this aberrant interlude, we find adjustments and bewilderment taking several shapes. Jane Williams, for example, is about to place her destiny in the hands of Hogg and so reduce its pains and splendors to one gray level of domesticity. Before that happens, Hogg must travel on the Continent—to fit himself for her company, it has been too prettily conjectured. He does, indeed, write her affectionate letters from Florence, Naples, Bruges, and other showplaces, but at the same time he is copying them, with journalistic embellishments, for Mr. Southern, to be published in the *London Magazine,* and later in a volume.[5] Peacock continues to wrestle sturdily with Whitton over the intractable Timothy's allowance to Mary, who is receiving two hundred pounds a year in "so strange and embarrassed a manner" that she hardly believes in the worth of it. The impacted situation is shown up by Peacock when he reports a difficulty in March, 1826: "the will and the deed are necessary for obtaining money, and . . . money is necessary for obtaining the will and the deed." If there is any outlet to that circle, it is not through Sir Tim's impliable mind; Mary has hardly published *The Last Man* when trouble threatens again. The Name has been brought before the public, and though she may get her money, she will be punished by a short delay. In vain Peacock argues to the baronet that the name is not on the title page, that the publisher only is to blame, that Mary is solitary and cannot reasonably be prevented from employing herself as taste and talent dictate in hope of bettering her condition. This might be, but "the name was the matter; it annoyed Sir Timothy."

There is a solace to authorship in June, when *Frankenstein,* now called *The Monster and the Magician,* is produced in Paris to a crowded house and rapturous applause. Mr. T. P. Cooke's "exertions" are again approved, the play continues to draw full houses, and, says the Paris correspondent of the *Literary Gazette,* "will restore the shattered finances of the Théatre de la Porte St. Martin." (It is unfortunate that its author's finances are not restored by it.) Leigh Hunt has struggled through an article on Shelley, for which Mary both

[5] *Two Hundred and Nine Days* (Hunt and Clarke, 1827). Trelawny commented on it to Mary (November 14, 1828): "Hogg's book is witty, clever, and amusing, but I think the nature of the animal is to be seen in it. It savours occasionally of the stye, the wash, and the grunt; it requires strong digestive powers, and a not over fastidious palate."

F

caresses and cudgels him, nursing some complicated sense of slight. The soreness is as much on Hunt's side: the *Westminster Review* has already rejected his paper as inaccurate on the authority of Peacock. These details Hunt has learned from Walter Coulson, who reports that Mary has accepted Peacock's judgment. No wonder the matter is awkward! She now corrects Hunt's statements (perhaps with Peacock's backing): Harriet had two hundred pounds a year, not half of Shelley's income—and she asks him to omit Claire and Edward's ashes from his narrative. For herself, she basks in the sun reading Virgil and Lord Shaftesbury; busier evidently than the superannuated Lamb, who, a gentleman at large, she relates, confines himself to a view of the New River, closed by houses. Maria Gisborne's long-nosed husband thrusts that organ momentarily into this narrative by an astonishing statement about the poet himself: "I asked Shelley," he tells B. R. Haydon on October 23, 1825, "if he did not think he might have done more if he had acted otherwise with his talents?" And that ardent reformer is supposed to have answered, "Certainly; he had made a mistake."[6]

Trelawny, the wild man in Greece, stammers out blurred sentiment between dashes, to each of the Pisan women in succession. To Mary, "If you love me,—*write*—write—write, for my heart yearns after you." To Jane a sort of roundel or recurring triolet: "I sadden and mourn amidst the wild confusion of my restless and active life amidst camps and battles. . . . there is now but three of us left—three are gone—we are held here by ties we cannot sunder—we must play our parts—fulfill our destiny—and then hope to rejoin them—nothing more—there are but three of us—and we should have remained together—for we are united by many ties—but alas who can control his fate?—we must play our parts." To Claire: "My heart is filled—at this period—with the same tenderness and deep affection—which filled it to bursting at our melancholy parting on the banks of the Arno—what can I say more?—indeed dear Claire I feel too much to say much." But he only ceased to say much in the autumn of 1825 when he was hit by two musket balls from a would-be assassin while defending the cavern fortress of Odysseus on Mount Parnassus. Then he sends Mary a short letter without dashes, only acquiring terseness

---

[6] *Benjamin Robert Haydon: Correspondence and Table-Talk,* ed. by F. W. Haydon (London, 1876, 2 vols.), II.

when his writing arm is "unfit for service." Claire bewails to Jane from Moscow: "Shall I ever see you and Mary in Italy again? My melancholy writes a 'no' to that! I am now going to the country, where I shall see nothing but marsh and heath, and where the circle of life grows ever lower at every step, and my fearful heart becomes as waste and desert as the wide common stretching all around me." Soon her "story" follows her to Moscow, and the friendly professor at the university, horrified at this germ from the Freethinkers' den, forbids her to educate the child of a rich family, for "God knows, he says, what Godwinish principles she might not instil." An Englishwoman has committed suicide rather than be a governess again; Claire contemplates the same course, despite her cultivated and intelligent German friend Hermann, with whom, however, she is not in love.[7] "Misery is the universal malady."

And one more mourner—the worse than widowed Contessa Guiccioli—writes from Rome to Mary: "*Io mi trovo sempre qui in Roma, in sufficiente stato di salute—senza desideri—senza speranza—ma abbastanza tranquillo d'animo. Ah perche non ci ha dato il Cielo la facoltà di dimenticare? ... Come contentarmi di vivere in un arido deserto dopo si sono conosciute le delizie del paradiso?*"[8] (Hogg had written to Jane, on Byron's death, "Why did he leave all his money to his silly sister, and nothing to the poor Countess, who, tho' she tore his night shirts and had thick ankles, was still a human being?") She has visited Shelley's tomb; so, too, has Hogg, who stands with his hat in his hand and some tears in his eyes, for Jane and the *London Magazine*. He had also visited the Contessa, who cross-questioned him too sharply for his comfort about Jane's matrimonial affairs. As she was "in the same situation," he nearly confided the truth, but "thought it more prudent to dissemble."[9]

A further misfortune, which no one appears to mourn more than Sir Timothy, occurs when Harriet's son Charles dies of consumption in September, 1826. He has been nursed at Field Place by his aunts

---

7 "What you [Jane] felt for Shelley I feel for him." But whether in spite of, or because of, this assertion, Jane later suspects she is in love.

8 "I am still here in Rome, fairly healthy—without desires—without hope—but peaceful enough in my mind. Ah, why did Heaven not give us the faculty of forgetfulness? ... How can I be content to live in an arid desert after having known the delights of paradise?"

9 *After Shelley: The Letters of Thomas Jefferson Hogg to Jane Williams*, ed. by Sylva Norman (London, 1934).

and grandmother, Sir Timothy anxiously keeping Whitton warned of danger and writing at last of "the death of poor dear little Charles without a struggle." Mary waits until the end of the month to record it, noting that "Percy is now Shelley's only son" (i.e., his heir). In October she performs an act of deferred generosity to Leigh Hunt, making herself his debtor for £2,000, the legacy Shelley had intended to leave him on rewriting his will.

The following summer (1827) she is again in torment: no sooner has Jane disappointed the disciples of Grief by settling down to live with Jefferson, than her unspiritual nature betrays itself in backbiting and conceit. It is that same old trouble about Mary's unfitness and her own preferment in the poet's household, which had almost wrecked friendship with Hunt in the Albaro days. Evidently Mary had not appreciated Jane's mischief-making, for the new "treachery" stirs her into "horror and despair." She feels the need of advice in her calamity. Even as it explodes, the sound of a singing voice that is "new and strange and beautiful" is in her ears; but alas, its warm and understanding owner has left town. So Mary keeps her bursting heart in fetters for seven whole months, until Tom Moore returns.

⊰⊱ III ⊰⊱

Moore had in June and July of this year been using Mary, as remorselessly as she had herself used John Howard Payne. Like the psychoanalyst who badgers his patient to remember, he importuned her for recollections of the "burnt materials" which he had sold without reading. She was deplorably amenable: "Mrs. S. disposed to give me every assistance in my 'Life of Byron'; promised to write out her recollections of the Memoirs."—"Seems to have known Byron thoroughly, and always winds up her account of his bad traits with 'but still he was very nice.' "—"She spoke of Byron's singing one of my melodies."—"Gave me, written down, her recollections of the 'Memoirs.' Told me all the circumstances of poor Shelley's death. Showed me a very clever letter of Lord Byron's to her on the subject of Hunt."—"Breakfasted with Mrs. Shelley. Mentioned the Grand Duke of Tuscany and his family walking past Byron's house at Pisa to get a glimpse of him." So runs the journal of Tom Moore; and in the following month comes the result of his peaceful penetration: "Received while at Benett's, two packets of Mrs. Shelley's communications relative to Lord Byron, which promise to be most useful to me: had to pay 8*s*. 6*d*. for their overweight." They were cheap at the money. But Mary thought herself well rewarded and singularly honored, as a glance at her journal shows:

> Moore breakfasted with me on Sunday. We talked of past times —of Shelley and Lord Byron. He was very agreeable, and I never felt myself so perfectly at my ease with anyone. I do not know why this is, he seems to understand and to like me. This is a new and unexpected pleasure. I have been so long exiled from the style of society in which I spent the better part of my life; it is an evanescent pleasure, but I will enjoy it while I can.

It is no unique perversity in Mary to have been prouder of the friend who flattered her for his own ends than of the admirer who rejoiced in selfless service. And after all, Mary did get some reward for her abetting of Moore's labors, though it came through his publisher, and not unasked. John Murray had considered buying the copyright of some of Shelley's poems. His application to Sir Timothy had been passed on to Mary, who wrote in January, 1827, to say the copyrights were hers to negotiate.[10] No more was done, but this communication, together with Moore's projected "Life," led her to apply to Murray in February, 1828, for a loan of one hundred pounds. To do Moore justice, he deemed her information worth fifty pounds from his own pocket, but was quick to thank John Murray for advancing the whole of it, assuring him that yet more letters of Shelley to Lord Byron might be drawn out of her. Mary, hoping to repay her advance as an author pays, attempted to interest Murray in her next novel (evidently *Perkin Warbeck,* for which Godwin was busy supplying historical information). The book when finished was declined, leaving Mary anxious to liquidate a debt which the publisher assured her was fully canceled by her services to Mr. Moore. Demurring, she wrote on November 12, 1829, ". . . besides, it would make me break a

---

10 It was not the only trouble Sir Timothy passed on. The question of an annuity for Percy so exhausted him that he wrote hopefully to Whitton on April 1, 1827, "Having completely conquered Gout etc without the aid of medical advisers, you will as readily conquer the case upon the like principle, Patience and well doing." (Ingpen, *Shelley in England*.)

vow I made, never to make money of my acquaintance with Lord Byron. His ghost would certainly come and taunt me if I did."

To return to 1828, Moore came back to town in February, and besides apologizing to John Murray for helping others "to draw blood" from him, listened to Mary's woe about the quarrel. He counseled her to have it out with Jane. Accusations, penitence, and tears were the result. While Mary's mind was on the subject, she thought, as she had often thought before, that she would never know peace again. In point of fact, as with Shelley and Hogg after the Harriet episode in Edinburgh, the two continued friendly, if less trusting than before. There was much to soften the blow: Jane was a housewife and had Hogg's meals to cook (a matter requiring great attention); Mary's pride was being duly nourished, during that autumn of waiting, by the acquisition of an admiring correspondent from America.

IV

This time it was a social reformer, who considered Mrs. Shelley's parentage and connection sufficient guarantee of a rebellious spirit. Frances Wright, a Scotswoman, born a few years before Mary, had been led by ideals of liberty and socialism to found a Negro settlement in Tennessee with the idea of solving the slavery question. Down the Mississippi, at Nashoba near Memphis, Miss Wright had established her settlement—a clearing in dense forest—where the Negroes were to be educated as white men, that is, with every respect for their potential intelligence. Unfortunately she made the idealist's common error of overestimating the material she worked with: the slaves showed every sign of remaining slavish, with the difference that they did no work. Anxiety produced brain fever in Miss Wright, who was restored by a sea voyage and found herself in Paris, whence she wrote to Mary introducing herself, her scheme for liberty and equality, and the name of her co-worker Robert Dale Owen, son of Robert Owen, the Socialist of Lanark.

Ten years her junior, Robert Dale Owen was connected through his father with a similar idealistic effort at New Harmony, Illinois. This community had already broken down in the spring of 1827, upon which Owen, going to Nashoba, had found both the settlement and Miss Wright's health in a poor state. They had traveled to Europe together, Frances, despite her illness, confident about the "congenial associates" they were bound to find. Her idea had been to collect kindred spirits from amongst the cultured souls in England and America, who would live at Nashoba in separate dwellings, contributing to a common fund and enjoying, in those backwoods, "lettered leisure." She hoped, undoubtedly, to collect Mary Shelley, whom she had pictured as an ardent radical reformer, fighting for principle against principle, at war with an apathetic world. It is just as well for the society-loving and depressed widow of Shelley that she never saw Nashoba, which even Shelley the hermit would have found too bleak. One Englishwoman saw it, led by its founder's glowing accounts to contemplate a long stay there with her children. Mrs. Trollope, who traveled to America with Miss Wright that winter, was appalled by what she found. "Desolation!" she described it, and published a faithful picture of gaunt, bare trees flanking a gloomy rectangular clearing edged by wooden huts and palisades.[11]

Its creator seemed blinded by her own vision to the wildness and discomfort she was offering her congenial spirits. An idea, once formed, obsessed her. At a time when women were inclined to shelter behind their femininity, Miss Wright was challengingly masculine, and expected those women she singled out for their interest to be masculine too. Robert Dale Owen brings out this hardness in describing her:

> . . . a tall commanding figure, somewhat slender and graceful, though the shoulders were a little bit too high; a face the outline of which, in profile, though delicately chiselled, was masculine rather than feminine, like that of an Antinous, or perhaps more nearly typifying Mercury; the forehead broad but not high; the short chestnut hair curling naturally all over a classic head; the large, blue eyes, not soft, but clear and earnest.

Owen, himself susceptible to more melting qualities, found much to admire in Frances, but nothing—emphatically nothing—to love. Accepting her composite theoretical portrait of Mary Shelley, he was to be agreeably surprised. We may take it that Frances herself would

11 See *Domestic Manners of the Americans* (1832).

have been surprised, had her opinion not been proof against event. In her second letter she was already overwhelming Mary with heartfelt friendship, and misled by the latter's customary bewailings, claimed her voraciously as a "bosom intimate." "You are the daughter of your mother." ("I am afraid you are a Wollstonecraft," Godwin was writing at the same period, referring only to her low spirits.) Mary was wandering that autumn—to Southend, Brighton, Arundel, even a brief trip to the Continent—but at last they met. "I found her very different from my preconceptions," Owen wrote later, drawing a careful and affectionate portrait, tinted with regret:

> Genial, gentle, sympathetic, thoughtful and matured in opinion beyond her years, for she was then but twenty-nine; essentially liberal in politics, ethics, and theology, indeed, yet devoid alike of stiff prejudice against the old or ill-considered prepossession in favour of the new; and, above all, womanly, in the best sense, in every sentiment and instinct; she impressed me also as a person with warm social feelings, dependent for happiness on loving encouragement, needing a guiding and sustaining hand.
>
> I felt all this, rather than reasoned it out, during our all too brief acquaintance; and few women have ever attracted me so much in so short a time. Had I remained in London I am sure we should have been dear friends. She wrote me several charming letters to America.
>
> In person, she was of middle height and graceful figure. Her face, though not regularly beautiful, was comely and spiritual, of winning expression, and with a look of inborn refinement as well as culture. It had a touch of sadness when at rest; yet when it woke up in animated conversation, one could see that underneath there was bright, cheerful, even playful nature, at variance, I thought, with depressing circumstances and isolated position.
>
> Looking back on those days, I feel assured that if fate had thrown Mary Shelley and myself together at that period of my life, instead of bringing me into contact with Frances Wright, the influence would have been much more salutary. I required to be restrained, not urged; needed not the spur, but the guiding rein.[12]

Owen the social worker is, one feels, within an ace of committing himself to a worship devout as that of Payne the dramatist or Edward

[12] Robert Dale Owen, *Threading My Way* (London, 1874).

Holmes, the musical friend of Keats. He was so far fascinated as to assert boldly that if the wrongheaded Shelley had lived on, "cherished and piloted by his noble wife," he might have borne comparison with the best poets of the century, Goethe and Byron not excluded!

Mary, aware of her own need of piloting, pretended to no sociological eagerness in the face of Fanny's enthusiasm. Some passages written in her journal eleven years later recall the trend of her talks with Owen. She had made it clear that she was a person of no strong opinions or argumentative powers, being inclined to see both sides and so remain inactive. To sociology she preferred society, believing that "living intercourse is the vital heat." Accused of worldliness and lukewarmness, she had yet befriended oppressed women and "supported victims to the social system." But Fanny Wright protested her need of friends as well as principles, gathered Mary hurriedly to her reforming heart, and when she and Owen sailed for America in November, gazed long from the boat on her "dear love's" little back, until it was lost sight of amongst the shipping.

Let us follow Miss Wright to the West for a moment. After conducting Mrs. Trollope to the Nashoba settlement and seeing her involuntary recoil, the rebel herself began soon to despair of Negroes and the wilderness. Her true vocation was among crowds, speaking in a public hall where, as Mrs. Trollope was herself to note in Cincinnati, her "extraordinary gift of eloquence, her almost unequalled command of words, and the wonderful power of her rich and thrilling voice" attracted multitudes, if not to her darling doctrines, at least to her startling personality. She toured America and then Europe as a public orator, appearing sometimes amid a bodyguard of Quaker ladies, her own white-clad figure impressive as a Greek statue. Her activities led to the formation of Fanny Wright societies, upholding women's emancipation and female suffrage. She married, perhaps surprisingly, in 1828, a French reformer, W. Phiquebal-D'Arusmont, but separated from him, perhaps less surprisingly.[13] She outlived Mary Shelley barely two years, dying on December 14, 1852.

Oddly enough, in the same year that Frances married a Frenchman, Mary when in Paris found a youthful admirer in Prosper

[13] By D'Arusmont, Frances had a daughter born in Paris in 1832, named Sylva; "delightful, precocious," but in the end hostile to her mother. Through Mary the family became friends with the de Boinvilles at Clichy. (See A. J. G. Perkins and T. Wolfson, *Frances Wright, Free Enquirer* [London and New York, 1939].)

Mérimée. They appear to have exchanged letters over a longish period, and a case has been made for Mérimée's—also—having fallen in love, after Mary had, perhaps, translated some pieces from his early work *La Guzla*. The relevant letter from Mary bears neither signature, date, nor name of the addressee who has been assumed as Mérimée on no better evidence than his sending an autograph of hers to a collector friend. The assumption is that Mérimée had made something near to a proposal in a letter which Mary now returned to him *"parce que je ne suis pas coquette. . . . Je ne voudrais pas garder l'expression des sentiments dont vous pourriez vous repentir après—ni le temoignage de ce que vous paraitra (il se peut) en réfléchissant, une faiblesse."* She assures him of her friendship if he wishes and shows himself worthy of it.

Mérimée, born six years after Mary and an enthusiast for the Romantic Movement, may have been dazzled by Shelley's widow; Mary may have felt maternal. But the incident is all too doubtfully authenticated to yield more than an imaginary conversation or a faint surmise.[14]

❧ v ☙

Continuing our rapid survey of the Pisan circle, we find the untamable Trelawny, while mourning the downfall of Greece and the death of Odysseus, giving rise to a scandal which has been fiercely denied and maliciously upheld in later years. When all is sorted out, malice must win; it seems impossible to clear him, and improbable that he was anxious to be cleared. A tale of monstrosity could hardly hurt a man who posed as a savage elemental, tortured like the lion into domestic intercourse with "forked animals." In April, 1824, Trelawny had married (as his second or possibly third wife) Tersitza Kamenov, the sister of Odysseus. By her he had a daughter named Zella.[15] But the

---

[14] See Dennis M. Healy on "Mary Shelley and Prosper Mérimée," *Modern Language Review*, Vol. XXXVI (July, 1941). The letters are included in F. L. Jones's collected edition (*The Letters of Mary W. Shelley* [Norman, Okla., 1944, 2 vols.]).

[15] The name seems to be a favorite among nomads; witness the gipsy chief in *Maria Marten*, who vowed vengeance on the villainous William Corder for seducing his daughter Zella. Trelawny's daughter was, of course, named after the Arab Zela of his *Younger Son*—if she, indeed, was more than a fiction.

marriage was of short duration. In October, 1827, Trelawny wrote to Mary Shelley that he had been detained in those Ionian islands for the last ten months by a "villainous law-suit." Tersitza had obtained a separation from him and, urged, it would seem, by a scheming family, stood out to get all the money she could from her former husband. She became entitled to an alimony of twenty-five dollars a month and went to live in a convent, where she gave birth to another child of Trelawny's, that died in a few months. So far, so good. It was not until 1892, when Sharp's *Life and Letters of Joseph Severn* was published, that a fumbling version of the terrible "box" story was let loose. It was contained in a letter of J. G. Cooke, who was answering, to the best of his ability, a request for gossip. "Did I ever tell you a wonderful story . . . ?" It was this: the Odysseus family, begging Trelawny to send back the child he had taken with him out of Greece, were told to apply to the Custom House at Zante. Here an offensive-smelling box was delivered to them which, when opened, was found to contain a child's body, dead some weeks. The infant having died, Trelawny was said to have chosen this savage way of ridding himself of the Odysseus circle.

The "wonderful story" appeared easy to refute by the simple proof that the child in question, assumed to be Zella, lived on to the age of eighty-one.[16] Even Trelawny's first biographer was compelled to recognize the existence of a second infant, the victim of these posthumous adventures. This child (he has it from the great-grandson of Trelawny) was indeed born in the convent, dispatched in a *basket* (airier variation) to its father, who at once returned the unusual postal packet, deeming, in unpiratical fashion, that the place for a new-born babe was with its mother. The strange game of bat and ball continuing, the unfortunate child was again volleyed—by the Mother Superior—at Trelawny, who, on opening the basket, box, or parcel, not surprisingly found the contents dead. It is considered "extremely probable" that he sent the corpse back to the convent, being on this showing a man provoked. The truth looks dark when a hero's great-grandson can vindicate his ancestor in no sweeter terms. And earlier confirmations are to hand: In November, 1827, a Mr. H. Robinson of Zante had written to the Deputy Collector of Customs at Corfu to

16 H. Buxton Forman, in his preface to Trelawny's *Letters* (London and New York, 1910), repudiates the "hideous calumny" on this argument alone.

introduce Trelawny—"a good fellow, though a singular one." A week later he was answering the Deputy Collector's inquiries about this very box story, by telling him "the real one." It was this (if Mr. H. Robinson is trustworthy): "During the time his wife was in the convent she was delivered of a daughter, whom she sent as soon as born to Trelawny. He put it out to nurse; it died, and he as a punishment for the mother's unfeeling conduct sent the dead body to the Castle monastery, where she was, in a box with her things and a message from him. The wife knew not what was in the box, and refused to open it, and there it lay until putrid. An examination took place with all the fuss which the Courts make about *suspicione d'infanticidio,* and ended by T. being fined ten dollars for improperly removing a dead body."[17]

Finally, a letter exists, written by Tersitza Trelawny herself in July, 1829, to the Lord High Commissioner asking permission to leave the convent and Zante, and complaining of her former husband's behavior. "The nature of the said Signor Trelawny is not unknown, and at the last, it is perhaps within Y.E.'s recollection that he brought grief to my very eyes by sending me while in the convent, with cunning and brutality, the dead body of my daughter and his."[18] There is no evading it. Nor does the story match badly with the cause of Tersitza's divorce, as related by the above-mentioned great-grandson to H. J. Massingham. Tersitza, proud of her lovely red-gold hair, was commanded by Trelawny to wear only national dress. Finding her giving a party clad in a Paris creation, he carried out a threat of revenge by cutting her tresses off, close to her head, with a dagger. The shorn Tersitza repaid his gallantry by leaving him next day and applying for a divorce.[19]

Fresh from such performances as these, the grave-digger and exhibitionist appeared in England in June, 1828, still, by letter, professing warm and exclusive love to both Mary Shelley and Claire Clairmont. Jane Williams he despaired of, on account of her "degrading connection . . . with a *hog*. . . . I cannot mingle up my feelings of

[17] "Pirate Trelawny," by T. C. Down, in *Nineteenth Century,* May, 1907.

[18] *Ibid.* Sir Harold Nicolson claims to have confirmed the tale through a different channel. See *Byron: The Last Journey* (London, 1924).

[19] Since the above was written, R. Glynn Grylls's new biography, *Trelawny* (London, 1950), has, while indulging the utmost sympathy for its hero, served to confirm these points, observing only that Tersitza's petition was unnecessary.

affection with coarse and gross animals." To Mary: "I love you sincerely, no one better"; to Claire: "I am unchanged, dear—at least in heart"; and at the same time there was a "sweet Alethea," faded and drooping, "her lips pale as marble, and her eyes dim with the shadows of death."[20] Trelawny went to Cornwall to look up his relatives (for whom he usually showed an adventurer's contempt), and delayed seeing Mary till late in the autumn.

Mary was not looking at her best. She was in fact never to look at her best again, for going to Paris that April to visit her friend Julia Robinson, she had at once developed smallpox, afterwards regaining buoyant health, though "a monster to look at." She hardly remained a monster, but her clear coloring was lost. To do her justice, this was a most bravely borne misfortune, hardly dwelt on even in the journal. She was more chagrined by the narrowness of her circle. Apart from Tom Moore's angel visits, whom did she see? "Lord Dillon, G. Paul, the Robinsons, voilà tout." Of these, Lord Dillon of Ditchley, author of a tremendously long poem, *Eccelino,* which was sent for Mary's approbation, must have gratified her pride, for he confessed she puzzled him; instead of an eccentric and indiscreet Sibyl, a sexless social reformer, he found, as Robert Dale Owen had, a creature of charming femininity, and told her so. Dillon was tall, fine, and handsome, according to a female contemporary. He was married. "G. Paul" was the son of Sir John Paul, the banker, and Mary was friendly with him and his wife. As for the Robinsons, they are notable, two years later, for having furnished a tiny scandal to the hopeful Sir Timothy.

The old baronet was getting thoroughly tired of the importuning Mary, who, when all financial settlements had been concluded, broke out again for an increased allowance because the wretched Percy Florence was to be sent to school. Sir Timothy wrote to Whitton on January 18, 1829, "I must entreat to leave this very troublesome woman to your judgment in respect to Finance. . . . What a wonderful assembly of animals I have to deal with." Knowing how he disliked her letters, her demands, and the whole subject, Whitton would have been glad enough to see him rid of it. Mary, staying with the Robinsons at Park Cottage, Paddington, wrote a letter to Whitton from that

---

[20] H. Buxton Forman, who might have helped us with Alethea's identity, cuts her out, as one of the numerous deterrents to a noble presentment of his hero. One cannot help regretting the number of illuminating facts and letters he suppressed.

address on September 1, 1830. The next move, whether genuine or ingenious, was a letter to Sir Timothy from Whitton, saying that a person had come into his room and told him that "Mrs. Bysshe Shelley had married a person named Robinson." Whitton, on inquiry, managed to get the impression that she had gone to live at this "person's" house. Sir Timothy himself, having been visited by Mary's friend Mrs. G. Paul, and given her a sovereign for Percy, was digesting a prim little letter from this young man, "artfully dictated," in his grandfather's opinion.[21] The death of Charles—no doubt in Sir Tim's eyes the only legitimate son—was supposed to have pained him into an extra aversion to Percy. It would be good news if Mary had gotten herself married (curious as it was that they should choose a quarter where the wind had never sat). Whitton asked straight out, in making the next payment. Mary replied that she was not married, and the flutter ended. There was to be no riddance of the tiresome dependent on the one hand, of the inheritance-blocking autocrat on the other. Claire Clairmont, who had also visited England this winter, concluded that his death was "an horizon which retreats as one advances." Trelawny, writing in March, 1829, hoped piously that the cold winter would "remove that old devil Sir Tim."

◦{ VI }◦

By that date Trelawny had removed himself as far as Florence, at which safe distance from her protests he broke the news to Mary that he too meant to join the worms that feed on scandal. The pirate, no doubt moved by the spectacle of remunerative scribbling he had seen in England, put aside the spade and dagger to take up the pen. Two obvious subjects were before him: first, himself; secondly, looking around that attractive obstacle, his relations with the poets in Italy, He chose both. The first was to be spurred on and criticized by Walter Savage Landor and Keats's friend Charles Armitage Brown, who were both on the spot to do it. The second—the life and *moral character* of Shelley, as he described it—was to depend on Mary's approval. Like Medwin, he began by flattery. She was the one to write it, but if she would not, then Trelawny, out of the great love he bore for

[21] Ingpen, *Shelley in England.*

Shelley and herself, would do his best to exhibit a Shelley-as-Trelawny-sees-him to the world. "Do you approve of this? . . . Will you give me documents, will you write anecdotes? or—be explicit on this, dear—give me your opinion, if you in the least dislike it, say so, and there is an end of it."

Mary was explicit. She disliked it thoroughly; not so much, it appears, through fear of caricature, as through fear of publicity for her shrinking self. "Could you write my husband's life without naming me it were something—but even then I should be terrified at the rousing the slumbering voice of the public. . . . You know me—or you do not, in which case I will tell you what I am—a silly goose—who, far from wishing to stand forward to assert myself in any way, now that I am alone in the world, have but the desire to wrap night and the obscurity of insignificance around me. . . . Shelley's life must be written—I hope one day to do it myself, but it must not be published now.—There are too many concerned to speak against him—it is still too sore a subject—"

This made Trelawny angry. If he had ever really meant to subject his plan to Mary's approval, he had long since buried that modesty under the conviction that he was indeed the man to save Shelley from "such mercenary literary vagabonds as Medwin, Moore and a host of others." She was being obstructive and unfair, and he arraigned her vehemently for supporting the literary vagabonds in preference to him. Mary wrote back (by this time it was December) objecting that Hunt had already slurred over the truth in relating the events of Shelley's life, the truth indeed being "hardly for the rude cold world to handle." Then why write fiction? "As to giving Moore materials for Lord Byron's life, I thought—I think—I did right. I think I have achieved a great good by it. . . . Did I uphold Medwin? I thought that I had always disliked him. I am sure I thought him a great annoyance, and he was always borrowing crowns which he never meant to pay and we could ill spare. He was Jane's friend more than any one's . . . ."

Between these parading, coy, and envious egotists, who is to hope for a clear vision of Shelley? Undoubtedly "there are too many concerned"—about their own poor selves. And this must excuse an apparent neglect of the central spirit in these present chapters of his after-history. They will have done no harm if they suggest how muddy and disturbed were the waters that drowned him, on account of the floundering efforts of the survivors to remain afloat.

Of the two immediate wranglers, Mary must after all claim our better sympathy. Hers was a wrecked, argumentative nature that bitterly knew its own faults and its own weakness in failing to conquer them. On the evidence of her more impersonal writings, she had been credited, by some admirers, with a "masculine" mind. In her complete make-up, she was as feminine as Lord Dillon and Robert Dale Owen had found her; but among the twistings of despair and vanity that governed her actions was a trace of something firm and straight and clearly independent. More than an ideal, it was a frustrated possession, and the glimpse of it, present but unworkable, threw up her intricate behavior into mocking relief, dooming her to an exquisite mental anguish on a plane inconceivable to Trelawny's cruder notions. For the most part in this chronicle we are watching Mary Shelley in her personal relationships, where her most vulnerable points are dragged into the foreground. But a writer, even of three-volume novels for an undiscriminating public, has a corner of her mind reserved from the ruthless battering of immediacy, a corner to which she can retreat, arranging its thoughts, perceptions, and philosophy into battle order without the dread of alarm and sudden invasion. Of Mary as an authoress I have written elsewhere,[22] and shall only add here a reminder that the authoress, for all her prolific and tedious redundancy, was modest, hard working, and given to relieving tortured feelings by repeated attempts to brighten her turgid narratives with figures copied (however imperfectly) from the ever beloved and wholly admired Shelley.

[22] "Mary Shelley, Novelist and Dramatist," in *On Shelley,* by Edmund Blunden, G. R. de Beer, and Sylva Norman (Oxford, 1938).

CHAPTER V

A Rally of Youth

-≪{ 1 }≫-

IT IS TIME to return to Shelley's poetry and person, taking a clear look at the development of their popularity as fostered by old friends and independent admirers. We have as yet seen little external evidence that the poet was anything but a temporary if fierce goad to controversy. Had that really been so, he would be fading at the very period we now reach, some six years after his death. Instead, the years 1828 to 1833 contain an outburst of interest, represented by a crop of literature which shows that the sensitive plant had been quietly taking root.

In 1828, Walter Savage Landor published Volume III of his *Imaginary Conversations*. The most personal of these—a talk in Florence between an English visitor, a Florentine, and Landor himself—brings in that writer's feelings about Shelley, whom he, though living in Italy, had never met. The reason becomes apparent here. As this section of the *Conversations* was cut out of all later editions, I transcribe the entire passage:

> Innocent and careless as a boy, he possessed all the delicate feelings of a gentleman, all the discrimination of a scholar, and united, in just degrees, the ardour of the poet with the patience and forbearance of the philosopher. His generosity and charity went far beyond those of any man (I believe) at present in existence. He was never known to speak evil of an enemy, unless that enemy had done some grievous injustice to another; and he divided his income of only one thousand pounds, with the fallen and afflicted. This is the man against whom such clamours have been raised by the religious à la mode, and by those who live and lap under their tables: this is the man whom, from one false story about his former wife, I refused to visit at Pisa. I blush in anguish at my prejudice and injustice, and ought hardly to feel it as a blessing or a consolation, that I regret him

less than I should have done if I had known him personally. As to
what remains of him now life is over, he occupies the third place
among the poets of our present age ... no humble station ... for no
other age since that of Sophocles has produced on the whole earth
so many of such merit ... and is incomparably the most elegant,
graceful, and harmonious of prose-writers.

A further testimony to Shelley's character is put into the mouth of
the English visitor, who is discussing Byron's astonishment that
Shelley should have risked his life in trying to save him from the
sword of the dragoon:[1]

> The answer was ... what Shelley did then, he would do again, and
> always. There is not a human creature, not even the most hostile,
> that he would hesitate to protect from injury, at the imminent
> hazard of life. And yet life, which he would throw forward so
> unguardedly, is somewhat more with him than with others: it is
> full of hopes and aspirations, it is teeming with warm feelings, it
> is rich and overrun with its own native simple enjoyments. In him
> every thing that ever gave pleasure, gives it still, with the same
> freshness, the same exuberance, the same earnestness to communi-
> cate and share it.

Such was Landor's estimate of Shelley.

We may note next that, apart from reaching literary men in
Florence, his fame has crossed the channel more publicly.[2] In 1827
there had appeared in England a collection published in Paris by
Galignani and a number of other names, of specimens of *The Living
Poets of England*. Volume II includes Shelley (living in poetry though
not in person). A careful memoir, signed A.P. (Amédée Pichot), is
followed by selections from *Alastor, The Revolt of Islam, Rosalind
and Helen, Lines Written Among the Euganean Hills,* the *Hymn to
Intellectual Beauty,* and a few complete poems. Two years later, cul-

---

[1] The incident is, in fact, inaccurately referred to, for Byron had ridden safely through the
gate of Pisa before the dragoon dealt his blows at Shelley and Captain Hay who were following.
(See *Journal* of E. E. Williams and article by Janet Ross in *Nineteenth Century,* November,
1891; also C. L. Cline, *Shelley, Byron, and Their Pisan Circle.*)

[2] His fame as a translator is still in the doldrums. Crabb Robinson, in a letter to Goethe,
rates him gently for omitting to note "the splendid fragments of Faust by Shelley, Lord
Byron's friend, a man of unquestionable genius, the perverse misdirections of whose powers
and early death are alike lamentable."

tured English speakers in France were to be given the whole for which these fragments had prepared them: in 1829 appeared the Galignani edition, in one volume, of the *Poetical Works of Coleridge, Shelley, and Keats*.[3] It seems to us a considerable achievement to have so soon assembled the main bulk of these poets' works; but the editors claim even more for the production; counting it "infinitely more perfect" than any of the editions published in London, "as they have been favoured, from private sources, with many original productions of these esteemed writers, which are now for the first time given to the public," besides items collected from periodicals. Naturally, these editions of the English poets were mainly prepared by Londoners. Cyrus Redding, a friend of Galignani, was applied to for a sketch of Shelley's life. Beginning the task with some idea of publishing new material, he wrote to Horace Smith asking for letters of Shelley to reproduce. Smith, however, answered that those letters he had were "of too confidential and hazardous a nature to be copper-plated." Several are requests for loans to himself and Godwin; some make private mention of Byron, Moore, and Hunt, that it might not be right to promulgate; and almost all are full of such heterodox notions as might horrify many good folks who might happen to see them. He advised Redding to apply, if he wanted "a mere fac-simile," to Mrs. Shelley or Mr. Peacock.[4]

To Mrs. Shelley, Redding accordingly applied, not for letters, but for an engraving of the poet, of which none existed, thanks to that deplorable dearth of portraits. He knew she had the "best and only resemblance," but unfinished—that is to say, the Curran portrait, as to whose merits Mary by now cherished no illusions. She wrote back warning him of its quality and suggesting that a first-rate engraver might yet make a good print of it. Redding took the hint, and she was persuaded to let P. R. Davis copy the portrait, to replace a "miserable representation" threatened by Galignani. "At any rate," she wrote, "it will be better than a likeness after the imagination of a Frenchman—that is the drollest, stupidest idea ever man, intent on selling an edition, hit upon."[5] An engraving was made from the draw-

---

[3] "Galignani is going to publish the poetical works of Coleridge, Shelley, and Keats in one large volume—a sort of 'Atheism made easy,' I conclude, for the pious public."—William Donne to R. C. Trench, December, 1829.

[4] Cyrus Redding, *Fifty Years' Recollections, Literary and Personal* (1858, 2 vols.), II.

[5] *Ibid.*

ing by J. T. Wedgwood; Shelley's features being thus published for the first time.[6] As for the memoir, Redding gave up the idea of an original production, and compiled his sketch from Mary Shelley's preface to the *Posthumous Poems,* coupled with liberal quotations and adaptations from an important work that had appeared in the previous year.

The work in question was Leigh Hunt's *Lord Byron and Some of His Contemporaries.* Written in haste to fulfill a promise to Colburn, it was an outlet for the author's anger against Byron, which was poured out in torrents of undisciplined prose. Resented warmly and read voraciously, the book boomed its stormy way to a kind of fame, and Shelley, playing in it the part of a contrasting angel, was heaved into general notice on Lord Byron's satanic shoulders. Visible at last from top to toe, he was seen to be attractive and not a little pitiable—for Hunt, friend and journalist, could praise dramatically. Some part at least of the Shelley myth we are tracing had its origin in these pages. The description of a saintly consumptive, subject to spasmodic pains, is surely an effort to call up sympathy from the outset. The insistence on those large and animated eyes, "with a dash of wildness in them," and on the aspect of a heavenly visitant have caused more mischief among the later skeptics than Hunt could have foreseen. Some of the prettier Shelley legends are launched: how the poet, ignoring the society ladies at a ball, chose for his dancing partner a woman of lost virtue—whose gay seducer was no doubt piloting a duchess. And how this Good Samaritan rescued a prostrate woman in Hampstead, when none of the proud dwellers would take her in. One of Trelawny's accounts of the cremation is presented, abridged from the original document sent by Trelawny to Hunt, and now in the British Museum.[7] The poet's "sympathy with the whole universe" becomes curiously delimited in the following passage, which was indeed addressed to the fair sex among readers:

We have heard of ladies falling in love with Lord Byron, upon the strength of *Don Juan.* These must be ladies in towns. If ever a more

[6] Mr. Andrew Boyle writes that, doubtless because of these difficulties, the first copies were issued without portraits. They contained a slip to say that an engraving of the three authors would be ready by January 15, when it would be delivered in exchange for the slip.

[7] See H. J. Massingham, *The Friend of Shelley, A Memoir of E. J. Trelawny* (London, 1930).

sequestered heroine could become enamoured of a poet out of the mere force of sentiment, or at least desire to give him exceeding comfort and consolation, it would be such a poet as Mr. Shelley. The most physical part of the passion acquires, from his treatment of it, a grace and purity inexpressible.

It was Hunt's misfortune that his most sincere and friendly tributes should frequently be marred by a lapse in taste or tone. Where he would praise most fulsomely, some goblin gave his pen a twist towards the absurd. Where he intended kindliness, offense was taken, plunging the voluble author into a tangle of explanations, justifications, or apologies. Further, his effort to make Shelley loved lost greatly by his acidity to Byron. But if it did not convince, it did in a manner noise the poet's fame, and Hunt was not altogether wrong when he closed his turbulent essay with the dignified words: "The friends whom he loved may now bid his brave and gentle spirit repose; for the human beings whom he laboured for, *begin to know him.*"

❧ II ❦

They were beginning to know him in one center of emerging art and intellect: the highly serious young men of Cambridge termed or nicknamed "The Apostles" had "discovered" Shelley, and with typical undergraduate enthusiasm proceeded to cry out their find. It was coupled with a revolt against Byron worship and an admiration of Wordsworth (whose academical brother, the Master of Trinity, was not considered the cause). To the query, "Have Shelley's poems an immoral tendency?" Tennyson for one voted the answer "No." Arthur Hallam, predestined victim of the longest funeral poem, but now a prospective poet in his own right, had brought from Italy a copy of the original and only edition of *Adonais,* printed at Pisa.[8] He and his friends reprinted it at Cambridge in 1829, thus claiming to have introduced the poem into British literature.[9] In June of this year

[8] In the following year the *Adonais* was translated into Italian by L. A. Damaso Pareto, and published (unaccountably) at Geneva.

[9] Newman I. White states that the Apostles issued *Epipsychidion.* I can find no confirmation of this, and he does not mention *Adonais* in this connection. I therefore assume he is in error.

Hallam's poem *Timbuctoo,* which failed to deflect the Chancellor's prize medal from Tennyson, included a long note on the author's borrowing from "a magnificent passage in Mr. Shelley's *Alastor . . .* that wonderful Poem, which cannot long remain in its present condition of neglect but would be marvelled at in time, for its great moral idea no less than for its poetic glory."

That same year the notable campaign was made, by invitation, into the enemy's camp, where the prophet had been dishonored and neglected.[10] Three delegates from the Cambridge Union—Arthur Hallam, Richard Monckton Milnes, and Thomas Sunderland—"drove manfully through the snow" on November 26 to meet the Oxford Union in a debate on the subject moved by Mr. Wilberforce, president of the Oxford Union, that "Shelley was a greater poet than Lord Byron." Milnes was a little uncertain how he applied to Dr. Wordsworth for an *exeat:* "I have always had a dim suspicion, though probably I did not do so, that I substituted the name of Wordsworth for Shelley." The arrival took place in some style, as befitted the solemnity of the subject. A contemporary print showed Mr. W. E. Gladstone welcoming the delegates as they descended from their coach, wearing top hats and greatcoats to the ankle. That evening the Union, with packed benches, is said to have "swarmed and murmured like a hive of bees." What the Cambridge men noticed, however, was the contrast from their own noisy, shuffling assembly to "a neat little square room, with eighty or ninety young gentlemen sprucely dressed, sitting on chairs or lounging about the fireplace, . . . enough to unnerve a more confident person than myself," says Milnes.

But the lounging was a key to Oxford's attitude. They had neither studied their Shelley nor intended to, preferring to ignore the atheist in cold superiority. (Cambridge maintained that the Oxford men hadn't heard his name.) When Sir Francis Doyle had mildly opened the debate, a flood of persuasive and bold oratory from the Cambridge specialists caused a mental panic. "We cowered like birds and ran like sheep," said Cardinal Manning, who took part in it. A gentleman from Oriel, Doyle reports, began in bluff and burly ignorance to pooh-pooh Shelley, when catching sight of "that terrible antagonist"

[10] Nearly sixty years later the Oxford Union Society will be seen clinging to its hostile attitude by voting against the payment of a guinea subscription to the newly formed Shelley Society.

Milnes, he faltered—and proceeded to record his vote in Shelley's favor. Milnes himself, cunningly banking on Oxford's innocence of the text, cited the chorus of Christian women from *Hellas,* without reference to its dramatic context, as a proof of Shelley's return to Christianity. "After him," Doyle relates,

> there was silence in the Union for several minutes, and then Mr. Manning of Balliol . . . with great propriety rose. . . . The framework of his argument amounted just to this: Byron is a great poet, we have all of us read Byron; but . . . if Shelley had been a great poet, we should have read him also; but we none of us have done so. Therefore Shelley is not a great poet—*a fortiori* he is not so great a poet as Byron. *In hanc sententiam* an immense majority of the Union went *pedibus:* the debate was over, and we all of us, including Mr. Gladstone, adjourned . . . to supper.[11]

Gladstone himself, who was to learn his Shelley by heart, as relaxation, when his Parliamentary career began, took no part in the debate, but afterwards commented humorously on "the invasion of barbarians among civilized men"—or was it "of civilized men among barbarians"? Whichever we prefer, it was a victory for Shelley—his first in any general court of appeal; but even so the record stands in Byron's favor, Oxford having doubtfully "honored the visitors" by voting for the Cambridge man.

J. W. Blakesley, commenting to R. C. Trench in January, 1830, on the Apostles' action, remarks, "They gained some converts, and spread the knowledge of the poet; so that some *illuminati* of the sister university, who at first took him for Shenstone, and then for 'the man that drives the black ponies in Hyde Park,' at last went away in the belief 'that he was a man whom Lord Byron *patronized,* and who was drowned a few years ago.' "[12]

It may have been this episode that convinced an Oxford man, the following year, that he could consistently pay his respects to Shelley and sing the praise of his university. Robert Montgomery's epic poem on *Oxford: or Alma Mater* was embellished at the end with a

---

[11] F. H. Doyle, *Reminiscences* (1886).

[12] Richard Chevenix Trench, Archbishop, *Letters and Memorials* (1888). Oscar Browning, in *Memories of Sixty Years at Eton, Cambridge, and Elsewhere* (London, 1910), writes: "[Milnes] always asserted that the Oxford Union Society had never heard of Shelley, and thought that the gentleman in question must be Shenstone. But this I believe to be a calumny."

biographical summary of eminent characters connected with the University." Shelley is picked out for a long note, the author upholding the authorities for expelling the blasphemer, and opining that the poet should be read "with mixed and mournful thought." He quotes a record from "one thoroughly acquainted with Shelley's life while at college." This intimate biographer is not Hogg, but the printer Henry Slatter, who had seen some trouble over the publication of Shelley's early works and was four hundred pounds down on a transaction with Shelley over the printing of a *History of Sweden,* by one Birde, or Browne. Slatter "sat down" to give his long-promised sketch on December 18, 1833, for Montgomery's third edition. It included, of course, some "pecuniary matters" which the editor wisely cut out. Slatter related how he was asked by Sir Timothy to indulge his son in his "printing freaks"; how *Leonora* was refused for its "free notions"; how the printer endeavored to turn Shelley from his wayward opinions; and how copies of *The Necessity of Atheism* being strewn about the windows and counters of his booksellers—"unknown to them"—a Fellow of a college advised their destruction, and they were burned in a back kitchen in his presence. On the whole, the loyal Montgomery managed to present Shelley as a freakish irruption rather than a great poet, and so did no virtual damage to the Oxford attitude.[13]

Throughout these years of Shelley's infant reputation, *Queen Mab* went out again to prove that whatever the intelligentsia might be learning, booksellers still found that "blasphemy" was salable. Besides, to the radicals it had become a creed.[14] This incompletely matured work continued to stand in a general way for Shelley's "philosophy."

[13] Reformers there were, though, even amongst rhymsters to whom Shelley was a beacon. In 1830, John Minter Morgan published a pedestrian but well-meaning poem on the distresses of the poor, entitled *The Reproof of Brutus*. In the course of it, most contemporary poets, including Coleridge, Scott, and Tom Moore, are reproved for not writing enough on the "worthy themes" of sociology and their country's wrongs. But Shelley is lauded as poet and reformer strikingly combined, and his rising fame welcomed as a symptom of the improving liberality of the age:

> *... When angry zealots vilify thy name*
> *And 'gainst thy conscientious doubts declaim ...*
> *May they from thee a Christian spirit learn,*
> *And true religion's surest sign discern.*

[14] The influence of *Queen Mab* on the Freethinkers forms a study in itself, and one that is out of my present scheme. K. N. Cameron, in *The Young Shelley* (New York, 1950), sums up some of the researches: "Between 1823 and 1841 White counted 140 items on Shelley (mainly on *Queen Mab*) in working-class or radical periodicals. In 1892 George Bernard Shaw

Leigh Hunt had tried to alter the balance. Possibly Trelawny hoped to do so, though his anger emerged rather as a personal jealousy of those recorders who had got in first. After Mary's refusal to help, he seems to have clung for a while to his intention; in November, 1830, the *New Monthly* announced (along with a translation of *Aeschylus* by Captain Medwin) that "a Memoir of the Life of the Poet Shelley during his residence in Italy, will shortly appear from the pen of his friend, Captain Trelawny." As we know, the pen of his friend was to dally another twenty-eight years before inditing that highly personal sketch of Shelley, Byron, and the impetuous author. In the interval the other Captain, freed from the classical bonds of Aeschylus, and from all obligation to placate the widow, scored again and yet again on the subject he had cunningly saved up And, running neck and neck with the journalistic cousin, there suddenly appeared that intimate friend of Shelley's Oxford days whom Robert Montgomery failed to provide just now—the fellow atheist, Hogg.

◄§{ III }§►

Both these opportunists used the medium of the journals for their publications, lest Shelley should not yet be popular enough to sell alone. True, his popularity and respectability were on the increase, as one might see that year (1832) by picking up a volume of his selected "Beauties" in its third edition. The accompanying memoir reassured "the generous reader" that "the remains of Mr. Shelley were attended to their final abode by some of the most respectable English residents in Rome." That made Shelley almost nice enough for the country vicarage, united as it was with kind quotations from the *Athenaeum*. This responsible paper is worth watching now. It reviews in the highest terms that revolutionary *Mask of Anarchy* held back cautiously from the *Examiner* in 1819, and now published by Leigh Hunt.[15] "Genius," writes the reviewer, "must eventually have its triumph." And in comes Medwin to supply this triumph by making Shelley a regular *Athenaeum* contributor for several weeks.

was informed by an old Chartist that 'Queen Mab was known as The Chartists' Bible,' a sphere of influence commented upon also, he found, by Karl Marx; and it was similarly regarded by Robert Owen and his followers."

15 Birth of another Shelley quotation: "What is the exact amount of the National Debt?"

The Captain had been holding a few Shelley pieces up his sleeve, and now placed them craftily, one after another, on the table, preceded by a memoir in installments. And how chattily amiable a memoir! On might learn at once that its modest author had lived from childhood in Shelley's pocket, "our mothers being relatives"; he remembers "no precocity of genius which he [Shelley] displayed." On the contrary *The Wandering Jew* was partly Medwin's, and *his* Cantos were preferred by *Fraser's Magazine.* Then for the cousinly revelation: Shelley's one and blighted love affair which he never got over, "even if he ever loved a second time." Harriet? the reader is meant to murmur. Yes, but Harriet *Grove.* They were "designed for each other"; Harriet wed another and broke Shelley's heart. This particular myth or novelette has gone down in the struggle for survival,[16] being less fit than the scandalous episodes of Mary and the later Harriet for argument and dismay. A more familiar myth comes next, concerning "his cracked voice, with its well-known pipe; 'Medwin, let me in; I am expelled for Atheism!'"; and then the picture of Shelley found sleeping by the railings in Leicester Square at 5:00 A.M. Little is said of Harriet the Second, except an implication that she never reigned like Harriet the First. Another myth—who knows if it is true?—is launched, of Shelley's being struck down as the atheist by a stranger in the post office at Pisa. "Insanity," cries Medwin, "hung as by a hair suspended over the head of Shelley."

This popular narrative is not without some praise of Shelley's beliefs; but on the whole it is a vote-catching performance, and the votes are sought, not, as in Hunt's account, for Shelley but for that skillful fisherman, Shelley's cousin. Two years later (1834) he was to display himself angling in Wales—an aristocratic sportsman haunting trout streams. But Wales and fishes could not fill two volumes; somehow Medwin switched himself to Italy and fished up copious reminiscences of Byron, with several of Shelley, under the thinnest of fictional disguises. Here too was a new myth—of almost biblical nature—concerning a young woman of high connections who came, renouncing husband, family, and friends, to throw herself at the feet of the master. According to Medwin, the uninvited disciple traced

16 Peacock disposed of it sternly and soundly in *Fraser's Magazine* in 1858, remarking, Medwin "was determined that on Shelley's part it should be an enduring passion, and pressed into its service as testimonies some matters which had nothing to do with it."

Shelley to Sécheron, followed him to Como, Venice, and Naples, and made a thorough nuisance of herself.[17]

To return to his 1832 performance: the memoir being completed in six numbers of the *Athenaeum,* the original "Poems and Papers" followed. The poems consisted of the *Invocation to Misery* and the *Magnetic Lady,* almost in their final form; two, as it were, decapitated poems with the titles *An Ariette for Music* and *With a Guitar.* In both these, and even in the *Magnetic Lady,* we find that Jane Williams has been removed from Shelley's verse. Whether the policy is intentional or accidental, it was to be followed by Mary in her first edition of the *Poetical Works* seven years later.[18] The prose papers were a mixed bag that included the essays on Florentine statuary.[19]

Now when these evidences of Shelley's versatility were collected in volume form in 1833, some additional verses appeared mysteriously among them. Like *The Flower and the Leafe* so long entangled with Chaucer's works, the lines *To the Queen of My Heart* have had a doubtful place among Shelley's since this date. Mary included them in her first edition of the *Poetical Works,* rejecting them from the second. Thomas Hutchinson, in the Oxford edition of 1904, prints them at the end of the Juvenilia with a note concerning their "doubtful authenticity." In 1851 the *Eclectic Review* published the following story of their origin: When Shelley's merits were being discussed by a party of literary men, one of them boasted that he could detect the poet's turn of mind among a thousand anonymous pieces. James

---

17 This mysterious lady has of late come into prominence again; she is suggested as the possible mother of the Naples baby, Elena Adelaide, whom the Hoppners had cited as being the child of Shelley and Claire.

18 The *Ariette,* better known as *To Jane: The Keen Stars Were Twinkling,* rhymes "Dear Jane" with "again" in its first stanza, the whole of which Medwin omits. *With a Guitar* is, of course, the "Ariel to Miranda" poem. Its opening passage, referring to Ferdinand, Miranda, and Ariel, too obviously stood for Williams, Jane, and Shelley to be allowed in print. In the *Magnetic Lady* only one line has had to suffer a change:

'Twould kill me what would cure my pain

should read:

What would cure, that would kill me, Jane.

One can hardly credit Medwin himself with the exercise of this discretion. The poems were in Jane's hands, and it seems probable that she passed them on to Medwin after doctoring them; not, perhaps, to spare the widow's feelings, but because she herself was—as far as might be—Mrs. T. J. Hogg.

19 The last poem printed in the *Athenaeum* with this series, *Lines Written During the Castlereagh Administration,* was not supplied by Medwin, but by T. F. Kelsall, who had it in 1824 from Mary. (See H. W. Donner, *The Browning Box* [Oxford, 1935].)

93

Augustus St. John, who had lately founded the *London Weekly Review,* decided to test the boaster. A few days later (May 3, 1828), *To the Queen of My Heart,* by Percy Bysshe Shelley, appeared in the *Weekly Review* and was at once acclaimed by the coterie. "The style of Shelley could not be mistaken," they maintained, "his soul breathed through it—it was himself." But it was St. John who had written the poem.

Medwin's book soon became a work of some importance in one country at least. The revolutionary representatives of "young Germany" seized eagerly on the account of Shelley's principles and personality, supplied to them for the first time by Medwin's memoir. They at once made use of the poet (or the idealized and melancholic picture of him they had built from Medwin's materials) as a reflection of themselves. Gustav Kuhne, in 1835, wrote a politico-philosophical novel wherein the lonely Shelley appeared as comforter of an equally lonely revolutionary. Gutzkov and others of the persecuted band wrote pamphlets and essays in defense of Shelley and themselves, in each case basing their opinions of Shelley, whose poems they had been unable to get, on Medwin's picture of him.[20] The ratio of Shelley to self-projection in their eager writings may be guessed. Still, we have to thank the Captain—whose own Germanophile tendencies were increasing with the years—for introducing some semblance of the image-breaker to these rebels abroad.

IV

Before the *Athenaeum* had begun to print Medwin's cousinly memoir, a more flashy and impressionistic account of Shelley at Oxford had broken out in the *New Monthly Magazine,* beginning in January, 1832. The articles being anonymous, some suspected Peacock, some Medwin; for, since *Two Hundred and Nine Days* had not been widely read, they could hardly be expected to recognize Hogg's style. According to that author's statement it was Mary Shelley who introduced him to Bulwer, the editor, with a view to his describing "those happy days" in the magazine. On this showing, Hogg, like Tom Moore, was among the privileged commentators in Mary's eyes. While

[20] Liptzin, *Shelley in Germany.*

Medwin and Trelawny were to be obstructed, Jefferson, whom she had once—how long ago and how foolishly—professed to love, was still to be encouraged. It was true that Jefferson was to write of Oxford—a period Mary could not know; while Trelawny and Medwin counted on painting her own familiar days in Italy.

Hogg plunged into his Oxford tale with such enormous gusto that Bulwer had to restrain his eloquence and cut him about a little. Twenty-six years later the offended author was still to be found smarting under the injustice that had forced him to subdue his tone. This "pearl within an oyster-shell" avowed himself "content at all times to throw pearls before swine," but they must be real pearls, "not glass beads and other worthless counterfeits, substitutes for my marine treasures."[21] If Hogg knew the difference between a pearl and a glass bead, his judgment interchanged the labels; it is certain that the edited glass bead of *Shelley at Oxford* is worth more to posterity's swine than is the pearly hailstorm of the surrounding chapters that make up his *Life*.

These Oxford papers, beginning with the sketch of the disputatious freshman met at dinner and ending with the expulsion of Shelley and friend, are so famous that we need only note what new aspects of the poet were shown in them, what further myths unburdened on the world. First, the picture of an ardent chemist, inquiring into galvanic batteries and burning holes in the carpet, had not been extensively displayed before. His impetuosity in mind and movement came out in numberless anecdotes. (The destruction of a dish of scalloped oysters was a matter Hogg could be trusted to recall with pain.) Pawning a solar microscope to help a beggar was in keeping with Hunt's anecdotes. Then, the challenge on Magdalen Bridge—"Will your baby tell us anything about pre-existence, madam?"—has attained celebrity, though one suspects pure Hoggery in the comment, "How provokingly close are these new-born babies." It was hard indeed for Hogg to restrain his pen, and given a good subject, only the strenuous prunings of a Bulwer could seek to prevent his making it a better one. By the time the uncensored *Life* was written, the better subject was undoubtedly T. J. Hogg; but in 1832 he was still able to concentrate for the most part on putting a lifelike Shelley before the public. The reader can even now go to Hogg's papers for a vision of

[21] Hogg, preface to *Life of Shelley* (1858).

the fragile youth who would burst in like a tornado, talk animatedly on science and poetry for hours, then abruptly curl up and sleep on the hearth rug with his tiny head exposed contentedly to the blaze.

The articles, Hogg noted, "were satisfactory to the poet's friends and admirers." Certainly they were much read and generally enjoyed. Copies were sent out to Claire Clairmont, then in Pisa, who gobbled them up and held out her spoon for more. "I am so delighted with the articles," she wrote to Jane, to whom it was in any case proper to compliment the author; "they recall Shelley perfectly. I wonder Jefferson did not praise his forehead, as it was so remarkably beautiful. . . . These articles will give reputation to Shelley, and particularly among the sober and the moral, who have imagined to themselves that he must have been in his private life most profligate and disagreeable." They reached their climax and conclusion in May, 1833, the same month that the *Athenaeum* ended its series of Shelley papers. While Medwin lost no time in reissuing his contributions as a volume, Hogg let his articles lie for the present. Neither the cousin nor the college friend had done with Shelley; and the pirate, though much preoccupied with his own affairs, still cherished his second project. It was now eleven years since the poet's death; and those companions who might have wondered at one time whether their freakish friend was only a private experience, knew beyond a doubt that however the world judged him it would not forget him. For them and their pens he had become, if not a gilt-edged security such as Byron, at least a sound investment which could be sold out when they chose without overmuch scrutiny of the market.

❧{ v }❧

To the general public, anecdoterie was, as ever, more attractive than philosophy. The casual reader was still warned away by that. Again and again we find Shelley's kindliest critics explaining his lack of popularity by the abstract and difficult nature of his verse. Shelley delights in visions of wind and sunbeams instead of Byron's earthly gusto, dissolves the corporeal into mist and wraith, pursues the untamed elements into regions beyond human knowledge, and employs an imagery and a phraseology that are all too remote from daily life. Neither *Swellfoot the Tyrant* nor *Peter Bell the Third* had yet been published to correct the notion of a rainbow-hunting bard. Hazlitt had written in 1824, "Instead of giving a language to thought, or lending the heart a tongue, he utters dark sayings, and deals in allegories and riddles." This was still the general view.

It is unexpected, then, and welcome, to find Macaulay, in 1830, digressing from an essay on Bunyan to point out a new and contrary aspect of Shelley's imagery. Shelley, like Bunyan, he claims, gave to the abstract the interest of the concrete; his imagination turned atheism itself into a rich mythology. "The spirit of Beauty, the Principle of Good, the Principle of Evil . . . were no longer mere words; but intelligible forms, fair humanities, objects of love, of adoration, or of fear." Although, Macaulay goes on, some of his metaphysical and ethical theories were absurd and pernicious, yet "his poetry seems not to have been an art, but an inspiration." Then comes the qualifying clause: "Had he lived to the full age of man, he might not improbably have given the world some great work of the very highest rank in design and execution." Even so, the passage is not only an answer to the "etherial" objectors, but also a counterblast to Hazlitt's latest dagger thrust in the *Atlas* of March, 1829: "Mr. Shelley, who felt the want of originality without the power to supply it, distorted every thing from what it was, and his pen produced only abortions."

❧ VI ❧

While the contemporaries were thus busy, gifted youths who had been children when Shelley died (we have already seen a few of them at Cambridge) discovered him now as the adolescent discovers beauty—a latent force that leaps suddenly into vividness, stabbing the soul with an almost painful joy. "Such writers as Byron and Shelley," Alfred Tennyson said in a letter to James Spedding in 1834, "however mistaken they may be, did yet give the world another heart and new pulses, and so are we kept going. Blessed be those that grease the wheels of the old world, insomuch as to move on is better than to stand still." In his early poetic years Tennyson loved his Shelley heartily. "We lived," he related nearly half a century afterwards,

97

near the most prosaic village in the world, a little beast! where they had never heard of anything. One day we went there to meet my brother Frederick, who was coming back from somewhere, and as we were driving home he whispered, "I've got a poet who's much grander than Byron," and repeated one line—

Waterfalls leap among wild islands green,

which I thought delicious. *Alastor* was the first poem of his I read. I said "This is what I want!"—and I still like it the best, though one can't tell how much these first loves are to be trusted.

It was only when Tennyson had qualified for the position of Grand Old Man of Letters in the eighties that his dictum went forth, "One must distinguish Keats, Shelley, and Byron from the great sage poets of all, who are both great thinkers and great artists, like Aeschylus, Shakespeare, Dante, and Goethe." By that time he had decided that there was "a great wind of words in a good deal of Shelley," but that "as a writer of blank verse he was perhaps the most skilful of the moderns." *The Revolt of Islam* was "splendid but gives me a head-ache—it's fatiguing—all mountain tops and glories."

The poet and artist William Bell Scott, born in 1811, became, as he put it, "thoroughly initiated in the poetry of Shelley, Keats, and Leigh Hunt." In 1831 he composed a poem *To the Memory of Percy Bysshe Shelley,* that began:

> *Where is Alastor gone—*
> *The fairy queen's own latest-born? . . .*

> *Few mourners have appeared;*
> *And meet it is; for he was ever grieved*
> *By others' grief. . . .*

Scott ended with the prophecy:

> *. . . Alastor, thou*
> *Shalt be our guide into the unknown*
> *   time;*
> *And we will bind about thy cenotaph*
> *The laurel and the olive, and the rose;*
> *The poppy and perennial ivy too;*

*Glow worms shall glimmer through the
  dark green leaves,
And great sphynx moths fly round it
  evermore.
And when our many chains are burst,
We'll say, "Alastor, thou wast first."*

The intention is fair enough, though it is hard to see why Shelley should be doomed to an eternity of sphynx moths. As for the binding of flowers and evergreens round the cenotaph, we shall be taking a look in time at the various gardening activities which were to succeed Trelawny's spadework in the Protestant Cemetery at Rome.[22] Meanwhile it is pleasant to find G. H. Lewes writing to Bell Scott six years later: "Sir—Leigh Hunt tells us that as cordial natures and as neighbors we ought to know each other. How far that is the case I know not, but this much I do know, that we both agree in loving Shelley."

The most ardent of the young poetical admirers, the one whose spirit became most passionately entangled at this time in the bright visions and beliefs of Shelley, was born a year later than W. B. Scott. Robert Browning was fourteen, fond of music, but largely untutored except at a local school in Camberwell, when the effulgent Shelley burst upon his view. The story goes—or did go—that he saw on a secondhand bookstall a volume advertised as "Mr. Shelley's Atheistical Poem: very scarce." (It must have been Clark's 1821 edition.) The schoolboy made inquiries, "learnt that there really was a poet called Shelley, that he had written several volumes; that he was dead." He then begged his mother to procure Shelley's works for him, which she did by visiting the Olliers. In later life Browning contradicted this tale of maternal solicitude.[23] And indeed, as the Olliers went out of business in 1823 and sent their Shelley stock to John Hunt, it lacks conviction.

From that time Shelley became the young poet's star and inspiration. Youth appealing to youth, it was *Queen Mab* that first attracted him. He went so far as to profess atheism for two years and practice vegetarianism. The latter course is said to have affected his eyesight, so

---

[22] See Chapter XIII below.

[23] See Mrs. Sutherland Orr, *Life and Letters of Robert Browning* (London, 1908).

H

99

he gave it up. The former he outgrew, long before he outgrew his faith in Shelley. This, too, was to happen, and the change of judgment (or policy) coupled with a wish to suppress his immature work, made him very much ashamed, in later life, of the curdled and enthusiastic poem *Pauline,* written before he was twenty-one and packed with Shelley worship. For all its muddle-headed extravagance it would be a great pity to have had *Pauline* obliterated, as he so strenuously tried to do, for it is not only an appealing record of a very young romantic spirit struggling to come to grips with the universe, it is also a glowing proof of the exciting influence Shelley could exert through his writings alone, apart from his magnetic person. In this poem Shelley is a god. The very pronoun that describes him must be written in capitals: "the glow I felt at HIS award"; and then that epithet which caused so much head-shaking:

> *Sun treader—life and light be thine for ever;*
> *Thou art gone from us—years go by—and spring*
> *Gladdens, and the young earth is beautiful,*
> *Yet thy songs come not—other bards arise,*
> *But none like thee—*

It seems a Miltonic echo—

> *Thus with the year*
> *Seasons return, but not to me returns*
> *Day, or the sweet approach of Ev'n or Morn....*

—and no doubt it was, for Shelley was indeed Light, Heaven's first offering, to the worshiping poet:

> *The air seems bright with thy past presence yet.*

Although he must rejoice that his idol was known to the world, "a star to men," yet he admitted to a "strange regret" that he was not, as he had once thought (reading those first editions by himself in Camberwell), a solitary lover.

There is no need to dwell longer on *Pauline;* yet it may still be read with fascination for its evidence of how the Shelleyan spirit had captured the young men (as Bernard Barton feared) and given them a star to follow:

. . . Soon the whole
Of his conceptions dawned on me; their praise
Is in the tongues of men; men's brows are high
When his name means a triumph and a pride. . . .

The poem, finished in 1832, was published anonymously the following February. Through Browning's friends Eliza and Sarah Flower, the attention of W. J. Fox, the Unitarian minister and editor of *The Monthly Repository,* was drawn to the poem. Fox professed to be no Shelley lover. In 1830 a request from Bowring for a contribution to the *Westminster* had evoked the retort: "I suppose you would not like me to do Shelley, else there is now an opportunity. Hunt has published *The Beauties of Shelley.*[24] Stuff! the only beauty he ever had was his wife."[25] But "Pauline" was suspected to stand for Eliza Flower, and Fox gave the poem his critical attention, even prophesying—alone among reviewers—a future poet of genius.[26] A few months later Fox wrote, in a description of a woodland picnic:

> Shelley and Tennyson are the best books for this place. They sort well with the richness, in every sense; with the warm mists, and the rustling of the woods, and the ceaseless melody of sound. They are natives of this soil; literally so; and if planted would grow as surely as a crowbar in Kentucky sprouts tenpenny nails. *Probatum est.* Last autumn Lizzie Flower dropped a poem of Shelley's down there in the wood, among the thick, damp, rotting leaves, and this spring someone found a delicate exotic looking plant growing wild on the very spot, with "Pauline" hanging from its slender stalk. Unripe fruit it may be, but of a pleasant flavour and promise, and a mellower produce, it may be hoped, will follow.

The mellower produce came, and *Pauline* went—so far as her author

[24] A mistake; Hunt was not guilty.

[25] Richard Garnett, *The Life of W. J. Fox* (London, 1910).

[26] Oscar Browning (who seems to have been capable of twisting a tale a little, just as he here twists a title) has a rival version of the fate of *Pauline* in what he terms the "London Depository." He says that J. S. Mill, wishing to review it there, was told it had been already noticed, and, on searching, found at the end of a column, "Pauline—balderdash." The explanation, O. B. adds, was that a single line was required to complete the page; the editor—Fox—took up the first book he found, thought it insignificant and pretentious, and wrote as above. Mill did, in fact, write an article on *Pauline* which was refused by the *Examiner* and shut out from *Tait's Edinburgh Magazine* "by the prior appearance in that magazine of a few words of the most contemptuous character." (*Life of W. J. Fox.*) This would seem to be the origin of Browning's tale.

could contrive to smother her;[27] until at last we have the quaint spectacle of W. M. Rossetti enthusiastically transcribing the entire poem from the anonymous copy in the British Museum.[28]

His deliberate repudiation of the Shelleyan influence appears to have cost Browning his intellectual unity. Mrs. Betty Miller has pointed out in a recent study[29] how the family's domination caused him to repress the fearless spiritual independence learned from Shelley, whom in *Sordello*—a study of his own divided mind—he could challenge defiantly:

> *—thou, spirit, come not near*
> *Now—nor this time desert thy cloudy place*
> *To scare me, thus employed, with that pure face!*
> *I need not fear this audience, I make free*
> *With them, but then this is no place for thee!*

Yet Shelley still haunted him. Living in Pisa after his marriage to Elizabeth Barrett, he could not forget that earlier household and its tribulations; and in the event his *Memorabilia* was to ring down the years, so that today the line

> *Ah, did you once see Shelley plain?*

has become a catchword even among those who have hardly seen a glimpse of either poet.

Two years later (1835) some of the most dignified verse efforts on Shelley were published by Thomas Wade in his *Mundi et Cordis Carmina.* Wade has sonnets on "Shelley and Keats, and their 'Reviewer,'" on "Julian and Maddalo," and on "Shelley." This last may be quoted here as summing the belief and ardor that had now been inspired:

> *Holy and mighty Poet of the Spirit*
> *That broods and breathes along the Universe!*

[27] "Only this crab remains of the shapely Tree of Life in my fool's paradise," he wrote in one copy. He inserted the poem "repugnantly" in his *Collected Works* (1868), and in the edition of 1888 wrote, "twenty years' endurance of an eyesore seems more than sufficient"—so he allowed himself to tinker with the style.

[28] But in 1896 a copy of the first edition sold for £175. (Letters of D. G. Rossetti to William Allingham, 1897.)

[29] *Robert Browning: A Portrait* (London, 1952).

In the least portion of whose starry verse
Is the great breath the sphered heavens inherit—
No human song is eloquent as thine;
For, by a reasoning instinct all divine,
Thou feel'st the soul of things; and thereof
*   singing,*
With all the madness of a skylark, springing
From earth to heaven, the intenseness of thy
*   strain,*
Like the lark's music all around us ringing,
Laps us in God's own heart, and we regain
Our primal life ethereal! Men profane
Blaspheme thee: I have heard thee Dreamer
*   styled—*
I've mused upon their wakefulness—and smiled.

VII

Now that we have taken a look at the broadening area of Shelley's influence, one circle—the narrowest and, it might have been, the nearest—remains to be glanced at. In a footnote to *Lord Byron and Some of His Contemporaries,* Hunt remarked that Gibbon "exhorted" the Spensers to consider the *Faerie Queen* as the brightest jewel in their coronet. The Shelleys included Sir Philip Sidney in their ancestry; "but," Hunt continues, "if I had a right to speak like Gibbon, and if affection might be allowed to anticipate the voice of posterity, I would 'exhort' in like manner the race of the Shelleys to pierce through the din of existing prejudices, and consider no sound so fair as the name of their aspiring kinsman."

Hunt might exhort, but the family at Field Place was not to be moved from its indifference into awe and admiration for the blackest sheep of its race. It may not be generally known, by the way, that Sir Timothy's existing prejudices—or shall we call them traditional piety or religious scruples?—were of a nicety that caused him to have each of his seven children twice baptized: first privately, within a day or two of their births, so that, if by any misfortune they should die before the date fixed for their public baptism a month or so later, they would still be sure of Christian burial, their rudimentary souls being saved already.[30] In 1806, Sir Timothy sent a detailed list of his children's births and baptisms to Whitton. We find from it that, Percy Bysshe being the eldest, his father's zeal was at its greatest. Born on August 4 at 10:00 P.M., he was privately baptized by the rector of West Grinstead at 11:00 o'clock the same night. Not every parent, surely, would think of calling in the rector so soon after the midwife!

That all this Christian caution should result in *The Necessity of Atheism, Queen Mab,* and a flagrant abuse of the marriage laws, cannot but have thrust Sir Timothy badly out of his stride. When we add to this the aggressive, dictatorial letters Shelley volleyed at his parents just after the marriage with Harriet—urging his father to turn from his errors and accusing his mother of impropriety—we may respect the outraged Timothy for his patience and excuse him for an intolerance far milder than his embittered son's. We have it from a lady who became intimate with the family at this time that the name of Percy Bysshe was a forbidden word at Field Place. In describing her acquaintance with the Shelleys, Mrs. M. C. Houstoun also gives us a hint of the attitude adopted towards the poet by strict and "well brought-up families in general.[31] Mrs. Houstoun herself was to become a popular novelist in the course of time;[32] but, writing, of eleven years after Shelley's death, she says, "I had hardly, I think, even heard more than the name of the man whose fame had already spread through the land. . . . The strict supervision exercised by my father over the 'reading' of his daughters, together with the fact that until my marriage the columns of the newspapers were to me as forbidden fruit, can alone account for the ignorance."

At Field Place, Mrs. Houstoun found two daughters—Hellen, spoken of as the elder, and Margaret.[33] (Elizabeth, that first love of T. J. Hogg's, had died in 1831, and Mary, the next daughter, was married.) These two lived with their parents, who were "excellent persons both," but, like the rest of the family, practical and prosaic, endowed with good sense but not a scrap of imaginative power; all

---

[30] Ingpen, *Shelley in England.* (It may be flippant to suggest, with Tristram Shandy, that *all* the children might have been—privately—baptized together at an earlier period, *"sans faire aucun tort au père."*)

[31] *A Woman's Memories of World-known Men* (3rd ed., London, 1883).

[32] There may be something of the novelist's fertility in her memoirs. They should be read with caution, but no doubt their general trend is true enough.

[33] "I hear that your old favourite, Margaret Shelley, is prettier than ever." (Mary to Trelawny, March 25, 1831.)

that, Mrs. Houstoun says, had been monopolized by Percy. Sir Timothy, "clad in his yeoman-like garb and his tanned leather gaiters," was forced during the midsummer holidays to suffer the presence of his "handsome" grandson, Percy Florence. Hellen Shelley, who "possessed great quickness of perception, and a very powerful autocratic will," became friendly enough with her visitor to talk a good deal about her brother, though never within the old gentleman's hearing. She recalled how he would tell ghost stories or impersonate the devil to alarm the younger children. She talked of Harriet Westbrook as being employed by her, at the Clapham "seminary," to take money surreptitiously to her brother when his supplies had been temporarily cut off. She gave, as a reason for his final exile from Field Place, that Sir Timothy had discovered him trying to inoculate her with his "peculiar tenets and opinions"; whereupon Percy was at once ejected and the rest of the family forbidden to mention his name to the outraged father.

We can picture these recollections and confessions going on in hushed voices behind carefully closed doors, while Mrs. Houston, child of reputable parents, wondered, not daring to inquire, what these outrageous tenets and opinions might be. As so often happens in the case of those who, "knowing the family," think all printed sources are superfluous, Mrs. Houstoun preserved her ignorance for years, until some inside information came her way. (That she was no reader of Shelleyana is clear, from her statement that *Queen Mab* caused Shelley's expulsion from Oxford. Her whole account is open to a like doubt.) The Horsham solicitor who had been employed by Shelley in the Westbrook lawsuit, dying, his daughter placed a collection of papers relating to the suit into Miss Shelley's hands. They included several letters from Shelley to Harriet. Mrs. Houstoun then read with horror, for the first time, some of the theories or heresies with which Harriet had been bombarded. The questionable existence of a Supreme Being she passed over as relatively familiar.

There were, however, other and far more revolting subjects on which the writer reasoned, insisted, and advised; and when it is remembered that these counsels were given, and these reasonings impressed upon the mind of a young wife who was the mother of his children, and whose purity of thought and conduct ought to have been a thing sacred in his eyes, the repulsion as well as the astonishment which the reading of those effusions called forth in the mind was great indeed.

She put it down to a "morbid condition of the brain" that prevented his distinguishing good from bad!

Despite this shock, Mrs. Houstoun (author of *Recommended to Mercy,* and perhaps practicing according to that title) bravely continued to admire Shelley's "transcendent genius" and deplore Hellen's blindness to its charm. One day she repeated from memory a passage from *Mont Blanc,* excitedly challenging her hostess as to whether ideas and words were not "prompted by a spirit that was more than human."

"Possibly, my dear," was the soberly spoken reply, "but if there *was* inspiration at all, I am afraid it proceeded from down there" (pointing with extended finger to the floor), "and not from the realms above."

In later years Hellen Shelley, with her sister Margaret, is to be seen at her nephew's house, having apparently become reconciled to the notion that her brother was a great poet. It is not to be wondered at. A man's own family is, as a rule, either the first or the last to rate him highly. It tends to be the first, and perhaps the only, encourager of a small sweet talent that hardly struggles into view beyond the home circle. Genius flares out independently, burns through the tidy, comfortable conceptions surrounding it, and reappears as a beacon in the outer world, while the home-dwellers are still sore against the accident that has damaged their domestic appurtenances.

CHAPTER VI

The Poet's Son and Others

⟨ I ⟩

AN ENTRY in Mary Shelley's journal will supply a clue to the personal side of our history at this date:

> January 22 [1830]   I have begun a new kind of life somewhat, going a little into society and forming a variety of acquaintances. People like me, and flatter and follow me, and then I am left alone again, poverty being a barrier I cannot pass. Still I am often amused and sometimes interested.

With her boy Percy she had moved from Kentish Town and was now living at 33 Somerset Street, Portman Square, giving and going to parties. Having relaxed her pose of tragic widowhood and ceased to expect deep satisfaction from any given individual, she had begun to know the pleasure of light acquaintanceship, stimulated by numbers, wit, and movement, unbroken by those hollow plunges into questioning agony which her egotism was inclined to force on her. Now she became a desirable and charming social adjunct; nor was she entirely a "man's woman." Amongst her new acquaintances two of her own sex have left us the most flattering—one might say loving—assessments of her that any woman so fearful of the world's neglect might hope for. Whether or not it was the link with Shelley that first attracted them, they remained, like Fanny Wright, Robert Dale Owen, John Howard Payne, and others besides, to honor Mary's personality and extol it.

On June 18 of this year Miss M. J. Jewsbury replied to an inquiry from her friend Anna Jameson, in these terms:

> . . . I rarely, if ever, met with a woman to whom I felt so disposed to apply the epithet "bewitching." . . . She struck me in the light of a matured child; a union of buoyancy and depth; a something that

brought to my remembrance Shelley's description of Beatrice in his preface to the *Cenci*. To those she loves her manners would be caressing; to a stranger they are kind and playful, less from a desire to please, than from a habit of amiable feeling. Her hilarity, contrasted with the almost sadly profound nature of some of her remarks, somewhat puzzled me. It is not the hilarity assumed by worn minds in society,—it is simple—natural—and like Spring full of sweetness, but I doubt her being a happy woman, and I also doubt her being one that can be distinctly termed melancholy. Looking over the *best* part of the writings of her father, mother, and husband, she is the kind of woman for them to love and describe. . . . She is not one to sit with and think ill of, even on authority.[1]

The second account comes from Elizabeth Rennie,[2] who had become an intimate friend of Mary's early in her own life, and gives some vivacious accounts of their London circle. Miss Rennie, not altogether in agreement with Miss Jewsbury concerning the special quality of Mary's charm, found that, although so young "she had none of the buoyancy or elasticity of youth about her. . . . There was a settled sadness, a grave, gentle melancholy in her face, and voice, and gait, which at once aroused your sympathy and elicited your interest in her." (Miss Rennie may be writing of an earlier year than 1830, or again the divergence may be simply explained by the former's having met Mary at parties, and the latter's knowing her at home.) She pictures Mary's personal appearance—her exquisitely fair skin, gray eyes, bright silky hair in ringlets, her figure inclining to *embonpoint*. Her admirer continues:

> She was not a mirthful—scarcely could be called a cheerful—person; and, at times, was subject to deep and profound fits of despondency, when she would shut herself up, and be quite inaccessible to all. Her undeviating love of truth was ever acted on—never swerved from. . . . Hence, she was most intolerant to deceit and falsehood. . . . "Since my boy learnt to lisp 'Mamma'" I have heard her say, "I have taught him, with his every accent—at all times, and in every circumstance—to tell the truth. There is nothing I would punish him for so severely as dissimulation."

[1] *Anna Jameson, Letters and Friendships (1812–1860)*, ed. by Mrs. Stuart Erskine (London, 1915).
[2] *Traits of Character: Being 25 Years Literary and Personal Recollections*, by a Contemporary (1860).

(Could Mary have hoped this would get around to Sir Timothy?) The last paragraph of Miss Rennie's account makes us wonder what, precisely—if there was anything precise—the gossipers were gossiping about this hater of dissimulation:

> Like all raised in supremacy above their fellows, either physically or mentally, Mrs. Shelley had her enemies and detractors. But none ever dared to impugn the correctness of her conduct. From the hour of her early widowhood to the period of her death, she might have married advantageously several times. But she often said—"I know not what temptation could make me change the name of Shelley."

Here, then, was Mary, whether melancholy or buoyant, at least in fair spirits, and solvent enough to hold receptions on Wednesday evenings in the Somerset Street house. To these soirées came the old friends and the new ones. Of those who could remind her of the earlier days there were Hunt, Peacock, Horace Smith, Jane, and Jefferson Hogg. (It may have been here that Hogg was introduced to Bulwer of the *New Monthly,* who was to give such off-hand treatment to his pearls.) The desirable Tom Moore was of course present whenever his intricate social program would allow. With him might come that much respected banker bard of the famous breakfast parties, Samuel Rogers—a charming companion with a bloodless, sickly-looking countenance, though destined to outlive the rosy-cheeked Irish poet. Another ornament to her parties was the captivating Lord Dillon, who had professed to be puzzled by Mary's character. Dillon was a great talker, loved his Italy, and knew everybody—that is to say, celebrities such as Byron, Mme de Staël, Lady Blessington, and Canova. He was of that pleasant type who can tease, or be twitted, delightfully in a crowd.

"Would you fight a duel for me, Lord Dillon, if you saw me insulted?" Mary asked. "Yes, I would," he answered, "—or for her," indicating Elizabeth Rennie, the recorder of this talk. But for some simpering beauty who told stories and would make out that he fought for love of her, he would not stir.[3] Dillon enjoyed meeting "oddities." One day, reports Miss Rennie, he burst in triumphantly and told her she *must* go to Mrs. Shelley's for "she has got such an extraordinary

[3] "She is the girl to start for the Derby!" he declared of a lady poetess whom he patronized patiently for two years before her book at last appeared.

person staying with her—a 'Miss Dods,' quite a character—so wonderfully clever and so queer looking." Miss Rennie went and duly found Miss Dods (or Dodds), with cropped curly hair and looking like a man dressed up. She had piercing black eyes, a disproportioned figure, and was dressed in white cambric like a close-fitting pillowcase. But "Doddy," as Mary and her circle called her, soon reconciled the scoffer by her fascinating manner and her mental endowments. She was a contributor to *Blackwood's* and author of *Tales of the Wild and Wonderful*. As a fellow writer, Mary must have enjoyed her company, which she was to lose when "Doddy" went to live in Paris.

Besides these, Mary mentions with affection Mrs. Hare, who "likes me, and is gentle and good. Her husband is clever and her set very agreeable, rendered so by the reunion of some of the best people about town." The husband, Francis Hare, was the elder brother of Augustus and Julius, who wrote the *Guesses at Truth*. It was a regretful day for Mary when this agreeable woman also deserted for Italy in the summer; and a sadder day still when the fascinating Dillon abruptly died in August, 1832. There were compensations for these social losses, as when, in July, a visit with Percy to Southend was broken by a scamper back to London to attend a ball given by the Speaker, Sir C. Manners Sutton.

A personality not to be forgotten here is Dr. Kitchiner—perhaps the only pedant who combined the rival hobbies of astronomy and gastronomy (or, as some would have it, stars and stomachs). Improvements—in the structure of the telescope and in methods of cooking— were his especial pleasure. Down in the kitchen he would produce a new dish; up in his observatory he would exhibit the telescope, and if you came in the evening, might show you a new star. Long, gawky, one-eyed, clad perpetually in a spencer, Dr. Kitchiner was celebrated no less for his odd and immutable habits than for his authorship. *Practical Observations on Telescopes* may have sold only to astronomical amateurs (though the scientific Shelley would have welcomed it); but three years later *The Cook's Oracle*—"the result of actual experiments made in the kitchen of a scientist"—brought him more general fame and perhaps a regular income.[4] It was at one of his typical,

---

[4] From stars Dr. Kitchiner had indeed come to stomachs, "every man's master and the mainspring of all our comfort." To this end recipe No. 568 of *The Cook's Oracle* is devoted to *Peristaltic Persuaders*, a preparation of his own that, tasting like gingerbread to encourage the children, would "gently increase the action of that grand organ the stomach."

tyrannical soirées that Elizabeth Rennie first met Mary Shelley. Tyrannical they were, according to the laws of Kitchiner. The women were asked to avoid finery, there was no supper, no card-playing, only conversation in which the Doctor played a leading part. There was also a strict "closing time" and no outstaying it; at five minutes to eleven the host would point smilingly at the hands of the clock, and all were obliged to leave. For all their simplicity, crowds attended them: authors, publishers, journalists, with professional singers to supply the music. One can picture the medley, and the rival egoisms that met and paraded until the guillotine hour. Miss Rennie noted an overdressed Hebrew singer, hung with jewelry, an editor of an evening paper, a co-editor who had produced a novel, a bard who dyed his hair from blazing red to bluish black, a female singer who promised one song only, being under medical care—and sang that song four times. Mary herself, observing two "small poets of the day," one of whom was humorless and ill tempered, whispered to her friend, "Is he not like my monster in *Frankenstein?*"

As for her prettier-mannered poet, Tom Moore, she might count herself fortunate to be still visited by that tiny lion. On the first of January, 1830, he had successfully launched the subject of his earlier calls on Mary—Volume I of Lord Byron's *Life and Letters*. The book was acclaimed (there was no such devil's advocate as Hunt at the back of it, nor so flighty a pen driver as Medwin), Lady Byron signified her pleasure, and a presentation copy was sent to Mary (small enough return for the "copy" she had given). On January 19 she wrote to Murray praising "the judicious arrangement and happy *tact* displayed by Mr. Moore," the elegant and forcible style, the strength and richness. She found in it *"our* Lord Byron—the fascinating, faulty, philosophical being—daring the world, docile to a private circle, impetuous and indolent, gloomy, and yet more gay than any other. ... Among its many other virtues, this book is accurate to a miracle. I have not stumbled on one mistake with regard either to time, place or feeling."[5] Besides being accurate, Mr. Moore was thorough, and planned to supplement his pounds with dollars by appointing the brilliant Washington Irving as his unpaid agent. Irving, who had been attempting the same office for Godwin, procured Moore three

[5] Samuel Smiles, *A Publisher and His Friends: Memoir and Correspondence of the Late John Murray* (London, 1891, 2 vols.).

hundred pounds for the advance sheets of both volumes. Since the light entanglement with John Howard Payne and Mary, this eligible American had been to Spain, survived the desirous glances of a French girl in the Russian minister's household, and returned with his bachelor freedom.

Perhaps Mary had outgrown her folly or else Irving had foresworn the paths of the susceptible fair, for we hear nothing of his presence in Somerset Street. Moore made up abundantly for the lack of him. There was an unforgettable occasion when he played and sang divinely (not unusual, that!) to the assembled company at Mrs. Shelley's. He sang new melodies, never yet performed, and one particular song, given with magnificent power and sentiment, thrilled all his hearers. They clamored to hear it through again. Moore repeated it while the rapt audience indulged in sobs and sniffs. When he had ended, the eyes of every woman streamed with tears. Worse still, a hearty young man of twenty-five was "compelled to leave the room to give vent to his emotion."[6] What was this magic that could so undermine the poise of a social gathering, affecting all its diverse members equally?

> *There's a song of the olden time,*
> *Falling sad o'er the ear . . .*

And so on. While the new prophet and singer fights for acceptance and arduously gains some ground, the little lyrist, without lifting a finger except to depress the piano keys, at once reduces the whole intelligent circle to enchanted tears. It was easier to adore Moore's sentiment than to appreciate Shelley's metaphysics.

❧{ 11 }❧

If Trelawny's zeal over the Shelley volume had been damped a little, his autobiography was proceeding at full steam. The two projects had merged now, in the pirate's mind, into a single history in two portions: first, Trelawny and his grand adventures; next, Trelawny and his remarkable friends. He had settled, that winter, in a villa near Galileo's tower above Florence, where his young Zella could be cured of intermittent fever. He was no hermit, as he made clear in his impulsive

[6] Sir John Rennie, *Autobiography* (London, 1875).

letters with their phrases thrown out jerkily between dashes. No, he went into society—had intimate friends—especially one interesting and admired—Lady Burghersh[7]—all heart and passion—she understood his feelings—was not earthy like the general mass. And on August 16, 1830, he looked across to England for aid, and wrote to Mary, whom he had previously vowed in pique to "do without," or speak of "according to her deserts." His book was nearly ready; Brown had testified to its financial value, so it must be disposed of to the highest bidder, who was not to omit or alter a single word, nor have the author's name disclosed to him. Mary, generous as her regretted Irving, fell into the office of voluntary agent, prepared to hawk the nameless manuscript to Murray, Colburn, or another. Besides this, she was to fill in mottoes from Byron, Shelley, and Keats at the heads of the chapters.

It was the prelude to a spate of altercation. Mary demurred at the coarseness of certain scenes and phrases; Trelawny replied with a list of notabilities who had approved them, and advised her to let Hogg or Horace Smith, and then the bookseller, be its judge. The title went through several alterations, while Trelawny, growing short of temper, took his childish revenge by mocking at Mary's friends, the Pauls, the Robinsons, and the Hares. In the spring of 1831, Trelawny accepted Colburn's offer of three hundred pounds on the first edition (he had hoped for six hundred) and had to agree to Horace Smith's employing the pruning knife. The book was on its way into print at last. On June 1 the *New Monthly* announced: "A work of fiction, from the pen of the companion of Lord Byron, of a most intensely interesting description, is about to appear, to be entitled *The History of a Discarded Son.*" That title also was discarded, though Trelawny at last accepted the "commonplace" *Adventures of a Younger Son* against his will. Yet he was confident about his book. Unlike poor Shelley's, his politics could be said to "go with the times."

The times were stirring. Reform was not only in the air but before Parliament. The bill was introduced, thrown out, ministries were falling; Wellington, prince of obstructionists, was to oppose it doggedly while the Whigs pressed it. Some of Shelley's lesser revolutionary principles did seem to have reached the practical world. In France they would have been manning the barricades by now, and

7 A correspondent of the Duke of Wellington, whose letters to her were published in 1903.

England was doubtfully content with a word war. The Manchester Massacres were not forgotten—Shelley's *Mask of Anarchy,* written red hot on the occasion, was still, in Hunt's practical journalistic hands, awaiting the safe moment for publication (although Castlereagh had killed himself three months after Shelley's death).[8] If the bill were to be finally thrown out, there might be further bloodshed. It was not surprising that the subject thrust itself into the correspondence of radical sympathizers, whether or not they were disposed to fight. Mary had written, "We are all here on the *qui vive* about the Reform Bill. . . . England will be free if it is carried." Back came Trelawny's thunder as one of the Titans, about the triumph of "such writers as I and the Poets of Liberty whom I have selected. . . . Would those glorious spirits, to whose genius the present age owes so much, could witness the triumphant success of their opinions. I think I see Shelley's fine eyes glisten, and faded cheek glow with fire unearthly. England, France and Belgium free, the rest of Europe must follow." All tyrants would inevitably fall. Meanwhile, Mary might perform several more commissions for the apostle of freedom, and was not to abandon him by "following the evil example of my other ladies. I should not wonder if fate, without our choice, united us; and who can control his fate?"

Mary could at least return a spirited bark to Trelawny's rumbles. "Will you come over and sit for the new parliament?" she asked ironically, when the bill had been forced through. Then, "Do you think that I shall marry? Never,—neither you nor anybody else. Mary Shelley shall be written on my tomb,—and why? I cannot tell, except that it is so pretty a name that though I were to preach to myself for years, I never should have the heart to get rid of it." To which Trelawny answered, "I was delighted with your resolve not to change your name. . . . Trelawny, too, is a good name, and sounds as well as Shelley; it fills the mouth as well, and will as soon raise a spirit." And Mary rejoined with the famous declaration: "My name will *never* be Trelawny. I am not so young as I was when you first knew me, but I am as proud. I must have the entire affection, devotion, and above all, the solicitous protection of anyone who would win me. You belong to womenkind in general, and Mary Shelley will *never* be yours."

----

[8] Admittedly we have already seen it published, in the previous chapter; but chronology, in this type of many-sided record, loosens up a little to give place to other groupings, and we are now back in an earlier year.

Thomas Moore

This talk of Trelawny and his womankind may have been exaggerated. Whoever might be his "Dulcineas," as Mary called them, his offspring at this date amounted to four only, of whom two were dead. One of these, as we know, was the box martyr. The other, named Eliza, was adopted by a Mr. Johnson who was ruined by an Indian bankruptcy in the spring of 1829, Eliza herself dying a few months later. There is news of the surviving daughters in the summer of 1831. The "little Greek girl Zella"—obviously Trelawny's favorite—had gone to live with an English lady, wife to the Marquis Boschella; under the fond father's roof she had been running wild. The elder (English) daughter Julia was living with Trelawny's mother at Old Brompton. Filial love was not Trelawny's virtue. In *The Younger Son* he was to show how badly he had been treated by his family and to imply that his mother had forgotten him. The plaint was hardly justified, considering that after the 1825 attempt to assassinate Trelawny, his mother, Maria Trelawny-Brereton, wrote anxiously to the Lord High Commissioner at Corfu, begging that his dreadful situation in the cavern of Mount Parnassus should be relieved.[9] Perhaps maternal exertions, being inglorious to the son, are better forgotten. He had long since given up writing to his mother, and by 1832 is found referring to "Julia's brutal grandmother . . . "I would have nothing to do with the old hag." Of other relatives, he was endowed with a fairly wealthy aunt, with whom he kept in touch.

The cast-off son had fought with all four elements and numberless human devils in the East, had developed into a swarthy Arab-faced tough, had loved, married, and lost the beautiful Zela, burning her dead body, according to his habit, on the beach. All this the world might gather when the book appeared in November, 1831. But the family, if his name were attached, would scent injustice, and some of his richest dilemmas would be labeled "lies." He was anything but quiescent, then, on finding that Mary's discretion had not been watertight. Somebody had leaked. In his dismay he let out the real cause of his need for secrecy: "Walter Scott says he trusted twenty people, and that they kept his secret. I have not been able to succeed with five, so it will be a dear book to me; my family will be indignant at my wanton and open aggression; my Aunt will disinherit me, as my Father did for a less offence." *My Aunt will disinherit me.* He may

9 T. C. Down, "Pirate Trelawny," *Nineteenth Century,* May, 1907.

have forgotten this protest by 1870 when he was to write to Claire, "The weak cling to their relations—I have always detested and avoided mine."[10]

✥ III ✥

Mary, with her own finances to consider, found little money in the literary world. Her other hope was Sir Timothy, who was reported to be "in a bad way" in the spring of 1831. In November he was well enough to refuse Mary's application for an advance on her three hundred pounds per annum for Percy's education. As the idea of Harrow was in her mind, Whitton's benevolent wish that she might manage a good education on the three hundred pounds was but cold comfort. Her personal view of these refusals was that Lady Shelley, rather than Sir Tim, was the real enemy, her motive being "the base one" of securing more money for herself, "and her terror was great lest I should see Sir Tim at one time. Now there is no fear, since the old gentleman never comes to town." Without coming to town, the old gentleman had been harried in August from another quarter. John Slatter, the Oxford plumber and landlord, having been silenced in 1823, the printer Henry Slatter now set up his wail. "Having suffered very much in consequence of an honest endeavour to save your son from flying to Jews for the purpose of obtaining money at an enormous rate of interest," he explained how the firm had lost money on Shelley's championship (through Slatter's) of a historical work. (He was, as we have seen, to pipe up to Robert Montgomery of *Alma Mater* when Sir Timothy failed him.) He asked now for some eight hundred pounds as representing the value of their bond and interest; and in fact he went on counting up his interest until the baronet's death, when a duly swollen claim was presented to Peacock.[11] Sir Timothy had only one reply to such demands. He might climb down for Percy Florence, who was after all his grandson, but not for a firm of printers.

Of our other stragglers from Italy, the beloved Jane was living tranquilly content with Hogg and children; Medwin had contrived

[10] Privately printed by T. J. Wise.
[11] See Ingpen, *Shelley in England*.

to be gazetted for full pay in the Guards—by employing his connection with the Shelleys, Mary thought; but a fortnight later was gazetted as retiring—cut by the officers at mess, she hazarded. Leigh Hunt, having published his *Collected Works* by subscription to keep his head above water, had now set up a penny daily paper, the *Tatler,* nearly all of which he wrote himself; but his health was bad, and his sons contributed nothing towards their support. Claire had written from Nice at the end of 1830, fearing her Byron connection might be exposed, as Lady Caroline Lamb's had been, by the French translation of Moore's *Life*. Since then she had been ill in Naples, quarreled with her mistress, Madame Kaiseroff, thought of going to Vienna, spent ten days in Florence where Trelawny found her looking "pale, thin, and haggard," and was threatened with a return to Russia. In Florence, Mary's much-loved Mrs. Hare had almost refused to notice Claire, being prejudiced by the stories she had heard. It was generally understood, among the circle, that Sir Timothy's speedy death was especially required for Claire's betterment. To be a governess was considered, and no doubt rightly, a worse fate than to struggle along with the pen.

Mary, persisting in the latter course, was in touch with one or two publishers on her own account as well as vicariously. She had sent some articles to Colburn for the *New Monthly,* and in March, 1831, while the Trelawny negotiations were still hanging fire, wrote to Charles Ollier inquiring, a little testily on both points. Although styling herself "the opposite of a business person," she is usually seen as an adroit and not too bashful handler of her own affairs, and a pretty good pleader for others She was soon to exercise the latter talent again to Murray, who had applied to her for personal notes on Byron, to enliven the projected edition of his complete works, edited, not unnaturally, by Tom Moore. Giving what she could in notes and suggestions, she followed it up with a petition for her father that required some courage. Godwin had published his novel *Cloudesley,* followed in 1830 by *Thoughts on Man.* Now he proposed the *Lives of the Necromancers,* and hoped that Murray would include it in his "Family Library." The Sage of Skinner Street was old, his patience was short, his ideas were running out, and his money had run out long ago. Mary was forced to appeal to Murray's pity. If Necromancers would not serve, Godwin could dish up "English Philosophers." But Murray would have none of them; the father's work was declined as firmly as the daughter's had been in 1829. Poor Godwin was in a sad "predicament"—to use his eloquent term. He had written two volumes and a quarter of his latest fiction, he told Mary in April, 1832, and was at a loss for materials for his third. Yet his brain and faculties were in excellent going order, and his mind in a state to improve on any raw material that might be offered him. "Do not teaze yourself about my calamity; but give it one serious thought." Mary was, then, to supply the invention as well as the money. Such was the outcome of his "mutual consolation" policy, as launched on Shelley's death.[12]

The family was to suffer another calamity in the autumn of 1832 when Godwin's son William died of cholera.[13] He had been Parliamentary reporter to the *Morning Post,* had left an unpublished novel, *Transfusion,* and an unproduced play, *The Sleeping Philosopher*— both of which negatives Godwin senior intended posthumously to reverse. As a member of "The Mulberries," a club for Shakespeare enthusiasts, William had known the dramatist Douglas Jerrold, who was just scoring a Drury Lane success at the time of his friend's death. Jerrold, consulted on the chances of the play, thought that, with some alteration, it might have a run at the Olympic. The matter was further discussed over a chop at Godwin's some months later; and there it rested. The novel proved an easier affair, for Godwin could supply an introduction and get it into print himself. If it gave him satisfaction, that was all he earned. Mary was right when she had written to Trelawny, "Money is scarce." She was even more specific to Mrs. Gisborne on January 16, 1833: "Money, of course, is the Alpha and Omega of my tale." We have seen it saturating Godwin's, Claire's, and Trelawny's circumstances, and now in the new year, Mary has gone to live at Harrow simply to cut down expenses in order to pay Percy's bills. As this recurrent money-baiting is a sordid business, let us take a turn into the sunshine by looking for the first time full into the face of Shelley's surviving son—who in any case is to have wealth enough for his hobbies before he reaches his middle years.

[12] The identity of this limping novel remains mysterious. In January, 1833, Mary wrote to Mrs. Gisborne, "My Father's novel is printed, and I suppose will come out soon." But except for the *Necromancers,* which found a publisher in 1834, no further volume appeared under Godwin's name.

[13] Percy Florence remembered William Godwin, Jr., as "a very good fellow, who used to take me to the play."

"It seldom falls to the lot of a child to have illustrious descent so heaped upon him," Leigh Hunt wrote of Percy Florence Shelley in *Lord Byron and Some of His Contemporaries;* "his mother a woman of talents, his father a man of genius, his grandfather, Mr. Godwin, a writer secure of immortality; his grandmother, Mr. Godwin's wife, the celebrated Mary Wollstonecraft; and on the side of Mr. Shelley's ancestors he takes of the blood of the intellectual as well as patrician family of the Sackvilles."

This illustrious descent was to dog poor Percy Florence throughout his life. Although it is a truism that genius is no mere fruit of heredity, but the product of a unique and inexplicable set of circumstances, yet it is always perversely hoped that the son of a genius will be "like" him, and therefore a genius in duplicate. There have, to be sure, been cases where the "chip of the old block" was pronounced to be "the old block itself," but the ways of politicians are not those of poets. Leigh Hunt was more understanding when he wrote of Percy Bysshe, "He was Shelley, and not merely a man of that name." The discovery being made, by those who met him, that Percy Florence *was* "a man of that name," he has been glibly dismissed as a stolid, uninteresting descendant of Sir Timothy. His own personality, because it was not Shelley's, has been slighted. He has been so far slighted that not nearly enough is remembered and recorded of him, although there have been, until recently, men living who had met him.

Born on November 12, 1819, Percy came as a compensation to Mary for the children she had lost. On November 13, Shelley wrote to Hunt: "Yesterday morning, Mary brought me a little boy. She suffered but two hours' pain, and is now so well that it seems a wonder that she stays in bed. The babe is also quite well, and has begun to suck." The following day he showed the infant to Sophia Stacey, remarking that "it could do no mischief now," but might some day or other be the "conqueror of provinces." Miss Stacey claimed to have suggested "Florence" as the child's second name. On December 1, Mary reported that he was nearly three times as big as when he was born. Of his father Percy remembered little, though his flitting recollection concerned the water—that source of pleasure to father and son alike. He could see Shelley standing with shoes and stockings off in the water at Lerici, pushing off the little canvas boat. Again, during a flood at Pisa, Shelley came to the house in a boat, and Percy remembered how he held up his arms to take the child to it from the window. There was a further recollection, but Percy was not sure about it in his later life. When Shelley left on his last trip to Pisa and Leghorn, little Percy was playing in the hall on hands and knees, and the poet took care not to walk on his son's hands as he went out. "But," Percy Florence added candidly, "I don't know if I remember this, or only remember my mother telling it me."[14] A nice point, and one not always so bravely faced by recorders of their childhood.[15]

In the month after Shelley's death, Mary wrote to Miss Curran, "My little Percy is well—not so beautiful as William, though there is some resemblance." He passed the winter with her at Albaro, playing, as we have seen, with the Hunt children and chattering only in Italian to them. During those months he was the principal object of Mary's financial efforts with Sir Timothy. When she left for England, she professed it was solely for the sake of him—whose "delicate constitution" must be watched on the journey. The following year he was already at school, learning to read and write in his own tongue and showing a talent for painting, besides playing at husbands and wives with Jane Williams's small daughter Dina. Kindergarten work kept him occupied till 1828 when, on March 25, he was sent to a school in Kensington kept by a Mr. Slater. As he was now heir to the Shelley estates, Sir Timothy took the trouble to visit him at school, while Mary was in Paris with smallpox. These meetings were an ordeal to the baronet, who had written to his solicitor in 1827, "I felt so unmann'd and unpleasant feelings at meeting the Little Boy." (Lady Shelley maintained in after years that—presumably on Percy's report—he "burst into tears.") It was almost a further annoyance that no fault could be found with the child and his upbringing (Peacock was said to have agreed with Whitton that "a Godwin education must be altogether avoided"). "He is really very good," Mary wrote to Whitton of the ten-year-old, "and above all tractable, which is not quite the virtue of his father's family." Under his mother's guidance

---

14 From recollections given me by the late Wilfrid Meynell, who knew the Shelleys at Boscombe.

15 We have also Trelawny's story of how in Pisa Shelley "sprang down the stairs . . . striding adroitly over a fair fat child" whom he failed to recognize as his own. As this is only one of those extra anecdotes introduced into the *Records* of 1876, it need not be taken seriously.

he was no doubt becoming childishly egotistical and priggish, besides developing some cleverer traits.

He had achieved the task of writing a letter to Claire. "Poor child!" she commented from Dresden on March 28, 1830, "he little thinks how much I am attached to him! When I first saw him I thought him cold, but afterwards I discovered so much intellect in all his speeches, and so much originality in his doings, that I willingly pardoned him for not being interested in anything but himself." It was later in the same year that Sir Timothy had his suspicions about the origin of the dutiful little letter Percy wrote on his birthday, on receipt of a bright sovereign. The "butter wouldn't melt" tone, with its final slithering into irony ("Some ladies, friends of Mama who know you, say I am very like you, so I am sure I ought to be good") no less than the prim little report of satisfactory schoolwork, all suggested the maternal mind attempting, with false emphasis, to placate the source of annuity, while itching to fly in his face and be done with him, as her more independent heroine in *Falkner* was to do when similarly placed. Concessions from Sir Tim were becoming doubly important, for the serious question of Percy's education was in her mind. She had known of Shelley's hardships at a public school, and could write with a vague eloquence, in her *Keepsake* stories, about something of the kind; but in practice it was different. As she confessed, she was innocent of reforming zeal. She loved convention and believed, now, in planing down the individual rather than altering the shape of the system. Within this framework she aimed high, and suggested Eton to Sir Timothy. The old gentleman at once objected. The place aroused painful memories, and "it would be highly improper, his Poor Father's being there would make life very unpleasant. From experience I am aware whatever a boy does at a Public School is remember'd for ages."[16] (The epithet "Poor Father" seems to be a nineteenth-century cliché rather than a personal sentiment. Percy Florence was in time to be heard, by the late Wilfrid Meynell and others, using it himself.)

Eton being negatived, Mary pinned her hopes on Harrow. The old man grumbled again at the expense and could not see why the widow's ambitions should fly so high when there were reputable and cheaper schools in London. But she carried her point, while he grumbled to Gregson, who had now replaced Whitton, about this

[16] Ingpen, *Shelley in England.*

"haughty dame"; and in September, 1832, Percy Florence duly entered, and remained till 1836. Harrow was then hardly in a line with Eton; the school was coming up and was, as Mary told John Murray in October, "in excellent report now." (After all, it had been good enough for Byron.) The headmaster since 1829 was C. T. Longley, D.D., subsequently Archbishop of Canterbury. He was followed in 1836 by Christopher Wordsworth. In the latter part of Percy's time, Bishop Colenso, the mathematician, was a master. Percy's housemaster in Large House (The Grove) was Benjamin Hall Kennedy, a classical master. Among possible school acquaintances of Percy's we may mention Anthony Trollope (whose mother we saw visiting Nashoba with Frances Wright). He had entered in 1823 and left in 1826, returning in 1831 for three years more—unhappy all the time. Another whom he certainly knew, for they were afterwards together at Trinity College, Cambridge, and then met in Italy, was Henry Hugh Pierson, the composer, who was to set some of Shelley's poems to music.[17]

Percy at once belied his father's school reputation by settling down happily at Harrow and rendering superfluous the morbid fears expressed in October by Claire. She was then staying in Pisa with the Masons, and enduring minor trials similar to Mary's in the Hunt household ten years earlier.

> I am very glad [she wrote] to hear that Percy likes Harrow, but I shudder from head to foot when I think of your boldness in sending him there. I think in certain things you are the most daring woman I ever knew. There are few mothers who, having suffered the misfortunes you have, and having such advantages depending upon the life of an only son, would venture to expose that life to the dangers of a public school.

Mary was not so sensitive. Her trouble was the expense (for it seems that finance must intrude again). It was more than she could do to pay for Percy. One must, to be sure, admire the parental pride that stints and starves and works itself to breaking point, rather than blush at the name of its son's school. Common sense tends rather to

[17] Others who overlapped with Percy were the Hon. Robert Grimston, president of the M. C. C., the Hon. George Anson Byron, who succeeded as eighth baron in 1870, A. R. Dallas, son of Byron's friend Dallas, and Beresford Hope, afterwards proprietor of the *Saturday Review* and writer of novels.

back up Sir Timothy's view—while admitting that Sir Tim himself ought to have placed snobbery before solvency and backed up Mary's. A single term was test enough for her; to scrape together the requisite sixty pounds, she was "hampered for the whole year." There had to be a sacrifice; mother and son shared it, though unevenly. For Percy it meant giving up the full experience of public school life, after two terms of it, and running the risk of growing up as a "mother's boy," by becoming a home boarder. For Mary the sacrifice was conscious and acute: she had to abandon London and its parties, leave those agreeable friends and distinguished circles, to live in Harrow. She consoled herself by arguing that "half the times I am asked out, I cannot go because of the expense, and I am suffering now for the times when I do go and so incur debt." The Reverend H. J. Torre, who was a Harrow boy at this time, tells us in his *Recollections,* "There were very few families then resident with a view to having their boys at the school; in fact home-boarders, as they were called, were rather looked down upon."[18] Another mortification for Mary! The same historian describes some of the rags and customs that Percy must partly have missed through his evening absence. For instance, beginning in the Fourth Form, Second Remove, and rising to the Head Remove the Easter quarter following, he seems just to have escaped the ceremony of being tossed into the Shell, as performed usually by some twenty boys with a blanket in Hall after evening prayers. We find him in the Upper Shell in April, 1834, a year later in the Fifth Form, Third Remove, and in 1836, his last year, he has reached the Second Remove, leaving at Easter, too soon to get into the Sixth Form.

On July 17, 1834, Mary wrote a long letter to Maria Gisborne, with the following close description of the growing boy:

> In person he is of a fair height, and excessively fat, his chest would remind you of a Bacchus; he has a florid complexion, blue eyes like his Father, and his looks and gestures and shape of his face would remind you of Shelley and his person before he grew fat; he is full of spirits and animation, but proud and reserved with strangers. There used to be a great want of sensibility—this lingers about him, but is rather concentrated than slight; he loves me more than he knows himself, and would not displease me for the world. If he sees

18 *Recollections of Schooldays at Harrow* (London, 1890).

me sad, he does all he can to comfort me, and would give up any pleasure for my benefit; his temper is a little defective, but he is neither violent nor sulky, but perfectly generous and true; he is trustworthy and thoughtful beyond his years—cautious though impetuous, and exceedingly constant, so that he now loves Edward and Dina better than any newer friends. He has the true Shelley hatred of society; he has no ambition, and little emulation, yet attentive to his lessons, and sufficiently diligent; he is the twentieth boy in a form of fifty boys; he has a great respect for truth and good faith. One day I said to him, "I suppose when you grow to be a man, you will leave me all alone." "Oh, Mamma!" he said, "how do you think I could be so shabby; that would be too bad!" To be *left all alone* seems to him the worst evil of all; he does not like any poetry except Percy's "Ancient Ballads," and Shelley's translation of Homer's "Hymn to Mercury," and the "Cyclops"; but he likes romances—any marvellous tales—and is a great story-teller; he is a little bitten by metaphysics; he is always occupied. He is very handsome, and a perfect child in all his notions, and quite obedient. He is better to me than any one, for he has no notion of giving up any whim to anybody but me, besides being very uncommunicative, except to his intimates. God help me if anything was to happen to him—I should not survive it a week.

All that had happened to Percy at the moment was a blow on the knee. Mary, fearing a tumor, "took him to Lawrence in a fright. . . . Overhealth, he said, was all his ailment, so he forbade him animal food; but the less he eats the more robust he grows. His contrast to Edward [Williams] is whimsical, both in complexion and stoutness; their height is the same." We might add that his contrast to his father is equally whimsical. Shelley chose vegetarianism and grew ill on it, according to Peacock. On the same authority, Shelley detested the theater, which was to be one of the two leading passions of his son. As to this animal health, it was grimly noticed by his Uncle John, Shelley's younger brother. John used to visit him at school, gaze at him, turn away with a grunt, saying "Well, Percy, you *do* look damned well." Percy, of course, stood between him and the inheritance.

A certain amount of hospitality went on in the Harrow house; there would be breakfast parties for six to eight, to keep the boy not unpopular, though only two friends had the freedom of the place.

"A strange mixture of Shelley and myself," said Mary, again noticing his want of sensibility. Another description of Percy, at secondhand, subtracts the compliments. John Watson Dalby, in one of his long series of manuscript notebooks, writes: "When I lived at Ruislip and he was at Harrow, all I could learn of him was that he was fat, florid, and of a mechanical turn. It was conjectured that Nature meant him for, and would leave him, a tolerable carpenter." Dalby, too, supports the easy view that Percy took after "the thick-headed 'Country Gentlemen' who preceded the great Poet." In truth, nobody seemed in agreement over poor Percy's family features, despite the several attempts to place him. In 1836, Trelawny, then in London, was to write to Claire, "Percy improves in his outside shell—he is thought handsome—in features and temperament more after the Godwins than his Father. Mary says he takes after his sire's family—which is not saying much in his favour—better for the Godwins—if we are not to have a Percy Shelley—let's have a Godwin—with a little of the father's leaven to upheave and quicken the good and wholesome somewhat slow and heavy stuff of which the philosopher is made—" In February, 1835, Mary reports him "in the fifth form, with a *tailed coat and watch,* and quite a man." Two years later she told Trelawny that he had "rather whetted than satisfied his appetite by going seven times to the play," and was performing like Apollo on the flageolet. "He is quite a child still, full of theatres and balloons and music, yet I think there is a gentleness about him which shows the advent of the reign of petticoats—how I dread it."

He had then left Harrow and was studying under a tutor, Mr. Morrison, vicar of Stoneleigh, near Leamington. If his passion for the theater had already asserted itself, the establishment of "the reign of petticoats" was a good ten years away. When it came, it was to be of a nature to delight Mary and to govern the reputation of Percy Bysshe Shelley rather than the recreations of his son.

❧{ v }❧

Percy's mother might idolize him and mangle her own pleasures for his schooling, but it was not incumbent on her to appear content. From the first she hated the "dull, inhospitable" Harrow. The friend she counted on had died of influenza, leaving her to brood over her loneliness and "pine for social festivity." She herself caught influenza her first summer there, "recovered youth and health" in Putney in September, walking for miles over the Heath and in Richmond Park with Julia Robinson; came back to her disagreeable lodging, worked hard with her pen, finishing *Lodore* and writing the lives of the Italian *literati* for Lardner's *Cabinet Cyclopaedia*. She was at least to be relieved of her father's maintenance when, in 1833, he obtained from Lord Grey's Ministry what Mary described as "a tiny shabby place under Government." The title "Yeoman Usher of the Exchequer" carried no duties with it and meant Godwin's removal to 13 New Palace Yard. His only real fear now was lest Parliamentary retrenchments should lead to abolition of the post. By one of those anomalies the glorious Whigs who had carried the Reform Bill were now little more accommodating than the Tories and did much to minimize their victory. A leopard cannot so easily change its spots, and in 1831 Grey's Whig Ministry, with Melbourne as home secretary, is said to have been more repressive than the Tories in its treatment of peasant revolts. Reform itself, though it abolished the Rotten Boroughs and in some measure eased industrial distress, was not the millenium Shelley saw ahead of him. That—like a star when we have passed the street lamps—came no nearer. It had, in his instance, one result, that his impassioned poetry, in the more human era, hardly seemed to date. (As we now see, looking on our twentieth-century tyrannies, it is unlikely ever to do so.)

In 1832 the Countess Guiccioli had visited Harrow, where she was sufficiently recognized as an item of the Byron menagerie to be invited to dine with the wife and family of his Lordship's tutor, Drury. While in London the Countess was a frequent guest of Lady Blessington, who reported her to be leading "a quiet, serious life, speaking all day the language of English people but finding it too formal, cold and restrained." She left England at the end of the year, and left it reluctantly, to Mary's surprise. "What she found to please her in this dingy land I cannot guess—not an *amanti,* I believe, as far as I could judge by the aspect of things." Whatever the attraction was, it brought the Countess back again in 1835. An acquaintance[19] who met her at Gore House in September described her in these terms: "Sweet, artless,

[19] Henry Fothergill Chorley, *Autobiography, Memoirs, and Letters* (London, 1873).

earnest, untidy, very guileless of mind, with a pearly white complexion, a huge foot, and profuse hair—the colour of a pale ripe nut—with all the gesticulation and *abandon* of an Italian woman, and something high-bred in spite of all."

At the Countess of Blessington's she might have met Trelawny, fresh from his latest exploit of attempting to swim across the Niagara rapids. In that wild scene the youthful Fanny Kemble had been captivated by her glamorous cavalier (she was long to be one of his favorites); but Trelawny professed himself scared and humiliated by his own performance, so near had he been to failure. Now he was back to enjoy the hum of high society, he who loved a lady as infallibly as Tom Moore loved a lord. He is heard of at Sir William Molesworth's, dining with political radicals, as a follower of the enchanting Caroline Norton (defier of scandal and challenger of an unjust law), besides attending regularly on Lady Blessington, whose own contribution to the memory of poets was now on the market. Her *Conversations with Lord Byron* concerns us here only for her report—whether well or ill remembered—of Byron's remarks on Shelley in 1823:

> "He was the most gentle, most amiable, and *least* worldly-minded person I ever met; full of delicacy, disinterested beyond all other men, and possessing a degree of genius, joined to a simplicity, as rare as it is admirable. He had formed to himself a *beau idéal* of all that is fine, high-minded, and noble, and he acted up to this ideal to the very letter. He had a most brilliant imagination, but a total want of world-wisdom. I have seen nothing like him, and never shall again, I am certain."

Remote from social gatherings, the unexcitable Jane Williams remained in peaceful domesticity with her chosen Hogg. After the storms of her early career, contentment seems to have set in almost permanently, as though the Magnetic Lady had, by the aid of children, house, and husband, herself been hypotized. Yet, if we look into Jane's affairs a little, it seems more probable she had the common sense and grace to come to terms with a life that had cheated her, no less than Mary's, and which might have left an equal melancholy. Rescued as she had been from her unworkable marriage to J. E. Johnson by Edward Williams, she was soon enough left with her two children to provide for. Like Mary, she had educational ambitions for her son. A lady who appears to have known descendants of the circle writes in 1935 (in her copy of Mrs. Marshall's *Life of Mary Shelley*) that Jane's grandson, J. Wheeler Williams, gave as a reason for her "marriage" to Hogg that she had hoped thereby to give her son a university education. The hope was forlorn. By this time committed to Jefferson's care, she must have seen that he had no intention, or no means, of complying. This commentator has it that the "excellent care" taken (as Mary told Mrs. Gisborne) of young Edward's education was due entirely to Trelawny, not to his stepfather. In fact, it was Peacock who later placed Edward in the India House. Jane seems to have resigned herself; and, with Edward and Dina growing up on reassuring lines, her only troublesome emotion was fretfulness when Jeff left her alone.

He did that for several months in the fall and winter of 1833. Brougham (perhaps to make up for disappointing him over a London University post he had applied for) appointed him as one of the Municipal Corporation commissioners. The late Sir Michael Sadler has given an excellent account of the commission and Hogg's behavior on it.[20] One writes "behavior" rather than "work" since Hogg neglected to investigate most of the boroughs entrusted to him, and ended by clumsily censuring the commissioners' report, after a far abler protest by Sir Francis Palgrave had been swept aside.[21] It was a typical piece of Hoggery; the unfortunate Jefferson, despite his miraculous capture of Jane Williams, never learned to accept life's smaller buffetings without a protest. Many concerned his literary works, many concerned his meals; he appeared to be fighting some general conspiracy to devalue him. If he saw the review of the Commissioners' first report in the *Quarterly* for July, 1835, he must have been mortified again to find himself listed among eighteen "obscure" names, of which the reviewer asked the public "whether they had so much as *heard of any of them* as a man of any professional practice, or even pretensions."

Mrs. Norton, besides flirting a little with Trelawny, had become

[20] "Shelley's College Friend, Thomas Jefferson Hogg: An Episode in His Later Life," University College *Record*, 1934.

[21] Since this was written, Hogg's work on the commission has been discussed in detail and represented in a kindlier light by his biographer, who finds his "independent attitude" more than justified. (See Winifred Scott, *Jefferson Hogg*.)

to some degree Mary's friend. She was drawn to her by sympathy in misfortune and those liberal tendencies that were always taken for granted in Shelley's widow. From Caroline Norton, Sheridan's vivacious and unhappy granddaughter, they flamed out in her fight to alter the laws of divorce and the custody of children. Like Shelley, she had been "legally" deprived of these. An irresistible personality, with a brute of a husband, she had magnetized the Duke of Devonshire, "Uncle Leopold," Macready, and Castlereagh. Trelawny himself had been named by rumor as George Norton's selected co-respondent in his suit for damages; but the pirate lacked the worth of a prime minister, and he chose Lord Melbourne. In 1836, Mary, conquering a certain shyness towards that brilliant spirit, begged from Mrs. Norton an unselfish favor for her stepmother, now a needy widow. Trelawny had written to Claire in the previous year: "Godwin is one of the immortals—I mean himself as well as his works: time passes without touching him." The following March he jocularly reassured her again: "Godwin and your mother are no more affected by time than the leaning tower of Pisa—bending with the weight of years— who can say when they are to fall?" Time was to give his final push to Godwin in a fortnight; on April 7 the Yeoman Usher became in another sense "one of the immortals," and his tottering post died with him. He was buried in St. Pancras Churchyard in the grave of his first wife, Mary Wollstonecraft, whose coffin, the *Times* reported, was "found nearly perfect." Young Percy was chief mourner, and Trelawny attended the funeral.

If Mary scanned the press for a more comforting estimate of her father than it had given of her husband, she was not to be altogether gratified. Where Shelley, by surviving forty years longer, might have reversed his reputation, this was very much what Godwin had done, but in the opposite direction, having sunk steadily in power and repute since the publication of *Political Justice*. Even if, as Hazlitt maintained, his had been "a sultry and unwholesome popularity," how much less stimulating was it to find himself "to all intents and purposes dead and buried"—forgotten in public, disliked on a casual encounter.[22] There was no revival of Godwinism on his physical death,

---

[22] "Truth to tell, I thought him one of the most disagreeable old men I ever met with," wrote Elizabeth Rennie (*Traits of Character*). To Thornton Hunt as a youth he appeared "a harsh and ungenial man."

only, as it were, the final gesture of dismissal to one who had so long ago sailed out of sight. "For many years he has been regarded as belonging to the past," wrote the *Court Journal,* though maintaining generously that his novels "analyze human character with an almost Shakespearean subtlety." But the June number of the *Gentleman's Magazine* thus delivered its verdict:

> In weighing well his merits with his moral imperfections, it is melancholy to discover how far the latter preponderated, and we are led to the very painful though certain conclusion, that it might have been far better for mankind had he never existed. . . . The opinions maintained by Mr. Godwin, on the existing state of society and actions of mankind, are sour and unhealthy. Pride was the basis and the root of his philosophy.

This double dying of Godwin left his somewhat sour and unhealthy widow ("crony—rheumy—rheumatic and phthisicky" was Trelawny's blunt description to her daughter Claire) in need of maintenance. Mary had thought Mrs. Godwin provided for; she had a hundred pounds in the house, there was a chance of publishing Godwin's posthumous manuscripts; the terms of his will required Mary to sort them, publishing and "consigning to the flames" as she thought fit; and she intended to write his life, which he had already begun himself. But this would not suffice; no doubt the hundred pounds, being in the hand, was gone, and the manuscripts, being in the bush, were useless. A kind literary society gave fifty pounds; but the only solid hope for the old lady was to secure for her a part of Godwin's pension on the strength of his doubtful services to the government. Mary begged Mrs. Norton to use her influence with the Prime Minister. She did use it, to such purpose that although the post was in fact abolished, Lord Melbourne made the Royal Bounty Fund available in Mrs. Godwin's case to the extent of three hundred pounds. Her troubles, and those of her supporters, were to begin again in 1838 after the sum had been withdrawn on King William's death. But for the moment the ailing widow seemed settled, and we find Trelawny crowing to Claire about his share in securing the money, thanks to his retaining "on our side the lady of song and beauty," Mrs. Norton.

Financial matters relating to Claire herself had been under

discussion the previous year. It had no doubt been a shock to Mary when she discovered that the legacy of £6,000 bequeathed to Claire by Shelley's will was duplicated—£6,000 appearing in the body of the will and another £6,000 in a codicil. Some hold that it was done designedly, but in that view one scents malice and a strong belief in the Hoppner scandal of "Elena Adelaide." In any case, the second sum was said to be dependent on her surviving Sir Timothy; the first had been put into the hands of trustees to purchase an annuity. Claire, in Florence, wrote a hysterical tract to Mary. She intended to leave half her legacy to Percy in her will, counting herself doomed to die of cholera; already she felt the preliminary pains. "As my end approaches," wrote this woman whose life was to approach the 1880's, Byron, the villain of her days, was not to be forgiven, above all for his treatment of Allegra. "He hated the child," raged Claire, "and was determined to be rid of her. . . . I knew how he hated Shelley, how he despised his poetry and his principles." This is typical "Clairishness"; it is remarkable how her whole mind bent towards malice— a malice so infectious that even Shelley in his letters to her may be found writing unusual, irritable detractions of his friends. Mary could probably smile, in her more patient moods, at these alarms and terrors. Almost every letter was a detonation that left the scenery unaltered when the smoke had cleared away.

Mary herself had been ill again, recovering this time on bark and port, helped by a visit to Dover, and still slogging at her Spanish and Portuguese lives. Harrow did not agree with her—either physically or spiritually. Her "disease," in Trelawny's words, was "pining after distinction and the distinguished of fortune." For some time a decided grudge against Mary had been growing on him. He told Claire he had met her at a party; "She lights up very well at night—and shows to advantage in society—for there she is happy—detesting solitude— in the country she does nothing but complain—she is now determined to fix her headquarters in Town—has a lodging near the Regents Park, and is seeking a small house to call her own. In the daylight the faded colour and chinks of time are observable, but not disproportionate to her years."

Be that as it may, illness and recuperation were expensive; *Lodore*, that curious tangle of mixed Shelleys and Byrons with their selected or impacted womenfolk, was not selling rapidly enough for its author's demands. Jane, without literary progeny, was happier in the birth, on February 4, 1836, of a flesh and blood daughter, to be named Prudentia Sarah, after her two paternal aunts whom Hogg sincerely hoped she might resemble. Mary, who was to stand godmother to the infant, had so far determined to work on her father's memoirs and correspondence that she wrote to Moxon offering him the book, and began sorting and collecting Godwin's papers and letters, applying, amongst others, to Hazlitt's son, who had just produced the memoirs of his father. "I wish I may perform my task as well as you have done yours," she complimented him.[23] A more important life than Godwin's had been asked of her. A year ago she had had the offer of six hundred pounds for an edition of Shelley's works, with "Life and Notes." This, obviously, was what the literary world required of Mary, rather than lives of foreign poets, which were anonymous, novels which could as well be written by someone else, and memoirs of Godwin who had been so long eclipsed. But she felt herself unprepared as yet for the edition, and as for the *Life,* it required another death before it could be presented. Old Time, or Eternity, as Sir Tim was often called in these latter days, lived on to uphold his nickname and his ban.

[23] Mary's project for Godwin advanced so far that in the *Literary Gazette* for Saturday, October 1, 1836, Henry Colburn announced as "in the press" the "Autobiography of William Godwin with his Correspondence, and a continuation of his memoirs to the time of his Death, By his Daughter Mrs. Shelley. 2 vols. 8vo."

Portraits or Distortions

✧ 1 ✧

LEIGH HUNT, whose friendship for Shelley as well as his personal
talent had just been surprisingly recognized in the pages of
his old enemy, *Blackwood's,* continued to love and honor the
poet through all his own vicissitudes.[1] Taking a long-due
holiday in Wales in August, 1836, where Mrs. Anna Maria Dashwood
was for a time his hostess, he was haunted by her startling resemblance
to Shelley. She had a look in her gray eyes "at times so very like him,"
he wrote to Marianne, "that I could shed tears at the sight"; and he
asked his wife to oblige their good friend with one of her profiles—
a full length. Marianne may have obliged the friend; but she was
doing better: the *Court Journal* for Saturday June 11, 1836, contained
this passage:

> We have just experienced a gratification of the highest kind in
> seeing a Bust of Shelley, that has been modelled from memory by
> Mrs. Leigh Hunt. It gave us for the first time a distinct idea of the
> personal appearance and character of the Poet. The face is radiant
> with sensibility and intellectual fervour. That etherial look which
> genius, that "o'er informs its tenement of clay" gives to the counte-
> nance, is finely expressed. The lips seem nerved with feeling; and
> we seem to see "the rapt soul sitting in the eyes" which gaze with all
> their orbs. The following extract from the prospectus announcing
> its publication gives a graphic idea of the original, and offers satis-
> factory testimony to the truth of the resemblance. We can only say
> that the bust answers to this description of the man. Mrs. Hunt says
> "it is pronounced by her husband, and others who knew Shelley, to
> be the only likeness *which does justice to the force and spirituality
> of his genius,* the portraits, hitherto published, having been made

[1] A modified version of this first section of Chapter VII appeared in the *Times Literary
Supplement* of May 18, 1951, under the title, "The Bust of Shelley: A Lost Prospectus." I am
indebted to the editor for permission to use it here.

up from unfinished sketches. The face of this distinguished Poet was remarkable for the sensitive and earnest play of its features, particularly about the mouth; and as emotion was as much a habit with him, as the reverse is with most men, Mrs. Hunt has presented his image to her mind, at the moment when he was conversing on the topics most interesting to his zeal. His eyes, with a very fine expression about the brow, were rounder and more open than with most; his nose very delicate and graceful; his chin soft and receding; his complexion flushed; his hair plentiful, and of a dark brown colour, though early tinged with grey. Altogether, though no heart was manlier than his, his aspect had in it something of that 'feminine' quality, which Coleridge has pronounced to be of the essence of 'genius'; and the artist has preserved it in this bust. Neither has she forgotten the singular prominence of the *larynx*,—the principal bone of the throat, which seemed, as he conversed, to partake of the earnestness of his emotion." The best compliment that we can pay to the extraordinary skill with which a recollection of the lineaments of one many years dead is made to assume a palpable shape in a bust, is to say, what is the fact, that it would do honour to any sculptor to produce such a breathing portrait, had it been modelled from the life, instead of being done from memory. Mr. Leigh Hunt has presented a cast to Mr. Serjeant Talfourd, with this striking inscription on it:

> *To him who gave the gods Ion's dear breath*
> *An Ion comes, whose whole life was a death.*[2]

Here is a notable announcement. It gives, as far as I can trace, the only available quotation from a prospectus of which no copy appears to have survived, its very existence being generally unknown. In it we have a new description of Shelley—probably a joint effort by Marianne and Leigh Hunt—which dwells for the first time on the receding chin and prominent larynx. It is also worth noticing that the *Court Journal* commentator, who had never seen Shelley, describes not the physical features of the bust, but the richness and expressiveness as of a radiant countenance, which would undoubtedly satisfy our ideas and ideals of the living poet. It reads like a description of the original in flesh and blood rather than of the bust as we now have it.

[2] Talfourd's tragedy *Ion* was produced at Covent Garden on May 26, 1836, and published the same year. In it the youthful Ion, king of Argos, sacrifices his life to rid his country of a pestilence. Hence, no doubt, the Hunts' analogy with Shelley.

There would seem to be some slight mystery in the matter. The bust has never been popular. The Curran sketch, girlish, weak, and as unconvincing as a mediocre Pre-Raphaelite, has held its own in reproduction after reproduction (it would be an interesting pastime to select the worst), for lack of a better portrait. Mrs. Hunt's bust, instead of giving "a gratification of the highest kind," has usually administered a shock. Had the Curran angel, we ask, so soon deteriorated into this fagged-out, wide-faced man of melancholy whose extravagantly drooping mouth expresses defeat and hopelessness and whose eyes seem veiled and dim? We know, in fact, that Shelley was never like the Curran picture, and we suspect that he was never like the bust. Marianne Hunt, modeling from memory, might so easily have failed. Yet she had seen Shelley in those last and harassed days before the drowning. And in the announcement there is testimony that the bust was, or *had been,* like Shelley. The lips nerved with feeling, the soul sitting in the eyes, the conversational zeal in his bright countenance—where have these vivacities fled?

On the other hand, we have the testimony of Leigh Hunt's friend and schoolfellow, Thomas Barnes, editor of the *Times,* to whom a copy of the bust was sent. Thanking Hunt for the gift on July 4, Barnes said he had only seen Shelley once, in his Oxford days, remembering him as a fine-looking youth with an ingenuous countenance that ought never to look old. "But I see by the bust that misfortune and disappointment had narrowed his features into an expression of disconsolate discontent. In spite of the beauty of the execution the bust inflicted on me as sharp a pang as I ever felt." It seems to have been as capable as Shelley's own mobile face of making different impressions on its several beholders. That countenance and character seemed to Leigh Hunt, when he greeted Shelley in Genoa, to be "the same as ever, with the exception of less hope." To Thornton Hunt, a small boy with a vivid recollection of the poet as he had been four years earlier, Shelley seemed, as it were, to have expanded, acquiring confidence, cheerfulness, and strength. Marianne has not recorded her own view; probably she saw both aspects in the short time they were together.

She appears to have worked apart on her undertaking, for we find no reference to it in letters before 1836. Mary had importuned her for silhouettes only, and Hunt himself, as we have seen, was asking for one as late as 1835; but in May, 1826, Charles Armitage Brown had written to Hunt from Florence, saying that W. S. Landor was anxious to know if there was a portrait of Shelley, and begging that Hunt would urge his wife to make one *either in clay* or in paper, if none existed. It may well be that she then adopted the idea, and had made an unsuccessful attempt by 1828 when Hunt asserted in his *Lord Byron* that Shelley's features "would not have told well in a bust." In any case, here in 1836, was the finished object, enabling many people to see Shelley, if not plain, yet certainly different, certainly less feminine. Hunt gave Marianne a public compliment in his *Blue-Stocking Revels, or The Feast of the Violets,* published in 1837. Apollo is receiving all the feminine talent of the day, colorful and abundant as a garden of flowers:

> *But what pleased me hugely, he called to my wife,*
> *And said, "You have done Shelley's mood to the life."*

Copies were "about" for several years. We know from his correspondence that in 1838 Hunt promised one to his friends the Dalbys,[3] since his wife was "to put two or three of the busts in presentable condition, for some friends, i.e. take the seams off and oil them; and one of them will come to you and Mrs. Dalby, by coach, with thanks for all kindness." The curious thing is that so few appear to have survived. We hear that one went to the Carlyles, that Browning possessed one, that William Bell Scott begged, borrowed, or was given one from which to make an etching. Further inquiry reveals all these as being, apparently, the same copy, which explains to some degree why the late Newman I. White, in his discussion on Shelley portraiture, refers to it as sculpture and treats it as being an object unique and unrepeatable.

To follow the fortunes of this cast a while, we find it given first by the Hunts to Carlyle. (His wife found the new arrival embellishing her "best room" in Chelsea on her return from traveling in September, 1836.) This although Carlyle was no admirer of Shelley[4] and his wife

---

[3] J. W. Dalby, who was so uncomplimentary to Percy Florence, used at one time to write an annual poem to Shelley on the poet's birthday. He has not be-rhymed the bust though. Hunt's promise is dated June 20, 1838.

[4] "A haggard existence, that of his!" Carlyle said to Southey, who paused and agreed earnestly, "It *is* a haggard existence." Southey, as might be expected, had been speaking of Shelley with "sorrow and aversion." He was still, in 1838, laboriously defending his own attitude against accusations of intolerance. "I took a great liking to him," he persists shrilly in a letter to J. E. Reade on June 12, "believed (most erroneously as it proved) that he would

found Marianne a torment. It was scrutinized with displeasure one day in 1839 by the fastidious and resplendent Count D'Orsay, who pronounced, "I dislike it very much; there is a sort of faces who seem to weesh to swallow their chins and this is one of them." So Mrs. Carlyle reported to her mother.[5] A story goes that Carlyle in old age turned angrily on Bell Scott who had been singing the poet's praises, and stamping on the ground exclaimed, "This Shelley of yours was a scoundrel and he ought to have been hanged."[6] Their walk proceeded in painful silence, but Carlyle, relenting, had hardly reached home when he dispatched the bust to Scott as a peace-offering. The tale appears to be apocryphal. I am indebted to Sir Shane Leslie for the information (which came to him from Wilfrid Meynell) that Browning almost certainly had his copy of the bust from Carlyle and lent it to Bell Scott who was to make a steel-cut of it.

The subsequent history of this cast belongs to a later point of our narrative. What strikes us now as odd, if not mysterious, is the virtual disappearance of every other cast of Marianne's bust. Mary must surely have possessed one. This would in time have joined the "Boscombe relics," but it has been said, no doubt correctly, that the poet's daughter-in-law Lady Shelley disliked the bust intensely—as Trelawny also did. When a question arose, years later, of using it for Shelley's tomb, he condemned it as "only fit for a scarecrow." Lady Shelley was to indulge her own taste in monuments, of a more high-flown order. Even so modern a critic as Newman Ivey White pronounced the bust a bad likeness because it differed so much from the Curran-and-Clint portraiture. We may take it that Lady Shelley and her school of biographers—Dowden, Garnett, Mrs. Marshall— were even more emphatic in this opinion. The bust evidently had no wide circulation; we may doubt whether any commercial orders were received. But there is still no clue to the loss of those copies given to

outgrow his extravagance, that his heart would bring him right, and that the difference between us was that at that time he was just nineteen and I was eight and thirty,—the observation appeared not to please him, for he would not allow that that could make any difference. Coleridge was equally mistaken in saying that the reports of Shelley's moral character and conduct were essentially false. I know them to be true, and the story is the most frightful tragedy that I have known in real life. . . ." (From an unpublished letter quoted by Anderson Galleries, New York, November 13, 1935.)

[5] Newman I. White ascribes a variant on this comment to Carlyle himself, but it is said that Browning had done so before White.

[6] *Pall Mall Gazette,* August 6, 1892.

Dalby, possibly Hunt's Mrs. Dashwood, and other friends, and more especially to Talfourd, who, thanking Hunt "for the resemblance of a dead yet immortal poet," added, "I never had the good fortune to see Shelley but I always cherished the deepest sense of his moral qualities."[7]

❦{ 11 }❦

At the same period as this portrait in clay we find the fiction writers, other than Mary, painting their distorted and fantastic pictures of the poet. In 1835—the year *Lodore* appeared—Henry Austen Driver published *Harold de Burun, a Semi-dramatic Poem* in six scenes, of which the *Gentleman's Magazine* noted, "Lord Byron is the hero of this poem, Percy, is Percy B. Shelley; and Teresa, we suppose, the Countess of Guiccioli." As the other characters were a hermit, a peasant, and a minstrel, the reviewer found them strange materials for a drama, but allowed that the author's genius had produced a clever and powerful poem. The next year, an anonymous three-decker, *Jerningham, or the Inconsistent Man,* came from a hard-working and catholic imitator of several schools of thought. The *Court Journal* was able to spot Godwin and Bulwer behind the "humanity," the Elizabethan dramatists behind the "passions," and Shelley behind the "poetic philosophy." The character of Everard Sinclair, an enthusiastic reformer, meant for Shelley, was "drawn with a true sense of poetry and a fine moral meaning." Taking *Harold* and *Jerningham* as read, we may move along the gallery to glance at the only one of these fictional pen portraits that is at all remembered in our day.

Crabb Robinson, making a New Year call at Lady Blessington's in 1837, nodded to the familiar faces of D'Orsay, Trelawny, Dr. Lardner, and Bulwer, and was held up before an unfamiliar visitor with whom he discussed German literature and the satires of Landor. This "stranger, whose conversation interested and pleased me," says the diarist, "I found to be young Disraeli." One might find almost anyone—with certain social limits—at Lady Blessington's; but the

---

[7] Quoted by Mr. Payson G. Gates, who points out that the relevant letters between Hunt and Talfourd are respectively in the Harvard College library and the Brewer Collection at the University of Iowa.

blossoming statesman and novelist was a close enough friend to write to his hostess that same spring, reporting on the developments in grace and stature of one who was to be Lady Blessington's goddaughter— "the fair *Venetia*." When this lovely offspring duly appeared in print, her begetter confessed in a dedication that he "had attempted to shadow forth, though as 'in a glass darkly' two of the most renowned and refined spirits that have adorned these our latter days." Disraeli had used his distorting glass to fit his story, and to provide that link-to-link arrangement of characters which Mary Shelley's fashionable novels have led us to expect.

His most striking adjustment was to separate Shelley and Byron by a generation, so that while the latter, as Lord Cadurcis, swaggers with boyish impudence and defiance through the narrative, the former poet's enterprise and reforming zeal are relegated to the American war of independence, and his abandoned daughter is of an age to provide Byron with a love match. This Marmion Herbert (a descendant of Herbert of Cherbury) is undoubtedly a "gentleman," for all that blot upon his past when he left Lady Annabel, his wife, and exiled himself in Geneva to write heretical books and take a mistress. (Byron is apparently mixed in with this.) He is a gentleman in spite of the apparent betrayal of king and country that marked his heroic gesture for republicanism. Why else should the deserted Lady Annabel have kept the scoundrel's memory green and ardent, locked up methodically in such a shrine as Lady Shelley was to install some twenty years later to the honor of her father-in-law the poet? (Even Disraeli could not have foreseen that worship.) So, in boldly, and not insensitively, declaring Shelley's worth, the diplomatic author made it clear that what he praised was wholly admirable. There was queer behavior in his Herbert, but there could not and should not be that undying query which will never allow Shelley to rest securely poised between the estimates of saint and villain. Disraeli's was a novel; his technique was right when he made Herbert reappear, a heretic still, but wise with years and experience, to be reconciled as in a Shakespearean comedy to his half-faithful wife and wholly loving daughter, to meet Lord Cadurcis, who had long admired his work and meant to be ever faithful to Venetia. Like their prototypes, the two must talk philosophy on the Italian coast between Genoa and Spezia, Herbert quoting from the *Defence of Poetry,* "poets are the unacknowledged legis-

lators of the world.''[8] Then the storm blows up, the young and the
elder poet are drowned together, and in time Venetia takes her idol's
name and title by a marriage with his cousin, Captain George.

What mainly delighted the reviewer in *Fraser's* (with its strong
Shelleyan interest) was the manly and "truly *English* spirit" of the
work. The characters could be recommended to provincials as a model
of aristocracy. "It was, indeed, a high and noble aspiration," said the
reviewer, "to attempt the placing of two such characters in a just light
before their countrymen." The whole review was intended as a leg-up
for the Tories, and we may smile again to think that Shelley the
reformer has fallen, in this twisted way, into the Conservative camp
for vindication.

⚜ III ⚜

Mary's determination to write Godwin's life hung fire. Her conscience
told her to bear the task in mind, her particular prudence and fear of
notoriety said "wait." "This year," she explained to Trelawny in
January, 1837, "I have to fight my poor Percy's battle, to try and get
him sent to College without further delapidation of his ruined prospects, and he has now to enter life at College. That this should be
undertaken at a moment when a cry was raised against his Mother,
and that not on the question of *politics* but *religion,* would mar all.
I must see him fairly launched before I commit myself to the fury of
the waves. A sense of duty towards my Father, whose passion was
posthumous fame, makes me ready, as far as I am concerned, to meet
the misery that must be mine if I become an object of scurrility and
attack . . ." and so to her habitual song of loneliness and obscurity,
ending with the practical request for a twenty-pound loan. No doubt
this vision of her hounded life played its part in steeling Mary for her
conquests. This time she was to see Percy go up to Cambridge on
July 7, as a pensioner of Trinity College, under the tutorship of Mr.
Thorp. She had published *Falkner,* for which she might to some extent
have thanked Trelawny, who rode unmistakably in another of those

---

[8] Lord Iddesleigh, writing an introduction to a later edition of *Venetia*, wound up with
the impressive assurance that this famous remark originated in the pages of the novel. It may
sometimes pay to quote.

truth-with-fiction circuses, and was seen to burn the corpse of a drowned girl. It was too mock-Shelleyan; Trelawny did not like it, nor can we feel anything better than a certain compassion for the woman who was driven to a kind of desperation, selling all she had and held, for this terrible fetish of orthodox progress through the mill of culture. It may have raised her spirits to receive a general compliment from Leigh Hunt in his *Feast of the Violets*—an appraisal of the feminine talent of the day:

> *And Shelley, four-famed—for her parents, her lord,*
> *And the poor lone impossible monster abhorred.*
> *(So sleek and so smiling she came, people stared,*
> *To think such fair clay should so darkly have dared;*
> *But Apollo the very name loved so, he turned*
> *To a glory all round her, which shook as it burned,*
> *And a whirlwind of music came sweet from the spheres).*

Hunt's mind was straying from the secondary back to the primary Shelley. He was to be given yet another opportunity for one of his untiring character studies when he was asked to provide notices of Keats and Shelley for C. S. Hall's anthology, the *Book of Gems* (1838). Shelley's poetry is praised with that facility of expression which is almost Hunt's downfall. It resembles creation, he affirms; "it hungers and thirsts after a certain beauty of perfection, as the orb rolls in loving attraction round the sun. He is remarkable . . . for being alike supernatural and human in his enthusiasm. . . . He not only

> *Relishes all things sharply,*
> *Passioned as we—*

he is far more passioned, and relishes them with a sharpness that makes him cry out like one constituted almost too delicately for existence."

More humanly constituted and less troubled by her mysterious father than the fictional Venetia was, Shelley's daughter Ianthe was preparing, in 1837, to make a comfortable marriage which should be solemnized with the good will of her one surviving grandfather (John Westbrook having died in 1835, leaving £60,000) and her property-owning aunt, Eliza Farthing Beauchamp. The chosen suitor was

Edward Jeffries Esdaile, who, as Gregson informed Sir Timothy in July, was "the eldest son of the eldest son of old Mr. Esdaile of the late firm of Esdaile & Co., bankers of Lombard Street." There was money on both sides of the family, the banker now living as a country gentleman at Cothelstone House, in Somersetshire, where the Beauchamps also resided at Walford House. The son, Gregson assured Sir Tim, would make a respectable match for the young lady, "upon whom report says that Mr. Beauchamp intends to bestow a fortune." A rumor, probably exaggerated, had it that Edward himself possessed some four thousand pounds a year. Decidedly, this reputable branch of the family was giving Sir Tim less trouble than the other. The two were married on September 27, and paid a visit to Sir Timothy's sister, Mrs. Parks, when Ianthe seemed well and happy, and "he behaved perfectly like a gentleman and very attentive to his wife. They promised to return and to write; and, in the manner of the young, did neither. But they made a dutiful appearance at Field Place.

While on the subject of marriage, we seem to have Trelawny to deal with again. The pirate had grown tired of society; in the summer of 1837 he departed to live for a while in "an old Cornish mansion" at Pencarrow, near Bodmin, prowling, as he put it, in narrower circles as he began to age. From here he went to Putney Hill, leading "the life of a recluse," wrote Lady Blessington, "never going to see a single acquaintance or friend, and scarcely ever visiting London." He made it appear so, maybe; but like any London fop he had his town addresses and was rapidly improving his friendship with one "Mrs. Goring," finding it perhaps more suitable to his character to drop her title as wife of Sir Harry Vane Goring. So he took society with him into the Putney wilderness and improved his friendship into an elopement, to the distaste of his daughter Zella, who was old enough by now to be his housekeeper. The unwanted daughter was packed off to the Continent, where she met and married a Mr. Olguin. Again Trelawny was to dodge the scandal of the courts; Lady Goring's divorce and, it is said, her marriage to him were procured by a "special Act of Parliament," all being done in privacy. She appears to have kept her barbaric spouse quiet for several years, with the exception of his sudden disposal of all the furniture in the London house, leaving only a few kitchen furnishings and a couple of beds—an act to parallel his hairdressing and baby-parceling escapades. Age, one may say, was

so far quelling the pirate that he confined his executions to the in-
organic. With or without furniture, the latest Mrs. Trelawny set about
providing three new children for the crooked ménage.

Mary, free now of her monster tales from *Frankenstein* to *Falkner,*
was working at last on a theme that was neither fantastical nor
machine made, but approached as near as she could make it to the
divine. The chance had come: Percy was safe at Cambridge; the
Godwin biography was shelved; novel writing was at a standstill—
was, in fact, never to be resumed. At the same time, selections and
piratical editions of Shelley's works with none to vouch for their
accuracy seemed likely to increase and multiply, and Moxon was keen
to publish a definitive edition. Mary, of course, must beg permission
to edit it. Gregson, as a "man of the world," was sympathetic, and
thus passed the case on to Sir Timothy: "The 'March of Intellect'
since 1815 has probably placed the rising generation in a situation to
be little damaged by this poetry, which I have read of, but never read."
The verdict of Field Place was: publish—but no memoir. We know
how skillfully Mary leaped that obstacle. The notes after each section
of the poems speak a more intimate and personal language than any
formal memoir would have done; and the arrangement must have
been congenial, giving her a chance to slip silently by those periods
and incidents she preferred to miss.

"Torn to pieces by memory," worried by her task, growing ill
before it was over, railing a little at her unsympathetic friends, Mary
struggled through the editing of the *Poetical Works,* using the final
notes to convey her own agony of recollection as much as the tragedy
of the poet she honored. *Queen Mab,* that had already caused so much
trouble and was to cause much more, became her stumbling-block.
First, she had difficulty in procuring a copy of the original edition,
even asked Moxon to try to get one from Southey, but was at last able
to borrow one—a valued relic of genius—from Mrs. de Boinville in
Paris. Then the publisher insisted on her cutting out the most "atheistical" portions, which would have injured his copyright. "I dislike
Atheism, but I shrink from mutilation," she wrote to Moxon; but
after consulting Hunt, Hogg, and Peacock, who seem to have favored
her own right to do as she pleased, she bowed to her publisher, and
Queen Mab appeared with the sting drawn from both text and notes.
On her own judgment Mary decided to drop the verses to Harriet,

remembering that Shelley had been glad to find "a foolish dedication to my late wife" omitted by the "piratical fellow" Clark in 1821.

For these mutilations the editor drew a storm down on her head. Trelawny, on seeing the tell-tale asterisks (Canto XII was printed with as much reticence as Chapters XVIII and XIX of the last volume of *Tristram Shandy*), "sent back the volume to Moxon in a rage." "How very much," Mary commented, "he must enjoy the opportunity thus afforded him of doing a rude and insolent act!" Hogg, too, wrote an insulting letter about that absent dedication. All this led the editor to exclaim bitterly. "In so arduous a task others might hope for encouragement and kindness from their friends—I know mine better." She had believed herself long suffering and detached enough, affirming, "There are other verses I should well like to obliterate for ever, but they will be printed." And certainly *Epipsychidion* made its brave appearance, without a word of comment; and the poems to Jane Williams were included, although, as in the Medwin papers, Jane's name was kept out of them.

⋯❀{ IV }❀⋯

The four-volume 1839 edition of the *Poetical Works* and Mary's notes to it are too well known to need description here. We may note the dedication to Percy Florence; also that Finden's engraving of the Curran portrait of Shelley, already familiar, found itself standardized as frontispiece, hardly to be released from duty throughout a century of Shelley books, except by those who preferred to go back to the elementary Curran or forward to the careful copyist Clint. Mary's notes everywhere supply a biographical and a spiritual clue to the poems, besides rendering Shelley's tragedy forever inseparable from his writings. The sympathy and intense emotion that drove her pen have given them a quality that is, on its own note, almost as lasting and unforgettable as the poetry itself. In this work Mary, without fictional barriers, wrote with deep sincerity and touched her zenith. However we may judge her other writings, it is these editorial notes which, appearing in the later "definitive" edition of the poems, establish her place in literature. *Frankenstein,* it is true, will be remembered as a more than ingenious romance; but so long as Shelley continues to be, in English poetry, the living force whose progress we are watching, so Mary's intimate editorship—personal, biased as it is in parts—must have its importance. We should honor her not only for performing it, but for submerging her own literary egotism while she did so, in the recognition that it could be more valuable to edit than to create. All her imperfect harmonies are reconciled here. Mary intrudes, and we welcome her intrusions, for she is a part of the totality. Her poignant, analytical story woven in with the poetry of the years is an indication—if any was needed—of why Shelley's life and writings can only be considered together, for either to be richly understood. Neither the conceit of a Medwin nor the exuberant egotism of a Hogg distort the picture; if Mary could not capture the entire Shelley, at least she did not project a mythical one.

The second edition of the *Poetical Works* appeared the same year in one volume, entirely reset. Apart from the workaday two-column arrangement of its printing, it was an improvement in every way. Not only had Mary, yielding to pressure from her hostile friends, restored the dedication to Harriet and all the missing passages of *Queen Mab,* but a more general conquest of editorial timidity served to swell the volume and exhibit Shelley in a further aspect. In the first edition Mary had been diffident and reserved to the point of cutting out an entire facet of the poet lest it should make enemies. Now she dared to present the brisk satirist and energetic critic of poetry and politics by publishing *Peter Bell the Third* and *Swellfoot the Tyrant.* Shelley is at last allowed his humor. Even so, she apologized for both as "playthings," while defending their views and sentiments to justify her decision. She was brave on a further point: for the first time the 1822 poems to Jane were printed in full, though still her name was prudently suppressed. "I now present this edition," Mary wound up her postscript, "as a complete collection of my husband's poetical works, and I do not foresee that I can hereafter add to or take away a word or line." It was hardly in her vision to foresee the files of anxious scholars who would busy themselves altering words or lines which their rivals had cunningly worked out as definitive.

But this scholarly era is as yet ahead of us. The critics of the first 1839 edition were indifferent to the finer textual problems. Most of them took this opportunity to place Shelley once more in the dock, pursue a thorough inquiry into his character and principles, and after a little head-shaking and a good deal of appreciation, acquit him with honor. Times had moved. For the rest, some of them chose to scratch their pens on Mary's notes. It was unfortunate for her that the *Examiner* was no longer under Hunt's editorship. Here, on February 3, she found herself in most unfriendly hands. The reviewer of Volume I declares:

> We will frankly say that we do not like the tone which pervades . . . Mrs. Shelley's remarks. There is throughout more of a cold and laboured effort to say what ought to be said, than of either the desire or the power to say it. We may be wrong, and we are very sorry if we are so, but it seems to us that there is, in her nicely-balanced phrases and well-rounded periods, far more of wordy affectation than of the gushing sympathy she professes. We feel this the more for the large need that Shelley's genius has of sympathy in its widest and most intense signification—and of the spirit that giveth life rather than of the letter that killeth.

The reviewer protests against the "emasculation" of *Queen Mab*. "It is a falsification of Shelley's nature and history. . . . Poets don't write for the instruction of boarding schools." Decidedly times have moved on. Shelley's genius is taken for granted here, and a knowledge of his work is assumed in the reader. The *Spectator*, reviewing the work in sheets on January 26, took a different view. Here was "another adventurous speculation of Mr. Moxon," for the "fanciful character" of Shelley's poetry, "like the puerile simplicity of much of Wordsworth's," would hardly amuse readers or attract those seeking a picture of man as he exists and hoping to deduce moral instruction therefrom. "But perhaps people buy who do not read"; already the suggestion seems to be that poor Shelley (in elegant form) is joining the ranks of reputable authors that a snob must place, and leave, on his bookshelf. The *Edinburgh Review,* in a long article in July, found cause to sanction the mutilation of *Queen Mab,* but not the secrecy of the act. The reviewer was minded, too, to rail against the inadequate biographical matter until, coming upon Mary's confession at the end— "I dislike speaking of myself, but cannot help apologizing to the dead, and to the public"—he accepted the apology in a gentlemanly way by quoting it.

The friendly *Court Journal,* on February 9, confidently upheld Shelley's "sublime powers," and heralded their universal acknowledg-

Letter from Mary Shelley to Douglas Jerrold, August 9, 1834,
requesting free passes for the theater.

MS in the author's possession

ment. True that some might still think him "nothing but 'a very clever gentleman, but so eccentric,' as old women observe." Yet (now comes the gem of it):

> —the fame of a *great poet* can only be posthumous inasmuch as he must always be in advance of his age. . . . Many a bygone linen-draper is obliterated though he sold elegant ribbons—but a meteor will rise up into the heavens from the tomb of Shelley—a meteor that shall last for ever to illuminate and etherialise all things on earth with the strength of its great heat.

(A phenomenon indeed! Linen-drapers should outlast meteors in the normal way. We are to watch plenty of activity at the tomb of Shelley, but no such rocket as this.)

We need not study the press further, except to note a slight development of attitude in the *Monthly Chronicle*. The previous year a discussion the "Present State of Poetry" (Monckton Milnes's poems were in the dock) had inspired a warning to the present generation against the dangerous influence of Shelley. "We cannot imagine a worse model for a young poet of genius, who has allowed his admiration for Shelley to suffuse his whole mind, than that most dazzling poet. . . . His heart was simple, his intellect was not." In 1839 the same paper saw the time arriving when justice would be done to Shelley's genius at the expense of Southey, Bowles, Ebenezer the Corn Law Rhymer, and other temporary godheads. As for the obstacles to his fame—we have met them portentously explained so often in prefaces, memoirs, and reviews that instead of quotations from these many journalists, the recurrent argument may as well go into a jingle:

> *His intricate obscurity*
> *Deferred his popularity,*
> *As also his profundity*
> *Of metaphysicality;*
> *His want of keen simplicity,*
> *His freedom from banality,*
> *Though lucid to posterity,*
> *Detracted from reality,*
> *And might induce hostility*
> *In those of small ability,*
> *Who hadn't the dexterity*
> *To grasp etherial verity. . . .*

To return more soberly to the *Monthly Chronicle*: "His spirit is embalmed in these elegant volumes," the reviewer ended with funereal gusto.

It is to be noted that although Mary had hoped, by her official edition, to suppress the pirates, such hardened performers as Benbow and Daly continued to publish their own partial and inaccurate versions, labeling them, as pleasure or business sense dictated, the "Complete Poetical Works."[9] Against these Mary could do nothing, but as a journalist she was not averse from getting her own back on the critics. There was an easy opportunity when she brought out the *Essays, Letters from Abroad, Translations and Fragments* in two volumes in 1840. In the preface she declared, "I am far from satisfied with the tone in which the criticisms of Shelley are written. Some among these writers praise the poetry with enthusiasm, and even discrimination, but none understand the man." Medwin received a special thrust at his *Shelley Papers*: "Generally speaking, his extracts are incorrect and incomplete." She gives one piece of practical news which we cannot afford to miss if the School of Divine Incompetence is to be countered; this is Shelley's project of a steamboat to ply between Marseilles and Leghorn. Some extracts from Edward Williams's diary were inserted as footnotes to Volume II. More than sixty years were to go by before it occurred to a Boscombe enthusiast to publish the journal. Even then it was strangely cut and mangled; only recently has a complete text appeared, and that not in England.[10] With Shelley's two memorandum books, the diary had been drowned on the fatal expedition and brought to the surface with the rescued *Don Juan*. It was worth redeeming, as being a record of the two men's movements before any hint of epitaphs and after-fame had arisen to induce self-consciousness in the writer. Apart from letters it remains the only perfectly spontaneous account of those final months, and after dwelling with the boastful, agonized, or in other ways sophisticated narratives of survivors, one may turn back to it with a cordial sense of freshness and relief.

[9] A dumpy little pocket-sized *Daly* of 1836 in my possession, claiming to be the first miniature edition, is distinguished by the misprint:

Vultures who build your bowels
High in the Future's towers.

[10] Edited (together with the Gisborne journals and letters) by Frederick L. Jones (Norman, Okla., 1951).

The troubles of *Queen Mab* were not yet over. Privately printed, rehandled by the author, published without his permission, banned by the Society for Suppression of Vice, reprinted and republished with piratical constancy after his death, used by every journalist to flay the atheist and by every revolutionary to support his argument, emasculated by Mary and her publisher, restored to quell the outcry of friends and critics alike, it reappeared in its entirety in time to raise a storm from a new quarter. In 1841, Moxon was indicted for publishing the "blasphemous and seditious works" of Percy B. Shelley. The history of that prosecution is one of the most curious chapters in Shelleyan after-fame, for the charge was a protest against the governmental forces of law and tyranny and was brought by the very type of reformer Shelley himself would have upheld. Not the slightest animosity to the poet was intended by a group who were even then publishing cheap accessible editions of Godwin, Robert Owen, and Frances Wright, and might very easily have been publishing Shelley, too. In fact, only his possession by a *gentlemanly* publisher laid him open to that particular attack. If the name of Hetherington—used so scornfully by Sergeant Talfourd in his famous "Speech for the Defendant"—has become dirt to hasty Shelleyans, they have only to look clearly at the man to see that his name does stand for liberty, courage, and enlightenment, in a more practical way than Shelley's own.

Born in the same year as the poet, Henry Hetherington, having set up as a printer and publisher, fought persistently for a free press and for the rights of the worker. He was the instigator of the "National Union of the Working Classes," which led eventually to Chartism. But his free-press campaign caused him the more personal trouble. At a time when a four-penny stamp duty was payable on all periodicals, when news, politics, and advertisements were taxed, with a heavy duty on paper, Hetherington fairly asked for prison by issuing *The Poor Man's Guardian* for the people, priced at one penny, with the announcement that it was "established contrary to law." Imprisonment, for him and his numerous vendors, followed at once, but the *Guardian* continued, while every variety of trick and disguise was used in order to distribute it. Publishing further unstamped weekly papers, in and out of prison, together with his loyal helpers to the number of some five hundred, organizing a fund for the victims, eagerly standing his trial and bearing his punishments, Hetherington won at last, when the Court of Exchequer declared the *Guardian* a "strictly legal publication," the four-penny tax was reduced to one-penny (which ruined the circulation of the unstamped papers) and later repealed.

This rebellion so far has little concern with Shelley. His part follows. The government was carefully watching its working-class opponents, and an indictment was preferred against Hetherington for selling blasphemous writings. The work, or pretext, was Haslem's *Letters to the Clergy of All Denominations,* which was charged as a libel on the Old Testament. Pending the trial, Hetherington determined, on the advice of his fellow reformers, to attempt retaliation and so find out if the law had an equal application to gentlemen and workmen. Accordingly, he himself turned prosecutor for blasphemy, the obvious work on which to try his experiment happening to be the second edition of the Shelley volume. A compositor named Holt was sent to apply for the book at several booksellers, and obtained it from Moxon and three others. Hetherington then indicted these four in June, 1841. He had been tried and served his own brief sentence before June 23, when the prosecution of the *Queen* v. *Moxon* came on for trial in the Court of Queen's Bench before Lord Denman. Thomas Noon Talfourd, in publishing his "Speech for the Defendant," has himself quoted for us the thunderous words of the indictment. It charged, he says, that Moxon,

> being an evil-disposed and wicked person disregarding the laws and religion of this realm, and wickedly and profanely devising and intending to bring the Holy Scriptures and the Christian religion into disbelief and contempt, unlawfully and wickedly, did falsely and maliciously publish a scandalous, impious, profane, and malicious libel of and concerning the Christian religion, and of and concerning the Holy Scriptures, and of and concerning Almighty God, in which were contained certain passages charged as blasphemous and profane. It then set forth a passage in blank verse, beginning, *"They have three words: well tyrants know their use, well pay them for the loan, with usury torn from a bleeding world!— God, Hell, and Heaven;"* and after adding an innuendo, *meaning thereby that God, Hell and Heaven, were merely words,* proceeded

to recite a few more lines applying very coarse and irreverent, but not very intelligible comments to each of those words.

There were further charges, relating to passages of verse and prose, all, of course from *Queen Mab.* A Mr. Thomas, for the prosecution, discovered still further passages, though he (magnanimously) "eulogized the genius of Shelley, and fairly admitted the respectability of the defendant." He called the compositor Holt, who proved the purchase of volumes at the desire of Hetherington. Then came Talfourd's speech, which for its insight and skillful marshaling of literary parallels, should have moved any court that was not wedded to the letter of its indictments.[11]

Talfourd had been Moxon's friend for many years, and on the occasion of the prosecution his first thoughts and feelings were not for Shelley, whom he had never met, not even for Moxon, whom he was defending, so much as for the dearest and most regretted friend of "early and happy days," by whom the publisher had been introduced to him. Let us forget certain exuberant writings about frogs and atheists, to appreciate Talfourd's heartfelt and deserving tribute to Charles Lamb. "Would to God that the spirit which pervaded his being could decide the fate of this strange prosecution—I should only have to pronounce his name and to receive your verdict!" He turned to the details of the charge. *Queen Mab,* wild, disjointed, visionary, difficult, yet contained "as much to ponder on, to weep over, as any half-formed work of genius which ever emanated from the vigour and the rashness of youth." Was it blasphemy to present the mistakes, struggles, depressions, and victories of such a spirit? He cited Fielding

11 I would urge some student of the nineteenth century to turn from the resounding names and raise a fitting memorial to Sir Thomas Noon Talfourd, judge, orator, dramatist, and writer of *belles lettres,* but loved and remembered not so keenly for these accomplishments as for his genius of personal friendship. If there have been more brilliant lawyers and sublimer tragedians (his *Ion,* in the classic manner, is still just readable), they have not always been— as the *Times* pointed out in its obituary—men of such rich personality, such warm-hearted loyalty and truth. Talfourd was an invaluable ally of many whose names and achievements are a by-word. Apart from his close connection with Lamb, we may recall that the *Pickwick Papers* and *Pippa Passes* were dedicated to him by their authors. When he writes in his sonnet *To the Memory of the Poets* of

> *The fame of those sweet bards, whose fancies lie*
> *Like glorious clouds on summer's holiest even—*

we feel that his rightful place is somewhere in their neighborhood, even though death caught him addressing the grand jury at Stafford in his scarlet robes.

and Richardson as authors whose works contain passages which would hardly be endured by the Society for the Suppression of Vice. But in every case the antidote was to be found with the bane, especially so with Shelley's "cold speculations of a wild infidelity." In *Queen Mab* itself atheism was neutralized and materialism contradicted on every page. For a parallel he turned to *Paradise Lost,* arguing that while Shelley faltered into piety, Milton, believing himself engaged on a pious work, was led by his imagination to enthrone God's enemy. "Do you not feel with me," Talfourd appealed, "that, as without a knowledge of the *Paradise Lost,* you could not absolve the publisher of Milton from the prosecution of 'some mute, inglorious' Hetherington; so neither can you, dare you, convict Mr. Moxon of a libel on God and Religion, in publishing the works of Shelley, without having read and studied them all?"

At this point we should like to record that the court adjourned to study the *Poetical Works* over its beefsteak; but Talfourd's speech went on, not quite on the lines the Shelley of *Queen Mab* would have appreciated, but none the less with brilliant eloquence. Poetry could not, by the very art of it, deny God. If "an undevout astronomer is mad," how much more truly is an atheist poet a contradiction in terms! Dealing with the prose passages, Talfourd described a genius of ethereal fancies struggling with a theory gross, material, and shallow. "His genius was pent up within the hard and bitter rind of his philosophy, as Ariel was in the rift of the cloven pine; and what wonder if a spirit there enthralled should send forth strange and discordant cries? Because the words which those strange voices syllabled are recorded here, will you say the record is a crime?" What could sellers of the *Decline and Fall,* with its two chapters against Christianity, hope for from the prosecutors of *Queen Mab?* Any Hetherington might obtain their suppression. Shakespeare himself might be placed at the mercy of an "insect abuser of the press." If Shelley, why not Byron, Goethe . . . "Protect our noble literature," Talfourd's peroration urged, "from the alternative of being either corrupted or enslaved!"

Since that was not unlike Hetherington's argument, the irony of the prosecution is enhanced. Both prosecutor and defendant fought for liberty, while the court, unmoved by threats to Gibbon, Shakespeare, Milton (who knows if Fielding and Richardson had ever been read?), gave judgment according to its custom, and found Moxon guilty. The curiosity of the workers had been satisfied; they saw that if the law was an ass, it was at least an impartial blockhead, lacking the wits, no less than the audacity, to discriminate. The next step was for the prosecutor to call up the convicted "blasphemer" for judgment. But the prosecutors were not interested. "We had gained enough," a friend of Hetherington's wrote;[12] "prosecutions for blasphemy were stopped."

❧ VI ❧

If the public could know the true facts of the case, then, this latest storm could do no harm to Shelley. (That he chanced to be a gentleman, published by a gentleman, was its practical cause.) Yet even in the present days of headlines, radio, and verbatim press reports, the public is often enough faced with a result, of cause unknown. In the first Victorian decade, and before Hetherington had secured his untaxed press, the chances of clarity were still slenderer. It appeared only that the blasphemous poem had been banned again. Besides, as luck would have it, electioneering and political topics had largely crowded out the episode and squeezed the reports down to a minimum. Appreciating these accidents of fortune, Talfourd decided (to posterity's gratitude) to publish his fine speech in pamphlet form, prefaced by an explanation of the case.[13] Naturally there was no explanation of Hetherington's good motives; but he reaped his own reward—or rather, his fellow men reaped it, for their leader was to die of cholera eight years later. The poet's true fame was beginning to glow through atmospheric resistance; Shelley at least was not to die again. At the point we have reached—almost twenty years after his drowning—we need only pause for a hasty glance around us to be confident of this.

---

12 W. J. Linton, *Memories* (London, 1895). The husband of Eliza Lynn Linton and a supporter of the prosecutors, he explained: "We knew, of course, that the Shelley volume would only be well advertized by the prosecution, we had no desire that it should be otherwise. . . . our purpose was to prevent the trial of Hetherington or to affect his sentence." In the first they were unsuccessful, but the sentence was only four months, seemingly reduced to six weeks.

13 The copy in the Bodleian Library, from which these facts are taken, is autographed "H. N. Coleridge from E. Moxon, July 1841."

153

Since the *Posthumous Poems,* which might have been the mere farewell of an ephemeral writer, we have seen selections, fragments, editions steadily appearing, noted his stirring influence on young poets, and the admission of that influence, whether for good or bad, by the critics. We have seen France and Germany discovering him, and the advocates of reform and freedom studying him as a worthy pioneer. His friends have found it paid to publish him or their accounts of him; essayists and journalists have discussed him seriously as both poet and philosopher, giving him equal place—or at least equal space—with Wordsworth, Coleridge, the idol Byron, and the Laureate Southey. His two volumes have reached America, where the man, rather than his poetry, is reviewed in the Boston *Dial.* Critics are still concerned with his philosophy more than his poetics; but the easy trouncings on *Queen Mab's* account are over, and a new tendency to magnify *The Cenci* has arisen. G. H. Lewes, for instance, in the course of a fine article in the *Westminster Review* of April, 1841, finds it "the greatest work of our poet." Great, that is, amongst works that all have greatness, if they lack perfection.

Naturally there are dissentient voices; the greatest poets (like the finest films, in our own day) are rarely applauded by the multitude. It is enough that Shelley after twenty years is honored and respected for his poetry, unread maybe by Tories, or even Whigs of Sir Timothy's mold, but admitted, even by some of these, as library furniture. All he lacks is the broader popularity. And yet, one is not so sure. Let us take up *Bentley's Miscellany* for 1839, and there be diverted by Mr. Dickens's *Oliver Twist* and Mr. Harrison Ainsworth's *Jack Sheppard* running serially with the adornment of Cruikshank's witty pictures. These thieves and rascals are not meant for intellectual pastime. Even the great author who prefers to sign himself T. M. (let us cogitate keenly and supply –om –oore), in handing out a contribution, allows it to be a light satiric letter to S[am] R[ogers] in rhyme. The whole magazine is filled with jest and brightness. And what do we find there, jostling Jack and Oliver, slung in the gap between one Cruikshank and the next? The name of Shelley, who died and was cremated (unlike Jack Sheppard, who forever escapes). He is a subject for a Bentley's versifier, who has done his work most nimbly. I give some extracts here, together with the marginalia of a later skeptic as found on one copy, since these seem to help the melody by providing a bass counterpoint.

The Cremation of Shelley, on the Coast of Tuscany,
Under the Directions of Lord Byron

A let-down for
poor Trelawny!

On a lonely and a foreign shore,
  By a wide and boundless sea

British Shores are Best.

Where the sea-borne gales come bounding o'er
  A plain of immensity;

(—to bound the boundless.)

A corpse was laid on a funeral pyre
  Where the flames were rising high,
And the sentinels paced by that grim watch-fire,
  With a hurried and awe-struck eye. . . .

How does an eye
hurry?

But calm was the face of the beautiful dead
  Though his eye was closed and dim. . . .

How known to be dim
if closed?

And they turned to behold the gift
            in death

O wondrous emanation,
Proceeding from cremation!

  That burnish'd glory gave,—
A funeral pile, and a faded wreath
  A verse, and a sculptured grave!

We thought to see but ash or
chaff,
And found a sculptured epitaph.

The rites are o'er—the train is gone,
  And the sea-breeze sweeps the plain,

Who was the engine-driver?

And the tideless ocean murmurs on
  In its hoarse and solemn strain;
But the spot is still upon the shore
  On the coast so bleak and bare,

Out, damnéd spot!

With a poet's ashes sprinkled o'er,—
  Tread lightly—tread softly there!
           W. D. B.

The new fertilizer.
Watch your step, too.

CHAPTER VIII

Of Death and Disenchantments

MARY, it will be remembered, had declared in some of the gloomier moments of her first year back in England that she had suffered a twin loss: first of Shelley, secondly of Italy. Shelley she could not, and finally would not, replace, despite some essays in her early widowhood. But Italy she kept as a bright star before her, while knowing that its real glamour was behind. She never despaired of a sentimental journey to the land whose name "has magic in its very syllables," where the mortal remains[1] of husband and children lay, and where, she felt confident, her health would be miraculously restored and her weary mind "array itself in a vesture all gay in fresh and glossy hues." (All this the shy spirit was to confide afterwards to her public.) In 1840 the chance came. For Percy it was to be a summer vacation ramble and reading party, in company with two friends from Trinity. For Mary, sweet and sad anticipations gilded the preceding months. "It seems as if I were never to be stationary—I who long so for a home," she wrote to Marianne. "I shall be back in the autumn. . . . "It is a hard world," she went on, with the inheritance in mind, "—and there are some Immortals in it. Yet . . . Lady Cook is dead at 95—so I have only 8 years more to wait."

Percy, Mary, and her maid set out, staying a night in Calais, and traveling to Paris in the diligence, not yet superseded, as in England, by railroads. Despite fatigue, the aging Mary now shook off her cares, began, as it seemed, to array her mind in the motley vesture described above, and to write down every sort of personal or objective detail she could accumulate, with a view to supplying her publisher later on. Hogg had done it; Talfourd was to do it, starting on his travels the

[1] Precious little in Shelley's case, and lost in little William's—but we use the conventional phraseology.

following year; and there was no reason—apart from the hundred or two similar productions—why the author of *Frankenstein* should not record her journey over the well-known tracks. In Paris they met by arrangement Percy's fellow travelers. These were Alexander Knox and Robert Leslie Ellis. Knox, who was reading for the Bar, was to take to journalism, working on the staff of the *Times* for fourteen years. Ellis, a mathematician of remarkable promise, was destined to be laid low with rheumatic fever in 1849, dying ten years later. One may say that Percy was not only happier than his father in his choice of college friends, but that his first Continental trip was made in easier company and circumstances than the runaway poet's.

Since the details of the trip—from Mary's angle—are to be found in her travel book, there is no need to trace them all out here. They went down the Moselle and up the Rhine, saw something of the Black Forest, entered Italy, to Mary's great joy and keen emotion (the very window curtains and washstands reminded her of "Italy long, long ago"); and settled down for two months in Cadenabbia. There, except for an alarm from a mad Englishman, Mary's chief anxiety concerned the arrival of Percy's little boat. "In shape it is something of a sea boat, and it has a keel, and a tiny sail; but it is too small to convey a feeling of safety. I look at it and shudder. . . . A tragedy has darkened my life; I endeavor, in vain, to cast aside the fears which are its offspring."

Steaming down Lake Leman, she caught a glimpse of their old haunts of twenty-four years ago—Diodati "and our humble dwelling Maison Chapuis . . . the terraces, the vineyards . . . the little port where our boat lay moored"; recollections and regrets surged up again.

On October 10 she reached Paris, where she settled down to spend the fall. A long letter to Abraham Hayward gives us an idea of her general interests in a society under the threat of war. Sainte-Beuve she had met and liked, but thought no Frenchman had a right to sigh over Waterloo. Louis Philippe, whose life had recently been attempted, was well received, and thawed to tears in the Chambre des Députés. "It was strange to see a King upon his throne cry"; so Mary cried herself in sympathy. In Soult's Gallery she saw an "Assumption of the Virgin" by Murillo and described it with a guidebook's attention to detail; but in a "Birth of St. John the Baptist" she noted a little dog "sniffing at and going to play with a young angel's wing." (If only Mary could have sniffed more often at angels' wings, her traveler's notes would have gained in lightness and independence.) Concluding, she sent her love to Mrs. Norton and to "dear Rogers." To that almost octogenarian poet who had sung her Italy, Mary now gave the allegiance once bestowed so despairingly on younger writers. Procter was married, Irving was out of reach, Beddoes (if she cared) was studying medicine and publishing political verse at Zurich. There remained then, only the pleasures of memory, and to their poet the disenchanted widow was to turn later, when her Italian volumes required a dedication.[2]

Meanwhile, Percy, with one of his friends and separated from his mother, had endured a perilous journey. After "picking up" a priest at Como, they plunged into an adventure with a raft on the Lake of Lugano, not unlike Benvenuto Cellini's expedition on the Lake of Wallenstadt. The wind howled, the waters rose, the priest prayed, the young travelers pulled and pushed at the diligence which, horses and all, was on the raft and threatened to be shortly in the lake. Percy's suggestion (plucky enough for his father and more practical) was, "Jump over and swim till the horses are drowned, and then swim back to the raft." But by good luck they made the shore without capsizing. Trouble on the Dazio Grande followed. The road was broken up and carried away by the tempest, and might be repaired at earliest in a month. Inquiries established the existence of a doubtful track across the mountains, but only one man knew the route. They set off with some thirty squabbling guides to carry their "lighter impediments," a larger detachment following with the "obstacles." Percy took the high road and his friend the low road, which soon proved to be no road. Percy's party took the wrong road. Footholds had to be cut and bridges improvised; an Italian in bright blue trousers began crying like a child. All arrived at last on a road in good condition, were revived by *kirsch-wasser,* and reached the inn at Airolo with its "jolly English-loving fat landlord and pretty daughters."[3]

[2] Crabb Robinson writes in July, 1845, ". . . I breakfasted at Sam: Rogers's (our oldest poet) with Mrs. Shelley, the *worthy* descendant of Godwin and Mrs. Wollstonecraft and the consort of a man who in poetic genius better deserves to be classed with Wordsworth and Coleridge than either Byron, Scott or Tom Moore." A concession from Crabb, who had previously found Shelley's atheism sticking in his throat.

[3] The account was sent to Mary by Percy's fellow traveler, and printed verbatim in her book.

❈{ 11 }❈

So ended Percy Florence's first Continental holiday—for we should be considering him at least as much as his mother by now. In the following year, 1841, he attained both his B.A. and his majority. An increase in Mary's allowance on the latter event brought her annual total up to four hundred pounds. It was sufficient for another trip abroad. They went in June, 1842, crossing to Antwerp, and enduring an egregious series of travelers' losses as they hurried through Belgium. First, Mary dropped her passport; secondly, her maid forgot her handbasket; thirdly, three items of their baggage were missing at Malines; fourthly *"encore un objet de perdu"* at Liège, this time the young men's money, possibly stolen by the boots of the hotel. There was a rumpus; the hotelkeeper was rude, his daughter sympathetic, and Mary remembered that her life was "stained by tragedy." A return to the Rhine made up for most of their troubles, and, at Kissingen, Mary remained to take the "cure." In Weimar they spent "two or three hours in running about to visit the lions"[4]—i.e., the great men's houses.

From Dresden they made an excursion to a wooded ravine where a musical friend, also from Trinity, had fled to work in solitude. This was Henry Hugh Pierson, son of the Dean of Salisbury, who besides composing operas and oratorios had set to music many of Shelley's poems.[5] "The fanciful wildness, the tender melancholy, the holy calm of the poet," wrote Mary, "have met a similar inspiration on the part of the musician. They have as much melody as the Italian, as much science as the German school." ("They are very difficult to play," she wrote to Hunt.) While they remained there, Knox, in spite of heart trouble, was moved to poetry by the vale of Rabenau, but the poet's widow took badly to the rural life. After three nights she dragged her son away to Dresden, leaving poet and musician to compose their

---

[4] We may bear in mind this expression "running about" when, in a few years, De Quincey quotes it from the lips of the young Harriet, and drops a tear over her "fawn-like playfulness" and gloomy death. Here is the forty-five-year-old Mary with her grown-up son, running about among the lions. She, too, will die eventually, though not by water. And will De Quincey weep?

[5] Pierson was a considerable figure in his day, composing on the grand scale, German fashion. Some of his oratorios were performed at the Norwich festivals, and his operas produced in Hamburg. For his incidental music to the second part of Goethe's *Faust*, he was given the gold medal for art and science by Leopold I of Belgium.

pieces undisturbed The road to Venice set Mary dreaming over her past tortures, recalling the nightmare journey when her child was dying. In Venice they passed under the walls of the madhouse Shelley's *Julian and Maddalo* described. So to Florence, where she spent the winter. In March, 1843, they arrived in Rome; "the bourne of a pious pilgrimage. The treasures of my youth lie buried here." Instead of them, she looked at a comet, and put in much laborious work at the picture galleries. In June they were at Sorrento, joined again by Leslie Ellis, and playing with a sailing boat that Percy had from Naples. A friend of Knox's[6] speaks of "the noontide picnics, graced by the intellectual enthusiasm of Mary Shelley." Knox himself was recalled from this idyll to England by the news of his father's business losses.

⊰ III ⊱

In the fall of 1843, Mary went to live in Putney, at the White Cottage, Lower Richmond Road—a house which she describes apologetically, according to her fashion. It is shabbily furnished, has no spare room, the "nice little garden" is sadly untrimmed, but the situation suits Percy, who has bought a boat. Here she prepared her *Rambles in Germany and Italy* for Moxon.[7] Another tale of trouble is mixed up with them. She hoped, by their publication, to provide money for a rascally Italian named Gatteschi. Mary's leaning towards the picturesque in gentlemen this time brought her near to disaster. Gatteschi had been introduced by Claire in Paris at the house of Lady Susan Lennox, whose title, with his professed "good birth," seemed to vouch for his integrity. Both Claire and Mary had an emotional faith in him. Meanwhile he was poor, accepted money given "delicately," supplied historical notes (Godwin's old function) for Mary's book, and lodged in England with Alexander Knox, who took to him better than Percy did. Mary's affections fell under his spell,[8] she poured her soul out in imprudent letters to which the cunning rogue responded with due

[6] Mrs. Andrew Crosse, *Red-Letter Days of My Life* (London, 1892).

[7] *Rambles in Germany and Italy in 1840, 1842, and 1843.* By Mrs. Shelley. 2 vols., 1844. Sir Timothy dying in this year, Mary uses her own name on the title page.

[8] "I am never afraid of loving a man who does not love me," she wrote to Claire on September 30, 1843, and professed herself indifferent to gossip.

sentiment, waiting for her to come into a fortune. Being "quenched of hope," like Iachimo's, Gatteschi's

> *Italian brain*
> *'Gan in our duller Britain operate*
> *Most vilely . . . .*

He took to blackmail, threatening to publish Mary's correspondence. Instead of saying, "Publish and be damned," Mary took fright and added further letters to his collection. The shy keeper of young Percy's reputation was in an awkward little trap. She bewailed her folly, so emphatically that it appeared even greater than it was. Eventually she was rescued: Knox took the matter in hand, and as Gatteschi had been mixed up in riots at Bologna, the political pretext served for a requisition by the French police. The dangerous letters were procured and, presumably, destroyed, for there is no record of anyone's having seen them. So runs the story of Mary's last and least fortunate *affaire du coeur*.

Her last work of the pen, written in the form of letters to a friend, was issued in 1844. The reviewers were polite but lukewarm about the travel book. Its eloquence was redundant, and the author voiced her personal sorrow too often. That last criticism probably surprised the author, who believed that in the public mind she and her tragedy still went coupled and inseparable. It never occurred to her that the public for light travel books and three-volume novels was not necessarily the public that read Shelley.[9] Mary herself called it, to Hunt, "a wretched piece of work." But it was lucky for her that her angriest critic was not writing for immediate publication. In September, 1845, Elizabeth Barrett sent the book to Browning "in disobedience to your commands." Browning read it and wrote back:

> Oh, that book—does one wake or sleep? The "Mary dear" with the brown eyes, and Godwin's daughter and Shelley's wife, and who surely was something better once upon a time—and to go through Rome and Florence and the rest, after what I suppose to be Lady Londonderry's fashion: the intrepidity of the commonplace quite

[9] An amusing example appears in a marginal note penciled by a contemporary of Mary's in my copy of the *Rambles*. Beside one of the earliest tirades on the beloved dead and the fear of shipwreck this exceptionally well-informed reader has written, "Alludes to Mr. Shelley who was drowned I think nr. Leghorn or Civita Vecchia."

astounds me. And then that way, when she and the like of her are put in a new place, with new flowers, new stones, faces, walls, all new—of looking wisely up at the sun, clouds, evening star, or mountain top and wisely saying "who shall describe *that* sight!"— Not *you*, we very well see—but why don't you tell us that at Rome they eat roasted chestnuts, and put the shells into their aprons, the women do, and calmly empty the whole on the heads of the passengers in the street below. . . . But once she travelled the country with Shelley on arm; now she plods it, Rogers in hand—to such things and uses may we come at last! Her remarks on art, once she lets go of Rio's skirts, are amazing. . . . but she is wrong every where, that is, not right, not seeing what is to see, speaking what one expects to hear—I quarrel with her, for ever, I think.

If the parade of his own vision (largely cut out here) mars Browning's comment, he is right about Rogers. What "Rogers" in this case stands for is middle age and the commonplace outlook. Mary recognized her loss of rapture, but she fondly hoped and half-believed Italian scenery was restoring it. The miracle would not happen; beauty, instead of kindling a new inspiration, only roused regret. The long effort of ordinary life had quelled her spirit, and she had no strong enough intellectual outlook to prevent a catalogue of trivialities. So her labored descriptions never catch the gold dust of felicity. Shelley's wings are lacking.

And it was Shelley, not his wife, for whom the Brownings cared. This same year Elizabeth Barrett had felt great anxiety about *The Rosicrucian*. Unbelievable that such trash should be the poet's! Not even "with a flood of boarding-school idiocy dashed in by way of dilution." Here was the mark: "printed for Stockdale 1822"—the year of Shelley's death. Didn't the innocence of the great poet stand proved? "For nobody will say that he published such a book in the last year of his life, in the maturity of his genius, and that Godwin's daughter helped him in it!" Browning had to damp her hopes in the "sad matter." . . . "It *is* by Shelley, if you will have the truth—as I happen to *know*—proof *last* being that Leigh Hunt told me he unearthed it in Shelley's own library at Marlow once, to the writer's horror and shame—'He snatched it out of my hands'—said H. Yet I thrust it into yours. . . . As for the date, that Stockdale was a notorious pirate and raker up of rash publications." (We have already noted

Stockdale hurrying out with his reissue of the 1811 novel as soon as he heard of its author's death.) But the name of Shelley began for the first time to annoy the rising poet. While Talfourd's *Ion* had been so popular, his own *Paracelsus* was treated with contempt, the *Athenaeum* saying "that it was not without talent but spoiled by obscurity and only an imitation of—Shelley"! (The punctuation is Browning's rather than his reviewer's.) Still, the subject had not lost its attraction. Two months later, writing deprecatingly of Wordsworth to Elizabeth, he recalled, "Did not Shelley say long ago 'He [Wordsworth] had no more imagination than a pint pot'—though in those days he used to walk about France and Flanders like a man?" And it was rather an outrage on perception when Tennyson bluntly asked Robert one evening, "What do you think of Shelley?"

⋇ IV ⊱

On April 24, 1844, the long-awaited financial event occurred: Sir Timothy Shelley died at Field Place at the age of ninety. The *Gentleman's Magazine,* that hive of obituaries, has no record of his death. But the *Annual Register* says he "was sincerly respected. As a landlord, as a practical agriculturist, he enjoyed a high reputation. In him the agricultural labourer has lost a kind benefactor and a constant rewarder of honest industry; in short he possessed, in a high degree, the best qualities of the English country gentleman." While we are being reminded for the last and almost the only time of Sir Tim's more generous attributes, it may not be amiss to look back on a local press report of one of our landlord's kind actions in 1795:

> Timothy Shelley, Esq., of Field Place, in the parish of Warnham, distributed, during the late inclement weather, among his indigent parishioners, forty stones of good beef, and a large quantity of pease soup; he also contributed liberally for the purchase of flour for the use of the poor, and sent a fat sheep to the prisoners in Horsham Gaol.

Once again we should insist that a country squire faced with such a Problem Extraordinary as Percy Bysshe has no title to mankind's eternal censure because he failed to throw over his canons of right and justice. Where they applied, he could be sufficiently open handed. It is simpler and handsomer to ease the concerted sufferings of a parish than to study the private demands of a lawless son and an importunate daughter-in-law. And even here, Sir Timothy was long suffering, as we may plainly see now that the Whitton papers have brought some of the poet's most peevish adolescent letters to light. In 1811 the Shelley of *The Rosicrucian,* however fair might be his principles, had been intolerably rude and overbearing towards his parents. While he assured his father of the error of his ways and insulted him for imaginary libels, he enclosed viperish letters to his mother, whom he virtually accused of misconduct with the music master. All this we now call on Timothy to forget. If he preferred to forget his son, it is hardly surprising. Could we also have forgotten him and ignored his later development, we might have agreed that the remains deposited in the family vault at Horsham were honorable in more than years and ancestry. As it is, Sir Tim has endless notoriety, but small fame.

The circle of legatees pronounced no funeral orations. Their utterances were in any case becoming testy. Claire Clairmont wrote from St. Germaine en Laye expressing her incredulity that the old immortal should be dead at last. As the recipient of £12,000 her mood was surprisingly sombre: "I have no occasion to rejoice. . . . it brings me no good; it will not add a penny to my income, and I shall have the bore of law affairs." Then came Hogg, to add his carping thanks for a legacy of £2,000, promptly paid, with the addition of interest. He was glad to hear that Byron had declined his legacy, making it clear that Hogg was in no position to indulge such gestures. He surmised that Mary, now so affluent, wished she were still richer, while he pitied and excused his scratchiness on the score of gout.

Mary did indeed wish herself richer, but not in the face of such affluence as Hogg pictured. The estate that came to her was heavily burdened; large sums were due to Lady Shelley and Bysshe's brother John; legacies, besides Claire's and Hogg's, included £6,000 to Ianthe and £2,500 to Peacock. Anticipating this state of affairs, Mary had written to Hunt on April 20 (Sir Tim's death being imminent) to explain and apologize. Twenty years since, she had promised Hunt £2,000. Now the matter was changed. The old man had lived too long; in all those years a debt, now due to Lady Shelley, was accumulating; Mary must pay back all her hardly won subsistence and the money borrowed for Percy's college fees. Percy himself now shared her rights, nor would she ask him to concur in her old promise until affairs were settled. So Hunt's legacy had to be reduced; his cheque would be honored for £30 a quarter, to be continued to Marianne should she survive him.

For Mary, then, the long-anticipated glory had materialized into a guttering candle end. Her consolation was that Percy was old enough to be consulted on every move and take the burden off her shoulders. Soon she visited Field Place and at last met Lady Shelley, who now wished she had known her daughter-in-law before. "Then why on earth didn't she?" Mary commented aside, with bitterness. She herself was nervous and ailing, and went to seek health in Brighton in 1845. It was not to be found, but restlessness had gripped her. The next year, while Percy, shaping as the country gentleman, became a lieutenant in the Fifty-third or Sussex Militia, Mary left her Putney cottage for a house in Chester Square, Belgravia.[10] In the summer, health was pursued as far as Baden, while in England, at the Shelleys' Berkshire property of Elcott House, the baronet's widow died at eighty-three. At last the stronghold of Field Place was in the rebels' hands; and like a town too long bombarded, it was not worth the taking. Out of repair, prohibitively damp (it had been built when a sheltered hollow rather than a well-drained upland was considered a fair site), Field Place had been endured through habit by the older gang. Mary tried to live in it, and tried to let it, gaining little satisfaction from either course. Undisturbed by its dignity and associations, the first tenants paid an annual rent of sixty pounds.

So the glorious candle end went on guttering. But a brighter flame leaped up in one home of impoverished talent, when in 1847 a pension was granted to Leigh Hunt. George Gilfillan (whose essay on Shelley is waiting to be glanced at) celebrated the Whigs' action by a paean of thanksgiving in *Tait's Edinburgh Magazine*. It seemed to him the final triumph of the ostracized Cockney School. "We glory in Hunt's pension, not merely for his sake, but for the sake of a class of men of whom he is the last living representative. Now may the injured shades of Hazlitt, Shelley, and Keats deem themselves in some measure

---

[10] 24 Chester Square still stands, one of a row with sturdy colonnaded porticoes. It is divided now into three flats and bears no plaque to commemorate Mary Shelley, who was to die there.

appeased. These all, as well as Hunt, had their errors; they all needed *counsel,* and, instead of counsel, received proscription—murder—under the judicial forms of criticism. They asked for bread, and received a stone, not over their graves, but in their foreheads!"

Mary, sending her congratulations from Brighton in June, doubtless breathed relief and never dreamed that the Hunt family, after this golden bounty, could be in need again. As the last of the injured writers, then, Hunt was provided for. The pen-wielding but uninjured friends of Shelley went on providing for themselves as best they might. Trelawny had gone, with his wife Augusta Goring, to Usk in Monmouthshire, where he began farming That wife was destined to stay with him long enough to rear the three children and help with his next book. Hogg, we have reason to suspect, was using his free time in writing down further anecdotes of himself and Shelley. Medwin, becoming more of a Germanophile and living in Heidelberg, kept his eye on a potential source of literary income, and matured a plan that was to plunge poor Mary into further tortures at the hands of rogues.

Deferring the Captain's mischief for a moment, we may note some fragments of publicity Shelley had received from other hands. Gilfillan, portraying the illustrious in *Tait's Edinburgh Magazine,* had decided (1845) that Shelley, despite his odious atheism, was worth a place in the Gallery. He proceeded to paint a picture, stormy, hazy, dramatic, and overcolored; Turnerlike in its play of lights and absence of outline, in which an occasional clear beam flashed across chaos. The usual discussion on obscurity introduced a topical simile. It concerned the planner of a railway, who might have carried it on in the light of heaven, but chose to "lead it through the darkness of a costly and ridiculous tunnel."[11] When the entire Gallery was issued in book form, De Quincey had the delicate task of reviewing it for the paper it had appeared in. Rather than criticize, he added his own gems. He coined a new phrase about Shelley: "an angel touched by lunacy"; and he told a story about Harriet at Keswick. She had replied to a visitor's query: "The garden is not ours; but then, you know, the people let us run about in it, whenever Percy and I are tired of sitting in the house." Here, De Quincey claimed, was the evidence of Harriet's "faun-like

[11] Railroad planning was in full vigor then. Sir Timothy had been troubled in his later years by the arrival of Stephenson's railway on a part of his property.

playfulness." How he sighed at "the gloomy death of this young creature, now frozen in a distant grave"! We have noticed the second Mrs. Shelley "running about to visit the lions" in Weimar at the age of forty-five; but De Quincey is not to be denied his ecstasies over children. He added a personal touch: he himself had been in Grasmere at the time of this garden episode; the youth Shelley might have profited by seeing Wordsworth and Wilson, and De Quincey's own library; but did he?—no, he left in a hurry.

Another attempt to picture Shelley had been made in 1845 when Joseph Severn chose to paint him writing *Prometheus Unbound* in the ruins of ancient Rome. The artist begged for Hunt's criticism; so did Mary, who was far from satisfied. Marianne's scissors were besought again. "The *nose* is anything but right . . . the mouth is defective—and so is the shape of the face—do look at it if you *can* contrive." The portrait, now in the Keats-Shelley Memorial House, Rome, belongs emphatically to the Romantic era. Towers and arches of the Baths of Caracalla make a Claudian setting for the musing figure—manuscript on knee and pen in hand—on its craggy perch.

> *To sit on rocks, to muse o'er flood and fells* . . .

it might equally well have gone for Byron composing *Childe Harold*. What it exhibits is Severn's attachment to the tradition of Claude and Poussin, rather than an attempt at the correct shape of Shelley's nose.

A pamphlet, political and now out of date, of Shelley's own was on the market. *We Pity the Plumage but Ignore the Dying Bird* was issued by Thomas Rodd as a facsimile reprint, probably in 1843. Of the original *Address on the Death of Princess Charlotte,* written in November, 1817, only twenty copies, said Rodd, were printed by the author. Not one of the twenty having been found, the suggestion is that Ollier, who had the manuscript, was too cautious to print; and even Rodd, issuing it after a quarter of a century, disclaimed responsibility by styling it a reprint. But the Princess and the executions were forgotten; the pamphlet came and went without a stir.

Out of his own country our prophet was making headway. The first "complete" American edition of the *Poetical Works,* edited and prefaced by G. S. Foster, was published in New York in 1845. Italy met the poet who had died off her shores through Marcello Manzoni's translations in 1844. Her real enthusiasm, induced largely by a feeling of partial possession, was to emerge in the eighties. The poets and political writers of "Young Germany" increased in excitement over this champion of democracy. Ripening for action against monarchical bondage, they raised the Shelleyan banner and continued to make him their own looking glass. Yet Julius Seybt's complete translation, appearing, like Manzoni's, in 1844, brought the chance of a closer knowledge of him than Medwin's anecdoterie had supplied. The younger poets wrote imaginatively on Shelley, Hervegh describing him in a sonnet as

Ein Elfingeist in einem Menschenleibe.[12]

⟐ v ⟐

And this brings us back to the naughty Captain, who was living amongst these enthusiasts. He flattered himself—perhaps not all inaccurately—that he had brought the seed. He could see by the tendencies around him and the tone of the English articles, that the hour had come to begin on the poet's life. He had not kept his own letters from Shelley, but in his clumsy, forthright way he wrote to Mary, asking of her what he most required. The subject he focused on was a thorn in Mary's side. He asked for details of the Chancery suit, Harriet's suicide, the question of Shelley's responsibility, discussion of his life and their relationship, his moral unfitness to retain the children —was all this torturing history to be spun out by the tough-skinned opportunist for the reading public? Mary's reply was reticent and pleading. She would give no details; the whole matter was too painful for Ianthe, and intolerable, she hinted, to herself. She begged him to publish nothing that could hurt the living. In face of this attitude, Medwin gave up wheedling, and determined to lay hands on all he could, not only of information but of cash. He came to England, pursued his own researches, went about seeking a publisher for his work, and wrote a villainous letter to Mary:

I have found in the Record Office, and made extracts of the pro-ceedings in Chancery regarding Shelley's children, which I have

[12] Liptzin, *Shelley in Germany.*

deemed an indispensable passage in his life. There are also other passages, I fear, whose discussion you would not approve of, but which justice to his memory has obliged me to dilate on.

It pains me much that I could not at once, on receipt of your letter, suppress the "Memoirs." The book occupied me eight months, and I have taken an expensive journey (have an expensive journey back), to bring it out, and have now disposed of it for £250. You are, I am sure, too reasonable to ask me, poor as I am, to make this great Sacrifice. If you are desirous that the "Life" should not be published, and will make me some indemnity for the losses I should sustain, I will give you up the MS., stipulating at the same time never to write anything more about Shelley.—This sacrifice of my own fame, and, in some degree, of Shelley's fame, I am ready to make, solely with a view of complying with your wishes.

As we are going to press immediately, let me have a reply by return of post.

Gatteschi again! Mary must have thought; and this time Shelley was in it. She began to imagine all manner of scandal and indiscretion stuffed into that nightmare work. But she found out something that, while establishing Medwin as an arrant rascal, made her hope she had heard the last of him. The very day he wrote to her, his book had been returned by Colburn, having already been refused by several publishers because it lacked her own approval. Nothing more was heard of it for months. Then, in the spring of 1847, Medwin wrote another insolent letter saying that it was on the eve of publication, that it was *slashing,* and would create a hubbub, that he was forced to write for the sake of money but would let Mary see the book—already printed—before publication if she liked. In May he was back in his and Shelley's town of Horsham, from which place he replied to her further objections, "When you say that you have vindicated the memory of Shelley, and spoken of him as he was, you seem to *imply that I shall take a different course.*" He had read Gilfillan and De Quincey, and his comment was, "I am disgusted with your English writers—with their accursed cant—their cold, false conventionalities—their abominable claptrap. They should take a lesson from the Germans." There followed praise of Germany—"you are 100 years behind the Germans" —and disgust of England, to which he only came to see his "dear old mother." "You cannot suppose," he returned to the attack, "that I shall undo the arrangement I have made for the publication, which will take place in about a month, or six weeks at latest, and you shall have a copy among the first. It will be translated in Germany by a friend of mine, a lady, Madame de Ploennies, who has admirably rendered some of Shelley's minor poems."

This time the threat was not an empty one; the much-traveled *Life of Shelley* had been accepted by Newby, and was indeed in print. Mary's nerves had been tried this way too often. Ready to believe the worst of Medwin's threats, she was in utter panic, and appealed desperately to Leigh Hunt for help. In her morbid imagination, all the good that had been done for Shelley in the quarter of a century since his death, all the honors that had accrued to him and the reputation he had earned, were in danger of collapse and reversal. Not only that, but the suffering survivors—Ianthe, Claire, and the retiring Mary—would all be called into the dock again to answer charges made by a perjured witness whose only gods were money and notoriety. Hunt's son Thornton, now gaining power in journalistic circles, volunteered to talk Newby over and prevent publication if he could.

His persuasions went for nothing; Newby soon began to advertise the book and Mary took fright again. Hunt tried to soothe her, and again she repeated to him the whole tale of Medwin's blackmailing effort to extort his £250. "If it be possible," she prayed, superbly confident of Hunt's potency, "contrive that no respectable paper and above all the *Examiner* should take the slightest notice of it." She was then at Brighton, and still "seeking health." "I am getting stronger but these things are not good for nervous disorders." Hunt continued to pacify Mary, writing in a tone of gentle sympathy that calmed her terrors. "I believe, as you say," she wrote back, "the Life was never so injuriously written, but for the sake of extorting money, he tried to frighten me—and a man who could commit that sort of low crime is capable of anything. Tho' not so injurious—I am sure the book will be a disgrace to dear Shelley's name and an annoyance to all connected with him—and that it should be passed over in silence is the most honourable way in which the press can act.... For myself, the man's letter and the advertisement disturbed me greatly, and nervous as I am made me ill.... I will not read a line—I will not look at the book if I can help it. I hope Mr. Newby will not send it to me for I dislike doing a rudeness but I should send it back directly...."

Mary was indeed in the low waters of despondency this year, and she let her friends perceive it. Her once-neat handwriting had now become an invalid's scrawl, and her gay epistolary braveries were crushed. She had been ill throughout the spring, and the long ordeal had induced self-pity, with a return to her former conviction that she had no friends. More than most people, on account of her frequent desolations, she seems to have built her estimate of friendship on the lines laid down in *The Passionate Pilgrim:*

> *He that is thy friend indeed,*
> *He will help thee in thy need;*
> *If thou sorrow, he will weep;*
> *If thou wake, he cannot sleep.*
> *Thus of every grief in heart*
> *He with thee doth bear a part.*
> *These are certain signs to know*
> *Faithful friend from flatt'ring foe.*

It was hard for her to look on the other side and appreciate that a friend, besides giving sympathy, asks companionship and some gaiety of spirit; the soul that is perpetually crying out for comfort soon exhausts its comforter by reducing his potential variety to a joyless monotone. Mary could be cheerful in company and was then admired and loved, but during her loneliest depressions she found a perverse satisfaction in condemning the society she normally knew and liked. Then she would pour out sorrow, either in her diary or to some distant and therefore guiltless sympathizer, as in the lines sent on April 17 of this year to her childhood's friend, Isabel Baxter, later Mrs. Booth:

> I never found a friend to be of any active use to me. When I think of my melancholy return to England in '23 and the natural interest one would suppose a young widow with an infant son—the heir to a good fortune, might have inspired—and the solitude and friend-liness of my position, when I think of the exertions I made when Percy was 21 to introduce him into active life—and not a human being wd. hold out a finger—nay wd. not show the inexpensive kindness of an invitation or a kind glance. You may guess that I never hope anything from the kindness and helpfulness of my fellow-creatures. . . .

It was not a good moment for the Captain's machinations.

He himself was equally indignant and railed furiously to their mutual friends. Groping back, in 1898, to the old battle, Jane Hogg's grandson Sylvan Leigh Hunt told of a letter of Medwin's to Mrs. Hogg that was very bitter against Mary and plainly hinted that he had "material for incriminating Shelley not only in the Viviani affair but also in something that happened at Naples."[13] His bark, in the end, was far worse than his bite. In discussing Emilia Viviani—whom he had visited with Shelley—he was to stress the "Platonic" nature of the poet's feeling. His only revelation was the subsequent history of the fair captive, who endured six years of an unhappy marriage and died of consumption brought on by malaria and a broken heart. On the Naples question, known as the "Hoppner scandal" until the twentieth century developed it, he was, in the event, to be still more reticent. His threats, we must suspect, were mainly bluff, and, although Jane's grandson thought he might have given Hogg sensational matter for his later—missing—volumes of his life of the poet, it is probable they were empty. Even Mary guessed at it; but gloom and pessimism had obscured her calmer judgment.

[13] Letter to Lady Shelley, February 19, 1898, in the Abinger Collection.

CHAPTER IX

New Lamps for Old

MEDWIN'S BOOK appeared in the early fall of 1847, and we never hear from Mary if her morbid curiosity did or did not defeat her resolution not to look at it. The *Life* was a typical Medwinian production—boastful, gossiping, charged with plunderings and inaccuracies, yet not without high spirits, and surprisingly penetrable, for all its fungus-and-brushwood style of writing. He swaggered before his readers in the preface, emphasizing his peculiar fitness for the task. His letters from Shelley, indeed, were missing; but what, after all, did letters signify in developing character? (What did anything signify that Medwin happened to lack?) He had decided to be no mere chronicler, but to discuss all important questions. The book, he claimed, had "been written with no indecorous haste" (in fact, it had taken him twice as long to publish as to write). As for appreciation of the genius Shelley, "I was the first to turn the tide of obloquy," he boasted; and having begun to familiarize the world with his gifted kinsman, the noble cousin took it on his shoulders to elaborate his good work in the form now offered.

A copy, heavily annotated by the author, fell in later years into the hands of H. Buxton Forman, who not only re-edited the imperfect biography incorporating those notes, but relentlessly pointed to all Medwin's misquotations, muddles, and inaccuracies. The amendments may there be studied with the original text. Medwin had certainly laid hands on all he could find for his confection, including of course the tastiest morsels of his earlier memoir: he tapped Hunt and Hogg and Mary, stirred De Quincey and Gilfillan into a purée of crushed plums, threw in more than a pinch of malice for Shelley's acquaintances, and flavored the whole with his own bias and mediocrity. If we want a lump of sugar, we may find it neatly deposited in Jane's teacup. "A purer being than Mrs. Williams cannot

exist. Not a breath of scandal could possibly attach to her fame."
Mary's worst fears went unjustified; anything "injurious" in the book
was due rather to negligence and stupidity than to a deliberate attempt
to wound. The Chancery papers concerning the custody of Charles
and Ianthe had indeed come into the Captain's hands, but his clumsiness misused and misinterpreted them. Nor need Mary have worried
much about the press. The *Athenaeum,* which had printed Medwin's
memoir fifteen years ago, now said bluntly, "We are not in any way
satisfied with this book. It is neither carefully written nor carefully
printed. It abounds in mistakes of all kinds. . . . Capt. Medwin has
here a great argument—and he has treated it in the style trivial." The
Spectator (influenced, maybe, by the kind offices of Thornton Hunt)
declared, "Medwin's labours . . . are chiefly remarkable for the art of
stuffing . . . nor does the author forget a scandal when he can pick
any up."

The *New Monthly* avoided critical treatment, finding itself, by a
coincidence, mainly interested in tracing a connection between Horace
Smith (as mentioned by Medwin) and the "Graybeard" whose
"Gossip about his Literary Acquaintances" had been devoted to
Shelley on the previous page. Smith's were graceful reminiscences of
an inspired Shelley talking on Hampstead Heath or pleading for
atheism in the natural cathedral of the Marlow woods, where "all
around was hushed, as if the earth itself were listening to the rapt
enthusiasts's voice." The reviewer flattered Medwin and no doubt
caused Hogg another grievance, by attributing the latter's *New
Monthly* papers on *Shelley in Oxford* to the Captain. The editor put
this right, but not until the following issue. So it was a tainted triumph
for the biographers; here was Hogg slighted and Medwin slated;
and we are bound to note that if the latter's book did make its way
to Germany, it seems not to have reached a second edition at home.[1]

Of the canny Captain we have now seen almost all we need to see.
He was to return from Germany to die eventually in 1869, in the house
of his solicitor relative, Pilfold Medwin, in the Carfax, Horsham.
Except for a journalistic flair, it is hard to say much in the man's favor.
In 1825 he had contrived to marry a lady of means and title, described

---

[1] But there is a fame of rarity as well as of merit. In a book catalogue of 1936 the latest
twentieth-century two-volume life of Shelley was going for 25*s.* while Medwin's original 1847
edition was valued at 35*s.*

as Anne Henrietta Baroness Hamilton of Sweden, by her first marriage Countess of Stainfort. Hogg, on his travels that year, had found them in Florence and taken tea with Medwin, "literally *in a family way,* for . . . the poor Countess was in bed in the next room, waiting, as the old women say, to get worse before she gets better." The excursion into family life was soon concluded; Medwin spent the Countess's money and left her with two daughters. His "career" in the Life Guards has already been noted. It seems probable that the episode was a mere money transaction—a matter of buying in order to resell at a premium. To his rank, or courtesy rank, of captain, he clung for the sake of swagger and respectability—much as others have done in later times. As an adventurer in the literary and journalistic worlds, Medwin is no uncommon type. We shall rarely find the scene free of the opportunists who bluff their hearty way into every circle, stressing their intimacy with famous men. "Friend of Byron"; "schoolfellow and collaborator with Shelley"; "confidante of the Poets (himself no mean performer)"—thus, with a wealth of dangerously readable gossip, does a Medwin push along his path. Such a reputation cannot hold, and the man knows it; hence his ceaseless exertions to grope for gold down every alley that shows its gleam. Thackeray understood something of his Medwin, but let him off good humoredly. In *Pendennis* (1849) we meet at a dinner of "literary gentlemen" a

> Captain Sumph, an ex-beau still about town, and related in some indistinct manner to Literature and the Peerage. He was said to have written a book once, to have been a friend of Lord Byron, to be related to Lord Sumphington; in fact, anecdotes of Byron formed his staple, and he seldom spoke but with the name of that poet or some of his contemporaries in his mouth, as thus: "I remember poor Shelley at school being sent up for good for a copy of verses, every line of which I wrote, by Jove."

And there, niched in Thackeray's light-hearted satire, we may leave the Captain, satisfied that at least one character in our comedy has gotten more than he deserves.

‹§ 11 §›

". . . They met at last, like two drops of water—like two flames of fire —like two beautiful clouds which have crossed the moon, the sky and all its stars, to hold their midnight assignation over a favourite and lonely river." It may have consoled Mary to have her love affair so hyperbolically hymned by that studious general songster George Gilfillan;[2] although he allowed her neither wit nor humor, and of dramatic talent very little. But she had written *Frankenstein,* and he respectfully reminded her of another duty—despite the effort by Medwyn [*sic*] to write Shelley's life. "She alone, we believe, after all fully understands him; . . . and we hope and believe, that her biography will be a monument to his memory as lasting as the Euganean Hills." Mary declined the invitation. As for monuments, we shall see them in the second half of the century springing up and toppling down as busily as the towers once did in Italian hill towns. Her own two spires, of differing designs, were to remain standing; the 1839 edition and *Frankenstein.* If a third spire, or say a tower, is demanded, we must seek it in Percy Florence, now becoming a most respectable gentleman, whose eccentricities are not of the type to break a mother's heart. So excellent a squire was Percy, the new owner of the unbeloved Field Place, that but for an intrusion of a curious nature (though in petticoats) he would have stood as Radical—"Blue"—candidate for Horsham at the 1848 election; and had he stood he would undoubtedly have won it.

The statement sounds rash, but the case was unusual. In 1847, Horsham had enjoyed a boisterous election, marked by general treating, bribery, intimidation, and even kidnapping of the electorate by both parties. Tradesmen and publicans shared in the corruption; there were free drinks, free joints, free suppers, and political punch meetings; every beer-house was either "Blue" or "Pink," and the party paid. In consequence, the Blue candidate, Jervis, though elected, was unseated on a petition by the supporters of his rival, Fitzgerald. He, having employed the same methods, could not claim the seat, and Horsham risked disfranchisement. However, another election followed in June, 1848, when the Pinks ran Fitzgerald again. It was then that Sir Percy was adopted as Blue candidate, and on March 24 issued

2 *Tait's Edinburgh Magazine,* December, 1847.

176

his election address. But on the same day as the motion for the writ was carried, Percy, on account of a domestic occurrence, decided not to stand. The rest of the story tells us why he would have succeeded. In his place Lord Edward Howard, second son of the Duke of Norfolk, was approached, and agreed to stand on condition he spent no more than the bare legal expenses. The Blues readily agreed, having thought out their policy. The election was a contrast to the previous one—no show, no flags, no meetings, and no treatings; only a placarding of the town with bills of protest against Fitzgerald's candidacy. Fitzgerald was elected, but on Lord Howard's petition was found guilty of treating in 1847, and unseated in favor of Howard, who continued to represent Horsham for four years, having gained his seat without trouble or expense.[3]

Percy appears to have had as much expense as Howard, without the triumph, or so Mary claimed in writing to Mrs. Hunt. Despite Hunt's pension, that family had faced trouble again—or was it merely that Marianne could not keep her money, but must be constantly overspending before her quarter? "I deeply grieved," Mary wrote on November 17, "over the account you send—we all hoped that Hunt was made comfortable for life. We have no command over sums of money—and just now are very much hampered by having to pay £500 for Percy's election expenses—when he thought of standing last spring—which must be paid out of what we may receive at Xmas— and will leave us quite bare—The estate is so much mortgaged and needs so much to be spent in repairs, totally neglected by Sir Tim, that it requires the utmost prudence to get on."

❈{ III }❈

And now at last we approach the reason of Percy's Parliamentary default. Of course, it was marriage. But here was no ordinary enchanting reign of petticoats. How pleasant it would be at this point to digress into the by-ways of a lover's idyll, forgetting Percy Bysshe while his offspring pays court to a young woman who delights in Percy Florence for his personality, and reads on his account for the first time

[3] See William Albery, *A Parliamentary History of Horsham, 1290–1885* (London, 1927).

because his father wrote it. If only the lady would allow us to digress! Instead, she makes of herself a central rallying point to which the faithful are almost forced to flock and extol the name and fame of Shelley, even if some slight bruisings of integrity are felt. Until now we have seen a reasonable chance of Shelley's finding his own level and being accepted with his genius and his failings as a human poet. But with the entry of Mrs. St. John myth becomes religion, hostility becomes neo-atheism, truth stumbles over her official robes and cuts some capers. If Mrs. St. John is not in every case the cause, she is certainly a formidable symptom. She heralds the livelier developments that belong to an era where biography is almost a means of self-expression, and the pursuit of a romantic poet—whether with haloes or brickbats—is an author's life work.

Her name, like Mrs. Williams's, was Jane, but she never loved her namesake. Born on February 24, 1820, she was the daughter of Thomas Gibson and had married, in 1841, the Hon. Charles Robert St. John, second son of the third Viscount Bolingbroke. He died on January 21, 1844. Three years later the young widow was staying with her sister in Chester Square. She was a Shelleyan already; not that she understood his poetry, but her sentimental nature was gripped by his romance to the point of taking a lively interest in that other widow who lived across the Square. What happened subsequently has been reported from her own account.[4] She heard that Sir Percy cared only for boats and sailing. Her friends urged her to meet Mrs. Shelley, but she felt shy of her cleverness. Then she met in Baden a young man to whom she piously offered her friendship as a substitute for the gaming table. Said the young man, "I wish you would do something for me." "Well," she asked, "what is it?" "I wish you would marry my best friend." She laughed and asked his name. "Sir Percy Shelley—such an awfully nice fellow. You would suit each other capitally, you would be so happy with him." Fatality was in it, though the lady indicates that she laughed it off, because she did not know the family. The next step was taken by Mary, who was also aware of the other widow (presumably from the rescued youth in Baden). She proposed to call on Mrs. St. John, sending a note which the younger woman

[4] Maud Rolleston, *Talks with Lady Shelley* (London, 1925).

Field Place, Warnham, Sussex, inherited by Percy Florence Shelley in 1844.

From Howard Dudley's *History of Horsham* (1836)

nearly threw away unopened. And when Mary did come, she seems to have risked a treatment parallel to the note's. Here is Mrs. St. John's reminiscence:

> I had been resting one afternoon in my bedroom after having suffered from one of my bad headaches. Feeling better towards the late afternoon, I wandered down to the drawing-room to find my book, not knowing that the maids had let in a visitor. As I opened the door I started back in surprise, for some one was sitting on the sofa, and I said to myself, "Who are you—you lovely being?" She must have seen my start of surprise, for, rising gently from the sofa, she came towards me and said very softly, "I am Mary Shelley." You ask what she was like. Well, she was tall and slim, and had the most beautiful deep-set eyes I have ever seen. They seemed to change in colour when she was animated and keen. She dressed as a rule in long soft grey material, simply and beautifully made. . . .[5]

It sounds exquisite. But as Mary was neither tall nor slim, we doubt even that long, soft gray material—the very stuff of vision and angel's wing. Mrs. St. John had fallen in love with Mary, and this is a lover's account. She was prepared to like Percy because he was Mary's son and Shelley was his father. There is no record of their meeting, nor of any mutual attraction. It was a *mariage de convenance* on novel lines. But at the time it suited Percy better than an election, and the event took place on June 22, 1848, at St. George's, Hanover Square. We must say this for the new Lady Shelley, that she never let Mary feel like a mother-in-law. Percy continued to have "all in common," and when they went to Nice the following year, she traveled with them. As Lady Shelley said, "She could not live without her boy," and she was not asked to do so, although they hardly suspected how short a time she had to live at all.

While they were at Field Place, Claire Clairmont came to stay. Claire had become something of a hysterical hooligan, whom Percy's wife had from the outset been unable to accept with the rest of the Shelley furniture. Besides, not only Claire, but her nephews and nieces —Charles Clairmont's children—had an idea that the Shelley furniture belonged to *them*. Lady Shelley, proposing to be absent, evoked from Mary the alleged outburst, "Don't leave me alone with her. She

[5] *Ibid.*

has been the bane of my life ever since I was two!" Claire brought her niece Clairey, and with her a welter of nerve storms and hysterics. Field Place begins to emulate a Dostoevsky household at this point. There is a scene; Clairey rushing upstairs and demanding to be saved from Claire, who is kneeling on the drawing-room floor and cursing her for refusing to take some crazy matrimonial advice. Mary, ill, is locked in her bedroom to prevent her from trying to settle the crisis. Claire is pushed off to bed, while Percy tries to comfort a sobbing niece; but the wild woman returns to hurl hysterical insults at the family, and is only calmed by the loud threat of a doctor, and perhaps an asylum. There was no peace in the house while she remained. As for the unhappy niece, she was eventually tied up with an equally unhappy friend who came to stay, and in spite of Mary's shivers about misery in the Clairmont blood and lack of love, the two did well enough together.

❦{ IV }❦

Field Place itself was not to be endured for long. The younger Shelleys turned their footsteps southward, and they, too, found a place of pine woods, barren shores, and beating waves. But where Shelley and Mary had chosen the Gulf of Spezia and the Casa Magni, Percy and his Jane felt no need to go further than the neighborhood of Bournemouth, and moving along the coast a little eastward, they settled at Boscombe Manor. Before letting this action invoke a cynical smile, we must sweep away the modern towns and look again. The shore was a wilderness of pines and cliffs and bracken, with a narrow tumbling river and a naked beach. In desolation and in grandeur it beat Shelley's Marlow. Here is a curious word on it by Matthew Arnold—another inhabitant of Chester Square—written that very year to his youngest sister:

> Bournemouth on the Sea is a very stupid place; a great moorland covered with furze and low pine woods comes down to the sea-shore, and breaks down towards it in a long sweep of cliff, half sand, half mud. There are no little bays and ins and outs as in the Isle of Man, but to the right and left you see one immense, gradually-curving line till the coast ends in two ordinary headlands at great

distances on each side of you. A little brook runs into the sea here . . . .

Development, and the health movement comparable to Dr. Brighton's, had not yet set in. Nor was there much competition over ground. Sir Percy might have acquired the entire sea-front from Boscombe Chine to the present Southbourne at the western end, but he decided that an estate of four hundred acres was enough. Boscombe itself consisted of a few thatched cottages and a wayside inn known as "The Ragged Cat," and later as the Palmeston Arms. It seemed a district of neglected beauties, although on Percy's own estate were mulberry trees planted by someone's enterprise in the time of the Stuarts.[6] The house, set well back from the cliff edge, looked across its own grounds to a shore happily devoid as yet of roads and bathing tents, and so out to sea. Not the site, but the use of it, supplied the contrast to Shelley's Italian choice. It was no refuge from the world that Percy planned, but a social dwelling place with a theater built in the garden, where humanity's artificial activities might have full scope. Boats there were certainly to be; not casually constructed freaks like the *Don Juan,* but yachts and schooners of orthodox design. Shelley's spirit visiting Boscombe would have been appalled by the noise and traffic of theatricals, which he hated. (In time the theater was constructed inside the house.) Avoiding these, he might have been equally appalled by the altar of the new religion set up and sanctified in his honor by a fervent daughter-in-law; and as the years went on, he must have mocked unmercifully at the learned literary biographers caught and struggling in the lady's noose and strangely contorting themselves to do him a warped justice.

It was arranged that Mary should come to Boscombe and live in a house by herself, like one of the heroines of her own short stories, on the edge of the cliff. But she never made the move from Chester Square, where she was to die on February 1, 1851. According to Thomas Hookham, as reported by the Reverend John Mitford, her disease was the painful one of cancer in the brain. Lady Shelley declares she died of no disease, but merely exhaustion. Both statements are unreliable, and we must go to Percy's letters for a truer version. His bulletins were sent at Mary's request to Isabel Booth. The first

6 See C. H. Mate and C. Riddle, *Bournemouth, 1810–1910* (London, 1910).

one, written from 24 Chester Square on January 3, 1851, said that his mother had been attended in her illness by a homeopathic doctor who did her no good. Then "She got a numbness in her left leg which gradually increased to paralysis. . . . At one time her speech was a little affected but that has entirely gone off." The next letter said Mary was no worse, the doctors were sanguine, and there was now no danger. But the third letter was deeply edged in black:

> You will be very much shocked to hear that my dear mother died last Saturday. Her illness puzzled the doctors so long, and presented so many different appearances that they could not make out what was the matter with her. At one time before and some time after I last wrote to you I was very hopeful about her—but about a fortnight ago she had a succession of fits, which ended in a sort of stupor in which she remained for a week—without any sign of life but her breathing which gradually ceased without any pain. And now she has left us most mournful and wretched.[7]

This stupor, or coma, was all that Mary's daughter-in-law could allow herself to record. In her official view, a heroine had to fade ethereally without mundane tortures to disturb her peace. So Mary, who is no longer the muddled, half-passionate, half-intellectual, all unharmonized woman we have seen her to be, now sinks into a being of infinite wisdom, purest vision and untroubled love. The myth necessitates it. "She lay for ten days without word. . . . She could not speak, but she turned her beautiful grey eyes on us and towards her desk so often with a longing and beseeching look in them." Her wish remained unspoken, and was discovered a year later when Percy could bear to go through her possessions. They opened her desk and found it full of relics. Here was the journal kept by her and Shelley in 1814, with other treasures of the kind. Lying apart was a copy of the Pisa *Adonais,* with a page torn loose and folded over in four. "We opened it reverently and found ashes—dust—and we then knew what Mary had so longed to tell us: all that was left of Shelley's heart lay there."[8] So here, if the keen worshiper has not mistaken her object, is the second appearance of that trophy so ardently discussed—and, like

---

[7] By Mary's wish Mrs. Booth was to have fifty pounds per annum and a suit of mourning.

[8] Ingpen says it was wrapped in a silken shroud, but nobody is in agreement about this organ.

Halley's eagerly awaited comet, considerably shrunk on its return. In the record of later years, when every conceivable theory on every Shelleyan detail was to be picked and pulled to pieces, we shall see doubts cast on the identity of this or any reappearing heart. For the present, let us allow that there are dust and ashes, that Lady Shelley has found them, and that, after this discovery of her reliquary, Mary is recognized more certainly than ever to have died a saint.

She was buried in St. Peter's Churchyard, Bournemouth. And once again we see Lady Shelley's glimmering mind at work. She tells us, no doubt truly, that Mary had rejected the offer of an Italian burial as causing too much trouble; she would rest in Bournemouth, but would like her father and mother near to her, their ashes being in consequence removed from London. Indeed they were removed, advisedly, had to be because St. Pancras Churchyard was to be dug up. But the fact is dull, and they certainly came to Bournemouth.[9]

The press piped Mary to her grave with prose and poetry. The *Athenaeum* quoted Shelley's dedication to *The Revolt of Islam*, pointing out in the light of it to what heights the genius of a young and gifted woman could be winged and nerved by the persuasions of such a spirit as Shelley's. *Frankenstein* was recalled with compliments, as being free from the "languor and melancholy" of her other books.

Another, yet another, snatched away—

began the *Leader's* blank-verse philosopher somewhat impersonally; but he made it apply to his "gifted sister" in the end by the usual method of referring her to her greater:

How doubly loved because entwined with Him!
Mourn her not, Earth! her spirit, disenthralled,
No more shall droop in lonely widowhood . . .

She was to rejoin the "bright-eyed child," the "Poet of the Soul," the "mighty Minstrel of the impassioned lay"; with only a brief farewell

Till friend clasps friend upon the silent shore.

And already the local bards of Sir Percy's new region (but the family had been in Hampshire long before) sprang to attention with their

---

9 A monument to them still stands in Old St. Pancras.

ready pens. A Fordingbridge correspondent of the *Poole Herald* sent in his contribution, ending with less optimism than the *Leader* poem:

> *Oh Mary, thou sleepest, far far from thy lover,*
> *The poet, thy husband, the dear one to thee;*
> *With kisses the zephyrs his smooth bed e'er cover*
> *Whilst thou hear'st the wail of the sombre pine tree.*
>
> . . .
>
> *Ay, sleep, with thy white palms press'd close to thy sides,*
> *While the heath purples o'er thy deathfrozen breast,*
> *Smooth palms, that a Shelley once clasp'd as his bride's,*
> *Soft breast that the lip of his infant once press'd.*
>
> *And know that the angels can watch o'er thy bed,*
> *Though seagulls flit round it, and wild tempests rave;*
> *While with lovely defiance each wave rears its head,*
> *To part thee for aye from that lov'd Southern grave.*

Five days after his mother's death, Sir Percy wrote and announced it to Leigh Hunt. Hunt, he said, was even now one of very few that he had written to; some question of "irritability" had come up in Hunt's last letter, requiring an assurance from Percy that he and his mother had both subscribed to that last and short-lived periodical, *Leigh Hunt's Journal,* had always thought everything good of him, and that Percy would continue so to do. Only Hunt's worries and exhaustion could have given rise to doubts. Essentially he also thought everything good of his young friend. The previous year, transferring some of his earlier accounts of Shelley to the *Autobiography,* he had added one phrase to the passage, written twenty-two years ago, on Percy's illustrious descent: "But, what is best of all, his own intelligent and liberal nature makes him worthy of all this lustre." It was a generous and deserved tribute to a man who would continue to be hampered, on certain encounters, by his grand descent.

In opposition, let us have Carlyle's judgment on Sir Percy's father, made at the same period, one day when he was breakfasting at the Dublin Zoo. (Was a comparison with the animals implied?) "Shelley is a poor, shrieking creature, who has said or done nothing worth a serious man being at the trouble of remembering." Yet Carlyle kept on recalling Shelley—that "windy phenomenon"—if only to give him another kick into the dust. Like Hazlitt, he could not resist scratching with a jealous paw whenever he spied an opportunity.[10] "Shelley is always mistaking spasmodic violence for strength," he carped. "I know no more *urned* books than his. . . . It is like the writing of a ghost, uttering infinite wail, into the night, unable to help itself or anyone else." Subtracting insult, something, even through the hostile words, remains. A spirit, a seer, or a revolutionary, the drowned Shelley still directs our narrative; the activities of his survivors only matter, after all, on his account. He has decisively outlived his generation. Now we may tentatively borrow the word "infinite," with acknowledgments to a generous enemy. These "urned" books will never be buried, but constantly revivified and blazed abroad. As we saw, he is now to have a priestess, but the fire is too great to be governed by her attentions. Some worship and much argument will go on around it, with the faces of rogues and innocents lit up by its glare.

Before entering on the new complexities, we may pause at one clear utterance that appeared in this year of Mary's death. The young George Meredith, having barely attained his majority, experiments with novel verse rhythms to catch, in four lines, the essential flavors of great English poets. Here, then, is Shelley's genius in his curious net:

> *See'st thou a Skylark whose glistening winglets ascending*
> *Quiver like pulses beneath the melodious dawn?*
> *Deep in the heart-yearning distance of heaven it flutters—*
> *Wisdom and beauty and love are the treasures it brings down at eve.*

[10] Writing to Browning about the latter's essay in 1852, he seized another of these chances: "I am not sure but you would excommunicate me if I told you all I thought of Shelley! Poor soul, he has always seemed to me an extremely weak creature, a poor, thin, spasmodic, hectic, shrill and pallid being. . . . The very voice of him (his style &c) shrill, shrieky, to my ear has too much of the ghost!"

PART TWO

The Shrine-Builders

1852–1899

"Even in modern times, no living poet ever arrived at the fullness of his fame; the jury which sits in judgment upon a poet, belonging as he does to all time, must be composed of his peers: it must be impannelled by time from the selectest of the wise of many generations."
—P. B. Shelley, *A Defence of Poetry*.

CHAPTER X

Beware of Roguery

S O LONG as the chief mourners trod the post-Shelleyan stage, an attempt was made to conduct this patchwork narrative in a sober chronological order suitable to their own ageing and decay. Some of them, to be sure, are still alive and have potential fight in them, even for two-score years and more; but as historian rather than biographer we cannot round our chronicle down to meet their sunset. It is Shelley, not his friends and relatives, who is our motive power; and since the poet, "belonging as he does to all time," is living more abundantly and in ever wider diffusion, either the story has to strain out and disintegrate, like a star under too high a pressure from within, or the historian must give up the pursuit of detail, content to note the landscape's general colorings and salient points. This is the more advisable in that many of these aspects have been lately under notice by scholars, theorists, editors of original documents, examiners of state archives, biographers of biographers, essayists plain and metaphysical, experts on handwriting, paper, and postmarks, poets, psychoanalysts and criminologists, thesis-writers aspirational or professional, and, in fine, every type of claimant to the controversial bones.

Yet we shall have to keep some track of these activities, for they become, increasingly, the story itself, as the years go on. Our next, and all-undodgeable episode, is a case in point. It has been much handled and demands attention on account of the lasting mischief it has caused and is still causing. Thanks to the tireless workings of an especial rascal, no Shelley or Byron letter, in the sales rooms or in private hands, is today immune from the suspicion of forgery. This man, who called himself George Gordon de Luna Byron and claimed to be the peer's natural son, began, not *un*naturally, on his "father," announcing his "Inedited Works," to include letters, journals, poems, and reminiscences by contributors ranging from Archdeacon Spencer to Augusta Leigh.[1] Now the curious thing is that although this rank imposture was shown up in the *Athenaeum,* "Major Byron" coolly persisted on his path and, thwarted of publication, tried the manuscript market. His real name, or an alias, was de Gibler. He appears to have had a genius for copying autographs, faking postmarks, inventing or borrowing passages that could pass as genuine, and then disseminating the result in a useful quarter.

So it happened that Murray and Moxon bought some autograph letters of Byron and Shelley respectively at Sotheby's. Moxon sent his twenty-five undistinguished specimens to Robert Browning, then in Paris, and asked for an introduction to the volume he proposed to issue. Browning found the letters good-natured, bare of revelation, rather dull—and drew attention to his own good office in commenting on these minor works. In truth, he never looked closely at the text before him—perhaps it was not before him—while he put down his chosen polysyllables; and if "George Gordon" had ascribed the letters of Julius Caesar to Shelley, it would have been all one.

The volume, published in February, 1852, was reviewed in all good faith. The *Athenaeum* found little in the letters and too much in the essay. It took up Browning's assertion that "a full life of Shelley should be written at once" and, dismissing Hogg, Hunt, Medwin, and the poet's widow, questioned who should write it. The *Literary Gazette* declared the letters "charming and valuable" and Browning's discourse conceited, obscure, and ungrammatical, standing in the way of the sunshine. Then it suddenly came out that the sunshine was spurious. Moxon had sent Tennyson a copy of the book; F. T. Palgrave, looking over it in his friend's house, paused at the letter to Godwin about Florentine art and recognized it as part of an article on Florence written by his father in 1840 for the *Quarterly Review.* Sir Francis was told at once. He compared the letter with the article and wrote to Moxon. A letter signed "Q" appeared on February 28 in the *Literary Gazette*: "Are you sure that the letters with which Mr. Moxon has favoured us are genuine?" and the Florentine extract was quoted in both its versions. Moxon could only point to the postmark of the letter. It was suggested, in its favor, that Sir Francis Palgrave

1 For a full account of the forger's life and knavery, see Theodore G. Ehrsam, *Major Byron: The Incredible Career of a Literary Forger* (New York and London, 1951).

might have seen the letter and then written his article, but that argument failed. The letters, bought at such high prices, were handed over to an autograph expert, who found the postmarks spurious. Murray's newly bought Byron letters and some Keats items also failed the test. Besides, there was a sameness about all of them—one forger had produced the lot.

They were hot on his trail now; journalism was agog with news and warnings about fraudulent letters. "The 'marvel' of the forgery," exclaimed the *Athenaeum,* "is not yet told." A series of intimate letters from Shelley to his wife had been catalogued for sale. They were said to reveal facts that a son might wish concealed; therefore, Sir Percy and his wife had bought the letters—now proved to be forgeries.[2] Other letters passing through the sale-rooms were undoubtedly false; such, for example, was a letter of Shelley's "containing an assertion against the fidelity of Harriet," which had sold for £6. 6. o.[3] "The forgery of Chatterton injured no one but an imaginary priest . . . but this forgery blackens the character of a great man, and, worse still, traduces female virtue."

Bit by bit the threads were unraveled and connections traced. Moxon and Murray had bought their letters from Sotheby's and from Puttick and Simpson's. They had them from a Mr. White, bookseller in Pall Mall near the Reform Club. White had them from two women and believed them genuine. The *Athenaeum* recalled its warning, three years past, against George Byron, and had it, on White's statement, that Mr. Byron had brought him the forged documents. At this point White, the innocent bookseller, became frightened and decided that the journal was bullying him. He issued a pamphlet describing in what romantic way he had acquired the letters, but he wrote it truculently, on the defensive. White told of a well-dressed, ladylike young person who brought him two unpublished Byron letters in the summer of 1848. He purchased them, and she brought him further letters, in twos and threes, reluctantly, to meet creditor's demands. They were the property of her sister at St. John's Wood, left

---

[2] "On three occasions in the last fourteen years forged letters have been presented to the family to purchase," Lady Shelley wrote in the preface to *Shelley Memorials* (1859).

[3] "I have just heard from Godwin that he has evidence that Harriet was unfaithful to me before I left England with you." (January 11, 1817.) It is a fake, but not far from the genuine letter, now owned by Lady Shelley-Rolls, which, in fact, says more explicitly, "four months before I left."

by their father, a deceased surgeon and autograph collector who had known Byron's valet, Fletcher. The Shelley letters, she intimated, were too precious to part with; but in time these followed the Byron books and letters into White's hands. He sent them to Puttick and Simpson, and on their sale was informed by a bookseller that one of the books had previously been sold by him to a Mr. Byron, who had never paid for it. White's suspicions were aroused; he accused the woman, she pleaded her husband's misfortunes, and the "husband" himself then called on Mr. White with excuses, and said he was writing (still) a life of his celebrated father. It was hard, by then, for White, if he did suspect the letters, to extricate himself and lose his property.

Much later it came out that Mary herself had been preyed on in her latter years. After Gatteschi, after Medwin, this one rogue more had found her vulnerable. A series of letters written by her to Thomas Hookham shows her reluctantly negotiating for the purchase of several letters represented to be those of Shelley that she had lost, and giving the importuner—even while she suspected his motives—a loan of thirty pounds.[4] Incapable to the last of detecting villainy at its source, Mary seems to have accepted the whole cock-and-bull tale of "Byron's son," paid liberally for the letters, perhaps before examining them (for if the forgeries deceived Mary, who had spent half a lifetime on Shelley's manuscripts, how shall the rest of us hope for a keener judgment?), and lent the man that money she could so ill afford that even her friend Leigh Hunt had had to be denied.

The intelligentsia, awake to the trick that had been played, now chattered appropriately. Browning was laughed at without mercy. Mary Russell Mitford—that ever ready gossip—told of a "son of Byron" with a chestful of manuscripts, bundles of letters, and an elegant young woman presented as his wife. The sensation spread to Paris. In London, Sir Frederick Madden, keeper of manuscripts in the British Museum, became caught up in a heated correspondence with the *Literary Gazette,* the *Athenaeum,* Murray, Sotheby, and White.

Gossip died out in time, and the incident seemed ended. Yet the forged Shelley letters have never cleared completely off the poet's

[4] Ehrsam, *Major Byron;* also Seymour de Ricci, *Bibliography of Shelley's Letters* (Paris, 1927).

pathway. They have edged into his published correspondence and influenced his biographers. One notorious document from Shelley to
Mary, written in December, 1816, and concerned with Harriet's suicide, remains as an unsolved puzzle, dividing present-day students
into opposite camps. Its first appearance was in itself suspicious, sent
as it was in 1859 to Leigh Hunt by one D. H. Taylor of the post office,
as having been returned, forty-two years ago, through the post, "unknown at the address." From first to last the letter has mystified.
Even the date has undergone various readings; and in the long run
it was to gain no honor by coming into the library of that fallen idol,
the unscrupulous bibliophile Thomas J. Wise. This, for a while, had
made it sacrosanct and safe against impudent attackers. Now, since
the unmasking, the sanctuary has proved a snare. In America and
England discussion has been raging, and it is no aim of this chronicle
to take up, in any detail, the strands of controversy.

And yet there was, and is, some urgency about the judgment on
that manuscript. It has a bearing on our narrative because, apart from
containing sensational biography, a strand of Shelley's reputation is
at stake in it. The text is now notorious: telling Mary of his distressing
day in London following the news, Shelley rails against the Westbrooks and gives such a report of Harriet's final actions and Eliza's
villainy as the biographer Dowden, under the searching eye of Lady
Shelley, was not to be permitted to print. Roger Ingpen, ruled by
Victorian sensibilities, respected his omission when publishing the
Letters of Shelley in 1912. The suppressed passage, as restored by a
later and freer generation, reads as follows:

> It seems that this poor woman, the most innocent of her abhorred
> and unnatural family, was driven from her father's, and descended
> the steps of prostitution until she lived with a groom of the name of
> Smith, who deserting her she killed herself.—There can be no ques-
> tion that the beastly viper, her sister, unable to gain profit from her
> connection with me, has secured to herself the fortune of the old
> man, who is now dying—by the murder of this poor creature.

(The "old man," as we saw, was to live till 1835.) We have said that
Shelley's reputation is at stake, but on which showing? On the face
of it these accusations by the poet are ugly, and the hysterical threats
that follow, against Eliza and the "detestable Westbrooks" are ugly,

too. Yet a couple of days later Shelley was writing quite otherwise to Eliza,[5] with fairness and control. Maybe he lost his temper in the moment of shock; maybe he was double-tongued, or simply afraid of Eliza.[6] None of these excuses flatters him, and we have a better Shelley, we should say, if the letter is false. The cunning argument that Lady Shelley thought otherwise and used it to whitewash her idolized poet by blackening Harriet's character, has been fully dealt with.[7] It is too specious to detain us now.

Let us only remark here that the groom named Smith seems designed to fit in with the inquest on the body of *Harriet Smith,* who has been—for what reason or with how much justification we can never fathom—assumed to be Harriet Shelley. The name of Harriet was common enough at the period, and so, perennially in England, is the name of Smith. Of Harriet Shelley's death by drowning we have only the evidence of the "suicide" letter she is supposed to have written to Eliza, begging her to take charge of Ianthe after her own impending death. And that leads to one more knot in the tangled skein; for if Harriet did not (and it is possible) commit suicide, then more than half the noise and clamor that pursued the poet as the Furies did Prometheus may be stilled at once. This, no doubt, is too much to expect:

The hope of torturing him smells like a heap
Of corpses, to a death-bird after battle.

[5] Leslie Hotson, *Shelley's Lost Letters to Harriet* (London, 1930). "I give no faith to any of the imputations generally cast on your conduct or that of Mr. Westbrook towards the unhappy victim. . . . I had the strongest wish to consult your feelings in this affair." (December 18, 1816.)

[6] In support of Shelley's wild assertion we have the opinion given in a letter to Byron, January 17, 1817, that Eliza "may be truly said (though not in law yet in fact) to have murdered her for the sake of her father's money." The suggestion that Harriet had been driven from home (by her sister) has been constantly denied. Of course, Shelley might be misinformed. He was, on the face of it, given to believing what he heard. When Godwin thought he had discovered on sound authority that Harriet had been unfaithful before the elopement with Mary, Shelley, as we saw above, repeated this to Mary as a fact, not as conjecture. Yet this last statement should not be stripped of its context. Shelley was discussing his chances of success in the pending Chancery suit over the children. He knew then that the Westbrooks were using every fair and foul means to make sure of dishonoring and so depriving him. They intended to drag Mary's name, and Godwin's, through the mud, while keeping back the circumstances of Harriet's death. It was to combat "this detestable conspiracy" that Shelley so readily repeated Godwin's news, with the comment, "If we can succeed in establishing this, our connection will receive an additional sanction, and plea be overborne." It was the legal advantage that concerned him when he wrote.

[7] In *An Examination of "The Shelley Legend,"* by Newman I. White, Frederick L. Jones, and Kenneth N. Cameron (Philadelphia, 1951).

Here, then, we shall leave the December, 1816, letter, which may continue, in spirit, to be torn in pieces and restored to wholeness while the body of it rests in the British Museum, *via,* we shall do well to remember, the Ashley Library of the late, the fallen, T. J. Wise.

⚜ { 11 } ⚜

Lady Shelley, that new keeper of a poet's reputation, looked round with some disquietude on the contemporary trend. If lies, frauds, and inaccuracies were to win a foothold, Shelley's fly-blown character might never again come clean. Like so many who preceded her, the enthusiast decided that his life—exhaustive, documentative, conclusive—must be written. And, unlike her more variously occupied predecessors, she had the will and the means to enforce her single aim. In Boscombe Manor a shrine had been erected. Sir Percy might spend his whole day in the theater or hanker freely after a yachtsman's life, but one corner of that seaside home was to be Shelley. Here, all the mementoes that came down from Mary were collected: his hair, his books, his manuscripts, his miniature (doubtful) as a fair-haired child, his wife's miniature, the books that were drowned with him, his very rattle, and, above all, that richer dust, his heart. Here, indeed, you might worship; nay, you must. As the entrant to a mosque removes his shoes, you took your hat off—man and woman alike—at the Shelley shrine (although Jane—Mrs. Jefferson Hogg—objected that "in church we put them on"; for the two Janes continued out of sympathy). But the shrine was a mere local incantation. If all evil could be shed away, in public, and all false criticism (i.e., adverse criticism) silenced, then the duty laid upon herself would be completed. Lady Shelley sought for the ideal biographer.

She found him in the person of the other Jane's husband, who, having ceded his claim to the family property to his younger brother,[8] still lived with his own unlegalized family in Maida Vale. There might have been others. Trelawny was not disposed to friendliness; in fact, he hated and despised the woman. Neither Hunt nor Peacock could bring himself to write a full life of Shelley. Hogg bounced in where these declined to tread. He had written vivaciously of the Ox-

[8] See Winifred Scott, *Jefferson Hogg.*

ford days, and Mary had approved him. So the Revising Barrister, with his Rabelaisian echoes and pert cynicism, his haunting suspicion that the world was slighting him—Hogg, the suburban guardian of a daughter and two step-children (now beyond his care), arrived at Boscombe in 1855 to be entrusted with the documents. It was not his first visit; in November, 1851 he had seen something of Sir Percy's special madness: "The Drama is all absorbing . . . we live and we breathe Theaters." However, it is not the Dramatic but the Biographical Era we are heralding. To say that from this date onwards there was always a biographer at Boscombe is perhaps beyond the literal truth; but there was always one in spirit, in intention, or in the offing—sometimes two or three. In later days a good deal of hectoring was to go on, and some jealousy to keep out the unwanted; but this first example, genially addressing his hostess as "Wrennie" and signing himself "Dah" in his correspondence, was left to pursue his secret whimsies, and, unsuspected by the trusting family, to develop his megalomania to the full.

Everyone now knows what happened: the hero became displaced although his name was on the title page; the expected life of Shelley turned out to be the rambling reminiscences and abundant inventive quips of Thomas Jefferson Hogg. Some parts of them made gay reading, some deplorable; but where was Shelley, apart from the Oxford episode? Shelley was usually round the corner. He had hurried off to Field Place, fled from Edinburgh, disappeared with flying coat-tails from the de Boinville's residence before the biographer arrived to sit munching bread and butter among the ladies, too late for both his dinner and the poet. This is no longer surprising, when we read in Chapter XV just what the "Divine Poet" did mean to his chronicler:

> He was a lovely, a graceful image, but fading, vanishing speedily from our sight, being portrayed in flying colours. He was a climber, a creeper, an elegant, beautiful, odoriferous parasitical plant; he could not support himself; he must be tied up fast to something of a firmer texture, harder and more rigid than his own pliant, yielding structure; to some person of a less flexible formation: he always required a prop. In order to write the history of his fragile, unconnected, interrupted life, it is necessary to describe that of some ordinary everyday person with whom he was familiar, and to introduce the real subject of the history, whenever a transitory glimpse of him can be caught.

196

The truth is that Hogg, whose *magnum opus* referred to Shelley in a conversational way as "the poor fellow" when it was not patronizingly dubbing him "Divine," was hopelessly incapable, from the outset, of putting his material into shape. The family papers he found unmanageable, partly through his failure to assess their relative values, and partly through his lack of mental balance where his own personality was concerned. He had been given, among other manuscripts, a small fragment of a biography Mary had begun. This he seized on as an opening for his preface, hoping no doubt to flutter the hasty imbiber who, taking the words for Hogg's, should read, "I was the chosen mate of a celestial spirit." After slinging a stone at the obstructive Timothy, Hogg was free to expand his warmer grievance against the editorial treatment of his Oxford Shelley Papers, ending his thunder with the surprising squeak that he proposed now to reprint them unaltered. Other pellets were hurled into the preface: the universities ought to be reformed—Shelley was a great poet and a lady's man—Sir Timothy (Hogg had suddenly come upon a letter to throw in) had objected to Mary's name on a novel—what was the difference between Whigs and Tories? . . . and finally a turgid peroration about Shelley's merits as recognized by Hogg with Boccaccio's backing. This analysis of the preface is enough to indicate the general non-method of the book. With infinite meanderings the second volume breaks off shortly after that admittedly memorable account of the "thrilling" voices in Skinner Street when Shelley darted out of the room after the pale, tartan-clad girl with the piercing look. It is perhaps the only specific Shelley myth Hogg then launched. Beyond that and the general suggestion that the poet was a buffoon, unable even to eat and drink with normal dignity, little can be seen or heard through the obstruction of pervading Hoggery. His decided wit and entertainment value have led several later critics to rate Jefferson highly. In doing so, they have increased his disservices to Shelleyan biography by trusting his false statements.

Had Hogg been merely incapable of strict accuracy, one might forgive him. But his faults were deliberate and studied, amounting almost to forgery, in the determination to spare his own good character at the expense of Shelley's, of truth, and almost of sanity itself. No wonder the heirs at Boscombe Manor were not to see the work in progress—"*our* book" though it was, in his letters to them, and theirs the material for so much of it. Hogg had materials of his own, as well; he had those early letters to himself from Shelley, now become notorious by his mangling of them. They are raw, fanatical, and rather silly letters at the kindest estimate, for Shelley was by no means at his mature best during his intimacy with Jefferson. But Hogg, too, had been absurd and indiscreet. He had tried a ragged courtship of Percy's sister Elizabeth; he had written a part, if not all, of the novel *Leonora;* and after his friend's knight-errantry with Harriet he had done his best to seduce the lovely wife. These are not incidents for a sober Revising Barrister to record. The letters might have been withheld, but the biographer knew a cleverer trick. He played a game of altering words, especially pronouns, so that Hogg, who had his living to earn as a respectable lawyer, was left intact; and Shelley, who was a mad, dead poet even if divine, had only a few more vagaries to answer for—not least among them being a passion for his sister. Not a line was wasted; even the letter of reproach for the Harriet episode could be used by the more impersonal trick of clapping it in, two years beyond its rightful context, as the fragment of a novel, "being an epistle from Albert to Werter," complete with Hogg's criticism of its style.

So the queer medley, like some Frankenstein's disharmonized monster, saw the light in April, 1858; and on the ninth of that month it brought dismay to Boscombe. Lies and inaccuracies, so far from being banished, had been perpetuated. The heirs were especially horrified because it seemed to have their sanction, being unctuously dedicated to "the Hon. Jane ... at whose request the delicate and difficult task was undertaken." On April 17, Sir Percy wrote an explanatory and disclaiming letter to Leigh Hunt. Hogg, he knew, "considered himself an aristocrat and wished to be thought orthodox"; yet they had trusted him, believing him Shelley's friend.

> He has written, I believe, with perfect good faith—and has produced the most disgusting book that can be conceived. That is my opinion, and I think it will be yours, though you may charitably use milder language to express the idea. . . . I am to blame for being such a fool as to trust such a narrow and unsympathetic creature. But the world would be different if there were no folly in it. But I am sorry that I am an example in my own person—and particularly on such a subject.

At this point Sir Percy held up his letter till May 1, intending, before opening the matter with anyone, to get back the materials he had sent Hogg and so prevent publication of the remaining two volumes. "I have now regained part of our materials," he then wrote, "and hope to get the rest—by law perhaps.—But as yet we are not declared foes." On July 2, Hunt wrote to Sir Percy the much-quoted letter suggesting that Hogg was "out of his wits" and referring to "this foolish book of an imbecile pretender."

The family were successful in removing their documents,[9] and decided that, instead of him, Lady Shelley herself should turn editor. The result was to be the *Shelley Memorials* published the following summer—and further words from the reviewers, who had not been over kind to Hogg.

◄{ III }►

A maze of biographical activity now confronts us, and it is hard to know which avenue to take. Pursuing our Hogg-track for the briefest scamper, we may see this unscrupulous egotist being gradually exposed. The Shelleys themselves knew only a fraction of his fraudulence. Leigh Hunt, on August 13, 1859, referred in the *Spectator* to "a heap of the most extraordinary mistakes and misrepresentations made respecting Shelley and others." Peacock, reviewing in *Fraser's Magazine* in June, 1858, had made some restrained corrections, but allowed his public estimate to appear more kindly than his private one. But within fifteen years an exceedingly keen mind had been at work on Hogg's and other biographers' details about Shelley's life. This was D. F. MacCarthy, who in 1872 fairly battered the now defunct Hogg on point after point, proving how many, even of his most vivid college stories, fell to the ground in the light of fact, or canceled one another out as contradictions.[10] Numerous instances of fictions and inaccuracies are revealed by MacCarthy's examination. They are

---

[9] The eventual success was due to Lady Shelley rather than her indolent husband. A letter among the Abinger papers (without date or address) shows her, in great anxiety and distress, urging Percy to go at once to Hogg and obtain the papers, postponing all interests in yachts, plays, or railways until this matter of far more consequence is settled. (The tone of it hints that she can bully when she pleases and is irritated by that very placidity in Percy which—had she paused to consider it—was the secret of their continued harmony.)

[10] Denis Florence MacCarthy, *Shelley's Early Life, from Original Sources* (London, 1872).

convincing and irrefutable. Even the "fragment of a novel" is seized on with an indication of its true significance. Hogg, one would say, leaves the court without a character, robbed even of his hearty pound of pigsflesh and ruined, as a biographer, for good.

But has he in fact been ruined? No, he is still secretly, when not openly, admired for his vivacity; he goes on, being alternately reviled and reinstated, rejected, reprinted, and rejoiced in to the end of the century. Edward Dowden, though he worked under the jealous eye of Lady Shelley, let his admiration openly appear. It was an admiration of opposites, for Dowden, painstaking, accurate, meticulous as he tried to be, poetical as he has been termed, and possessed of a searing conscience about truth, had never a spark of that free gaiety that his flashing predecessor everywhere displayed. On this score Dowden thought he knew his better. "We should spoil his narrative," he wrote, "if we were to interrupt it with cross-questioning or rebuke. The veracity of the historian and the veracity of the artist are not identical. Allowing for Hogg's peculiar point of view, for his egotism, and for the fact that at all hazards he must be witty, we may assert that in his chapters on Shelley at Oxford he has painted an admirable portrait, true in the essential qualities of being characteristic and living." W. M. Rossetti, writing his own memoir of Shelley, referred to Hogg's irresistibly amusing book." In the twentieth century Hogg is again reprinted (with an editorial warning), because men enjoy his hearty clumsiness as they would a post-impressionistic picture, glowing and distorted. Hogg is, in fact, reissued as a modernist, while continuing to bemuse those biographers who forget to disbelieve him.

By now we have the matter put before us with reasonable clarity; Mr. W. S. Scott, who married into the Hogg family, has published not only the correct versions of some of the known letters, but a further series written to Hogg by Mary in 1815, that show the floundering young unmarried wife, in her distress at Shelley's apparent preference for Claire Clairmont, trying with a pathetic application of Shelley's or the early Godwin's principles to love Hogg.[11] This, too, has given rise to a new "scandal"—unjustified, we may safely say, when the conditions and circumstances have been all weighed up. It is generally agreed that Hogg, for all Boscombe's withdrawal of the relevant documents, did write his third and fourth volumes of the *Life of Shel-*

[11] *New Shelley Letters,* ed by W. S. Scott.

ley. Mr. Scott was at one time confident of finding them, and nearly every British and American Shelley student has at some moment or another joined in the pursuit.

❦ IV ❦

How refreshing, in this clatter, are the reverent interludes where a poetic spirit sings to its own lyre in the solitude; loving, devoted, innocently ignorant of the worshiped deity but casting its own dreaming aspiration into the hero's form. After Browning with the *Pauline* so mercilessly smothered, we have an eager young radical, Bessie Rayner Parkes. She was to marry the Frenchman Louis Swanton Belloc and become the mother of Hilaire Belloc and Marie Belloc Lowndes. Before this, she had been taken up by those Pre-Raphaelite Shelleyans we are soon to meet with, who noted her conversion to the Church of Rome. Her long poem *Gabriel* may well have been a step towards it; her whole approach to the chosen theme is that of veneration. It was written in 1856 as an Easter offering and is prefaced thus:

TO A GRAVE IN ROME

TO AN IMMORTAL FAME IN ENGLAND,

AND

TO ONE WHO LOVES AND HONOURS

THE GENIUS OF

PERCY BYSSHE SHELLEY

I DEDICATE THIS POEM.

There follows an idealized picture of the life of Shelley as a heavenly visitant due for martyrdom. She quotes St. Luke's "The Angel Gabriel was sent from God." After an account of the stately home and birth of the visitant with Sydney's blood in him, Gabriel is shown conversant with Greek literature, awakening to strife with the world's evils and determined "to wrest the meaning out of life." Some think him mad, but he is "Dieu-Donné," and his college career, wherein religion seems entirely to have replaced the traditional atheism, possibly catches out the authoress sublimating some private inhibitions, and even remodeling Shelley according to the desires of a faithful heart.

201

Besides, the women in Percy's life are absent; after "Bisham beeches" we go to Italy for some gentle description;

> *But one dire grief each Venice wave repeats,*
> *And one we buried by the grave of Keats.*

Gabriel, "poet of the future," sings of his decision not to return to England. Then come shipwreck, death, and burning. At the last,

> *He stands a type of what our race may be*
> *When life and love and thought are just and free.*

The poem falls short of *Pauline's* passion and impelling power; but Bessie Parkes was not a Browning, even though some passages of explorative freedom recall Elizabeth Barrett's *Aurora Leigh*. It has, with the dignity of real worship, the imperfect sincerity of a mind entranced by its own symbols. At least this Shelley is not the ineffectual angel that is soon to obsess the later Victorians; it is easy enough to see behind Bessie Rayner Parkes's figure of Gabriel to the figure of Christ, which was her real analogy. If she lacked the philosophical reasoning to make of the poet a Promethean symbol, she was not wanting in the missionary fervor that could present him with all confidence as a god.

Browning, as we noted, had revoked his faith in a mode to induce anger when anyone should so much as remind him of the early confession that was *Pauline*. Tennyson, too, as years and responsibilities grew on him, had lost his early rapture. If we look closely on the staunch adherents in the later nineteenth century, an uneasy suspicion creeps in that those who stuck to Shelley did so in the way of business, because the editing and probing and biographizing of a chosen poet could set a man up with a title to distinction and transform a miscellaneous journalist into an authority. Would, then, the author of *Gabriel,* having no call to be professional over Shelley, drift away? It is a pleasure to have been reassured, on the evidence of her son, Hilaire Belloc, that she "continued in her admiration of Shelley all through her long life." Nor was there any revulsion on her children's part. Maturing early enough to be clear of the present century's cult of anti-romanticism, Hilaire Belloc, never afterwards swayed by literary fashions, knew Shelley for a great poet from the outset, and in this opinion he was confirmed throughout his long life.

Now essentially—as it seems to us—Bessie Parkes knew and understood her Shelley very much better than did the author of a fifty-page grinding critical essay published the same year in the *National Review*.[12] Author was also editor: no one could reject him, though he saw in Shelley "a poet as to whom our information is but scanty."[13] Humility requires a "my" instead of "our," but we could let that pass if intuition would make up for it. This dweller in the literary backwoods, being by profession an economist and by preference a politician, is Walter Bagehot, who retains a name for his excursions into letters. Now there is no harm in an economist's looking at a poet— or even being a poet if he is able. (Shelley the poet had all too many calls to function as a practical economist!) But there was more poetry in the late J. M. Keynes's little finger than in the brain of Bagehot— who not unexpectedly quotes Hazlitt on Shelley's having a *maggot* in his brain. As text or journalistic excuse for an essay in 1856, he takes late editions of Mary Shelley's *Poetical* and *Prose Works* of Shelley, bracketed with Medwin's *Life* of 1847. These works, that is to say, are listed in a footnote, not reviewed. Mary had supplied him with a text of Shelley from which he could quote long, misinterpreted passages; Medwin had led him into error with his tale of Shelley's outstanding love for Harriet Grove. It matters little, since his Shelley is of the headiest burlesque vintage—a pitiable windy object swayed by impulse only, innocent of reason, unfit to grapple with the world of men. Forever fanciful and foolish, playing with light and loveliness as a child with toys, Bagehot's phantom invents its own delectable program of regeneration, "is cheered on his way by a beautiful dream" (though presumably haunted in all his poems by the death of Harriet Westbrook) and scorns all earthly ordering. "The essential feelings he hoped to change; the eternal facts he struggled to remove."

This visionary, floating in his own Elysium, fashions one interchangeable loved being from Cythna to Emilia, with a fairy's passion, for "his verse runs quick and chill." As excuse for such a condition the economist offers the plea that Shelley's works are "in the strictest

---

[12] Published in *Literary Studies*, ed. by Richard Holt Hutton, Vol. I (1895), and many times reprinted, such was the literary economist's popularity.
[13] As to that, let anyone judge who has battled through our survey to this point.

sense 'remains' " and that no long work of excellence could be expected from a man who died at thirty. That Shelley was three times thirty in his inner life is all too hair-fine a perception for this critic, who does, however, give him marks on language. "There is much more," he concludes, "which might be said, and which ought to be said, of Shelley; but our limits are reached."

There is always much more to be said, whether or not it ought to be. In contrast to both Bessie Parkes's deification and Walter Bagehot's decorporation, we have, three years later, his heartily rough treatment at a cleric's hands. Charles Kingsley, appointed in 1859 Chaplain in Ordinary to Her Majesty, broke out in print in his *Miscellany* with a monitory sermon. "Hysterical Rousseaus, hysterical Shelleys, uttering words like the East Wind." Byron's good qualities (of manly diabolism) "condemn him in the eyes of a mesmerizing, table-turning, spirit-rapping, spiritualizing, Romanizing generation who read Shelley in secret, and delight in his bad taste, mysticism, extravagance, and vague and pompous sentimentalism. The age is an effeminate one [an age of water-babies, to be sure], and it can well afford to pardon the lewdness of the gentle and sensitive vegetarian, while it has no mercy for that of the sturdy peer." The Chaplain held out some hope for humanity: "Thousands, doubtless, have read Byron and Shelley, and worse books, and have risen from them as pure as they sat down." And before Kingsley sits down after his own hysterical outburst, he gives a parting shot: Shelley never wrote a genuine drama; "Beatrice Cenci is really none other than Percy Bysshe Shelley himself in petticoats." (The position of Count Cenci in this dilemma is unspecified.)

CHAPTER XI

Lives of "Me Old Father"

OR ALL THAT, Shelley is on the flood tide, and no Canute-like efforts of the Queen's Chaplain will delay him now. As that essay showed, he has supplanted Byron in the public's preference, and to judge by the forthcoming supply of literature, the demand is inexhaustible. During the same few months that saw Hogg's *Life* appear, two other accounts had been presented. First came Charles S. Middleton's *Shelley and His Writings*. The priority was perhaps fortunate for a young man who, while so many were able to write personal reminiscences, could not pretend to be anything but a stranger. Middleton was at least attracted to his subject for the good reason that he had poetic longings in him.[1] His book gives a few fragments picked up from interviews in Marlow. (Shelley is said to have doled out blankets for charity, with his name in large letters in the center to prevent their being disposed of. This argues a certain horse sense in the visionary.) But it is mainly remarkable for a grand myth of Sir Timothy as the wicked father. The baronet, we are told, was distinguished "by the hardness of his heart and the vindictiveness of his disposition. His ruling passion appears to have been the love of money—the most odious, perhaps, of all the vices which degrade humanity." Nobody now reads Middleton, except for research purposes. He was too handicapped in the competition against Hogg, Peacock, and Trelawny. Nor could he even apply to them for detail: they would have been sparing of it.

Trelawny had been busy on his own narrative of his "first meeting with poets." Here was firsthand evidence—story and confession and character study—by one of the heroes of the famous circle: the cele-

---

[1] In 1848 he had published *Hours of Recreation*, a collection of poems written at the age of twenty-one, and including quotations from Shelley. (It is of interest to note that he spotted and reprinted from the *Bedford Times* John Clare's *I Am*, and wrote a verse reply to it.)

brated grave-digger himself. Trelawny was no mere researcher, no
mere observer even, as Medwin might be, but a leading actor. And
his memoirs are those of a leading actor, full of natural egotism and
bombast, but lively, vivid, close to the event, and conversational. He
wrote to Claire for some scraps of information (keeping his purpose
dark), but for the most part trusted to his erratic memory and his
sense of dramatic fitness. Where the two came into conflict, the latter
won; but it had been so animated a life in Italy that for the most
part truth and drama danced with even steps, or so little out of time
as to make no odds to the bandmaster. The *Recollections of the Last
Days of Shelley and Byron* was, as we foresaw, intended as a sequel
to the *Younger Son*. But it inverted the usual rule of sequels—to be
flatter than its forerunner. Fine as Trelawny might be as a hero, his
reinforcement by the two great poets must be trebly fine. In fact there
is no comparison. The *Younger Son* is reprinted in adventure classics,
but the fame of the *Recollections* is such that we may almost be let
off describing it here at all. If Trelawny's meeting with the "strip-
ling" Shelley has been quoted once, it has been quoted fifty times;
and the myths and anecdotes bravely launched defy all listing. The
book could hardly have evaded popularity; it has precisely that air
of picturesque charlatanism and (to borrow from Dowden on Hogg)
artistic truth that sends a shiver of delight through the awakened
reader, and makes him sigh involuntarily, "At last!"

Of course the sensation is illusory; there is no more finality about
Trelawny's picture of the Pisan circle than there can be about any
autobiographer's account, especially so disjointed an account as this.
Trelawny had meant to rewrite it "in connected form," but in the
end he sent the rough draft to the printer "in 'most admirable dis-
order.'" But compared with Hogg's meanderings it is autobiography
with a difference. What could be more effective than the "preparation" of the first brief chapter: the priest at Lausanne railing at *Queen
Mab,* and the "self-confident and dogmatic" English walking tourist
who turns out to be William Wordsworth and pronounces so emphatically that Shelley is no poet and the *Cenci* "won't do"? He
prints, too, for the first time (but for Mary's footnotes in her *Prose
Works*) quotations from the journal of Edward Williams, giving as
appealing and sympathetic an estimate of Shelley as can ever have
been penned before or since. Williams—himself shown, in Trelawny's

narrative, to be a charming personality—found Shelley "of most astonishing genius, in appearance extraordinarily young, of manners mild and amiable, but withal full of life and fun. . . . His ordinary conversation is akin to poetry, for he sees things in the most singular and pleasing light; if he wrote as he talked, he would be popular enough. Lord Byron and others think him by far the most imaginative poet of the day." Shelley, in Trelawny's pages, is undoubtedly a very lovable human being, and undoubtedly a poet. We may note that the most readily accessible of the Pirate's several accounts of Shelley's cremation is to be found here. ("One word for Byron, two words for Shelley, and ten for Trelawny," the *Athenaeum* commented, stressing the hero's self-importance.)

❧ II ❧

The three books—Middleton's, Trelawny's, and Hogg's—formed an obvious group on which a writer for the leisurely periodical might base an essay. Two men were living who could write such an essay from firsthand knowledge. Of these, Leigh Hunt attempted no general survey. His writings on Shelley had been numerous, and he had only a year more to live. It was left to Peacock, who had always been averse from using his pen on this subject, to overcome reluctance, and to do so with no half-measure. He had not been with Shelley at Oxford, nor in Italy, but he had known him well in the years between, at Marlow, besides possessing a detailed correspondence from abroad. The memoirs he now wrote place him instead of Middleton in the trilogy. The first section appeared in *Fraser's Magazine* for June, 1858. The second was to dally a couple of years.

Unlike Hogg and Trelawny, Peacock was free of the anxiety to cut a figure. All that he tells us in the line of personal narrative has the authentic ring in it. When Shelley is seen holding his first babe, Ianthe, in his arms, while he croons the monotonous lullaby "Yahmani, yahmani, yahmani," we feel confident that Peacock is remembering, hearing, seeing; no less when it comes to the poet's passion for sailing paper boats. There was, too, that haunting nightmare (too much scoffed at) of incipient elephantiasis—a monstrous imaginative growth from the sight of a fat old woman in a mail coach. Comic, ridiculous, poignant, it is something that happens to defenseless genius in a body-haunted mind. Shelley, so frequently in pain in his later years, spoke then of his spirit's imprisonment in a feeble frame. At best the mind could escape into creation; too often it was driven back on itself, frustrated by the physical barrier. Never glorying in it as a healthier, more animal organism would, he was driven always to the dangerous brink where the slightest call to shuffle off mortality could attract him. His close contact with the sea was always dangerous; he would not (could not) swim, would lie in the bottom of the boat, stay motionless, content to sink heedlessly when danger threatened. We can only surmise that in the end he gave his body to the sea with readiness, but cried out against the cessation, if it was to be such, of his mental faculties.

This, to be sure, is a digression. But to Peacock the incident in the mail coach was significant, too, though of other symptoms. It chimed with one of his two prejudices about Shelley—the poet's propensity to hallucinations. On this account, backed up with further myths, he plunged with vigor, in his second installment, into the famous midnight attack at the farmhouse at Tan-yr-allt. Many have since "proved" that Shelley was attacked, and many disproved it. To Peacock it was clear that the poet was misled by his imaginings, and was his own and only attacker. It seems now that we shall never know.[2] However, a critic in the *Spectator* of August 6, 1859 went all out for the theory of hallucination, pursuing it so far as to hint that if Shelley's mind and nerves could so delude him, then none of his other acts or movements were to be trusted, and, in short, that he was mad.

Boscombe was not pleased; neither was Leigh Hunt. The failing but still warm-hearted champion of Romantic poets set out, under difficulties, to make a protest. Already the cold shades of night were falling on him, and his friend Charles Reynell had decided to carry him off, together with the books and papers he was working on, to Putney. But he forgot the *Spectator* notice and had to rack his weakened memory for the phrases used in it. Even so, his paper, "The Occasional," contributed on August 13 to the *Spectator,* was a spirited answer to the charges of invention, hallucination, and aberration. As

[2] Peacock backed his hallucination theory by two further incidents: Shelley's vision of a woman with four eyes while Byron was reading *Christabel;* and a long tale of how Williams of Tremadoc did not, as Shelley affirmed, pay a visit to Marlow—a tale in which all Peacock's reasoning was based dizzily on an interchange of ill-fitting hats. It is unconvincing.

it was to be Hunt's last public utterance of any length, it is significant that Shelley was again, as he had so often been, its subject. The reviewer answered, drawing from Hunt a laborious rejoinder on August 20, the evident work of a sick man and a tired mind. On August 19 he found he had missed Lady Shelley, who had been to town and now begged Hunt to come to Boscombe. In the great internal pain that now beset him Hunt remembered her and Sir Percy with gratitude and tears of pleasure. His last letter, of August 24, was written to her. He was to live only four days longer. Thus the memory of his friend, upheld in journalism and embodied in relatives, was with him to the last.

Peacock the memoir writer had a second, more important prejudice—the prejudice that, one suspects, had led to his reluctance to begin writing on Shelley at all. Loyalty to his friend must for him be tempered by loyalty to Harriet. Much as he might wish to reconcile them, it was impossible when the tragedy came to be discussed. In his first installment he had hinted the situation, describing how Shelley, torn between Mary and Harriet, had seized a laudanum bottle and had declared his hatred for Eliza the ever present sister. Peacock promised himself more discussion on the subject when Hogg's further volumes should appear.

He might have waited till his death for these; but the appearance of the *Shelley Memorials* in 1859 warned him that there was no more to expect. It showed him, too, that "chatter about Harriet"—a phrase to be coined by the later Victorian biographers who indulged in it so mercilessly—was already acidulated. Between the Regency and the twentieth century had come the strictly ethical outlook of this era that could not allow for compromise or base a broader understanding on psychology. The sheep were black or white. So Lady Shelley is seen rallying the old hands and the young enthusiasts to fight her battle against Hogg and Peacock. She and her husband are to miss Hunt's backing; but there are rumors of a very young literary aspirant from the British Museum who, having pronounced with eagerness on Shelley,[3] is called to Boscombe to assist in a ghostly capacity with the production of *Shelley Memorials*. The twenty-four-year-old Richard Garnett will be out in the open soon as a scholarly recruit to Shelleyana. For the moment this future author of *The Twilight of the*

[3] Richard Garnett's poems *Io in Egypt* (1859) include a sonnet *To the Memory of Shelley*.

Gods may see the dusk of those survivors from the Romantic Age of Shelley, Keats, and Byron. Hunt, as we noted, is to write once more on his poet and pass away; Hogg has another five undistinguished years to live; Peacock, in his quiet home at Chertsey, a few more; Medwin a decade of complete obscurity. Only Trelawny, that unquenchable Titan, is to go on, growing more titanic and less veracious, settling down to a monstrous lease of life and swagger, amongst Victorian biographers, wives who join and leave him, pre-Raphaelite poets and painters crowding in to see, admire—and pump.

❦ III ❦

The *Memorials,* edited at least nominally by Lady Shelley at Boscombe, was a modest volume setting out to give the documents Hogg might have retained for use had he been a more obedient pupil. As it was, the initial anxiety was to wash off all Hogg's effluvia. This was done in the preface. Among the manuscript materials were Shelley's *Letter to Lord Ellenborough* and the *Essay on Christianity,* now first published. Presentation of the Harriet question was clever by reticence: "Estrangements," at the end of 1813, had reached a climax that led to separation; Harriet's death was in no way due to Shelley. The deplorable incident ends a chapter, and Mary first appears in the next. Dates are withheld, so that the innocent reader, if there was one, might suppose that the poet, being left unmated, met and later married his second wife.

Peacock had been patient with Hogg; he was angry with Lady Shelley, showed up her trickery, and declared there was no thought of separation until Shelley met Mary, who had been described to Peacock by Harriet herself. Harriet he speaks of in the most favorable terms. But still he keeps his head about this question; during the bickering that was to follow it would have been well to remember his rational, almost modern argument. So much bellicosity might have been avoided, so much printer's ink and paper saved!

> Some of Shelley's friends [he wrote] have spoken and written of Harriet as if to vindicate him it were necessary to disparage her. They might, I think, be content to rest the explanation of his con-

"The Poet's Son"—Sir Percy Florence Shelley

From a cartoon by "Ape" in *Vanity Fair*, December 13, 1879

duct on the ground on which he rested it himself—that he had found in another the intellectual qualities which constituted his ideality of the partner of his life. But Harriet's untimely fate occasioned him deep agony of mind, which he felt the more because for a long time he kept the feeling to himself.

A ding-dong battle followed, too tedious by now to trace over in detail: Richard Garnett, hand in glove with the Boscombe family, had returned to the matter in *Macmillan's Magazine*.[4] Peacock tried some sleuthing, searching already for the lost letters that were to be discovered by Leslie Hotson so long after his time. He wrote a "subsidiary Notice" in 1862, upon which Garnett, about to publish his *Relics of Shelley* under Boscombe auspices, hastily added a section on the subject. It is notable for a piece of rank dishonesty. In order to prove that Shelley was "through" with Harriet, he quoted, thus, a letter written to Hogg on March 16, 1814, while Shelley was staying with the Boinvilles:

> . . . is still with us,—not here!—but will be with me when the infinite malice of Destiny forces me to depart. I am now but little inclined to contest this point. I certainly hate her with all my heart and soul. It is a sight that awakens an inexpressible sensation of disgust and horror, to see her caress my poor little Ianthe, in whom I may hereafter find the consolation of sympathy.

Garnett's readers would almost certainly fill up the blank with the name "Harriet." In Hogg's *Life* it was actually "Eliza." Instead of a bald statement that he hated his wife, Shelley was only asserting that she had beaten him over her sister's presence. It is as poor a trick as a disinterested literary man could play. But we should not be over hard on Garnett; he was young, he was a little overawed by his position as spokesman for the Boscombe family, and it would have been embarrassing and ungrateful, in the face of Lady Shelley's ardent promptings, to have questioned her accuracy. He was the first but not the only Boscombe biographer to glimpse this awkwardness; Dowden was to have a tussle for liberty, and Mrs. Julian Marshall to be led obediently along the route prescribed. But it indicates the curious influence emanating from the Boscombe shrine that Peacock,

4 "Shelley in Pall Mall," June, 1860.

who, of all these controversialists, was Shelley's friend, should have
been driven into an attitude resembling hostility through his efforts—
only a trifle tinged by sentiment for Harriet—to present the truth.

For the moment we may escape from this Harriet chatter by quoting a pretty conceit from one of Shelley's end-of-century admirers. Sir
William Watson, whose poem *Wordsworth's Grave* was to bring him
a momentary fame, was born in this very year that launched the three
biographies. Later he confessed to Dowden on receiving a copy of
his *Life of Shelley*:

> *In my young days of fervid poesy*
> *He drew me to him with his strange far light—*
> *He held me in a world all clouds and gleams*
> *And vasty phantoms . . .*[5]

Another poem, on the 1892 Centenary, referred to "Shelley, the cloud-
begot" hurrying to greet the Great Perhaps with *Why?* and *Whence?*
(Fitzgerald's *Rubaiyat* seems to lurk behind it) ; and amongst a series
of *Epigrams* of 1884 we rediscover:

> *Shelley and Harriet*
> *A star look'd down from heaven and loved a flower*
> *Grown in earth's garden—loved it for an hour.*
> *Let eyes that trace his orbit in the spheres*
> *Refuse not, to a ruin'd rosebud, tears.*

This is to leap on a little. But the year of biographies, 1858, had seen
a fictional life in German, by Wilhelm Hamm, who had met Mrs.
Shelley on her travels in Germany in 1846.[6] His attempt to rescue
Shelley from oblivion (as it appeared to him then) concentrated,
ironically enough for Mary, on the Emilia Viviani episode. Shelley's
struggle between love and loyalty was expressed in passionate utterances cut and repatched from *Epipsychidion*. The Mary of the tale
tried poison, but grew reconciled, and the crisis ended with Shelley's
welcoming his death as a release. This hybrid bloom was something
of a lone shoot at its period: on the Continent, the 1848 revolution
had failed, and that meant Shelley's doctrines had failed, also—or they

---

[5] William Watson, *Poems* (1904).
[6] *Shelley, eine biographische Novelle* (Leipzig, 1858). See Liptzin, *Shelley in Germany*.

had not been persuasive enough to win through. Hopes that were built on the reformer fell away, and the tired aspirants turned to earthly things. For so much is Shelley now responsible.

⊰⊱ IV ⊰⊱

"There seems to be a decree that we shall have no good life of Shelley," the *Athenaeum* reviewer wrote when the *Memorials* came out in 1859. He was looking back at Mary Shelley's notes, and probably, without mentioning them by name, at the works of Medwin, Trelawny, Hogg, and Middleton. In the *Memorials* he found as little satisfaction. "The whole book is as mournful a one as

> '*a sound and a dream from the moaning sea,—*'

nor can we imagine any, written on its subject, to have more health and hopefulness in its tone. We presume that it is to be accepted as the final memorial of him whose ashes lie under the shadow of the Pyramid of Caius Cestius, and of her who toiled on with a broken wing and a weary heart." In this he was a poor prophet.[7] One who appeared to agree was Leigh Hunt's son Thornton, who, writing in the *Atlantic Monthly*, dismissed all Shelley's associates as "mere tourists or acquaintances."[8] Youngest of contacts, he had been six years old during the Marlow period, and precocious enough, it would seem, to look critically at the undeveloped Mary, who "did not do justice to herself either in her aspect or in the tone of her conversation." To Peacock's picture of sailing paper boats he added one of those notes of dark foreshadowing that so many were to find in Shelley after the event (not that we need doubt Thornton's *bona fides*): when the boats capsized, the poet had wished playfully to get into one of them and be shipwrecked—"a death he should like better than any other." A curious passage suggesting that Shelley (no less than Keats) was affected by "venal pleasures" at Oxford seems to have escaped Lady Shelley's vigilant eye, or perhaps she was reluctant to attack Hunt's son.

[7] The *Atlantic Monthly* described the book less sweepingly as a "feminine offering of tender admiration and grief laid upon the grave of departed genius."
[8] "Shelley; by One Who Knew Him," *Atlantic Monthly*, February, 1863.

This was a random utterance; Thornton wrote no life; and another non-starter was George Eliot's G. H. Lewes, who, it was reported, had assembled, from Hunt and others, materials for a biography which he was never to produce. But the five years, 1858 to 1862, have seen the personal Shelleyans in their autumnal flowering, while the new crop of professional literary men begins to sprout. Here, then, is young Garnett, half sprouting on his own, half gleaning, as he rescues the Prologue to *Hellas* and the lovely *Lines Written in the Bay of Lerici* for his *Relics of Shelley*. The volume is unhappily titled, at least from the angle of the present compilation wherein relics—thick as autumnal leaves—are generally of a more material nature, sometimes so intimately material as to be not a little ghoulish.

The great marble monument Lady Shelley had commissioned from the sculptor Henry Weekes could hardly be called a relic, though it takes its place, not without a hitch, among other memorials. This fanciful effigy of Mary supporting the naked corpse of the drowned Shelley may be guessed to derive its inspiration from Michelangelo's *pietà* in St. Peter's, Rome, with its Virgin Mary supporting the dead Christ. (Perhaps this was as near as Lady Shelley would come publicly to subscribing to the attitude of Bessie Parkes.) Be that as it may, the vicar of St. Peter's, Bournemouth, for which church it was intended, would have none of it.[9] He objected that it would make his church a showplace. It is better housed now, under the tower of the lovely old priory of Christchurch, some few miles along the coast. A copy was made for Lady Shelley's sanctum. The effect of this "Chapel" must, one suspects, have been "High Church" or theatrical, with its domed ceiling of dull turquoise set with clusters of gold stars. It was built to impress. It became a *mystique,* to be remembered as a strange experience, or, when possible, to wring tears from the heart.

For the first, we have the evidence of a lady, so long afterwards as 1925. "Albinia Locke" of Wick wrote in the *Christchurch Priory Magazine*:

> When I was a little girl I well remember my mother, who was a great friend of old Lady Shelley, taking me to Boscombe Manor,

---

[9] This vicar, the Reverend A. M. Bennett, now lies next to the Shelley grave in St. Peter's Churchyard.

and in a corner of the beautiful drawing room there seeing an alcove fitted with silken curtains and a red lamp which was always kept burning and standing before it an urn containing, she told me, the heart of the poet, the greatest and most revered treasure of the house of Shelley.[10]

This heart theory is one of the many and spurious. We shall look at them later. But wringing tears from the heart was what the votaress required of Shelley's only living daughter, Ianthe Esdaile. She came, we are told, with her children at Boscombe's pressing invitation; came with her own heart hardened by her family, asking that no allusion to her father should be made. She was taken to the sanctum and left for an hour with letters, journals, and relics. At the end of it, sobbing bitterly, she said, "Send my children to me; let them come and love him too." But all this, on her return home, was discountenanced by her clergyman, a "narrow episcopalian," who assured her she had been led astray. Nor did the early poems in manuscript that she had promised in her melting mood, reach Boscombe. So runs Lady Shelley's story, twice recorded.[11]

What part Sir Percy Florence plays in all this reverence is doubtful. He has become entirely a gentleman of hobbies. They are strenuous ones. As we saw, he has his own theatricals; he paints his backcloths (one of them representing the Bay of Lerici), and wounds the dignity of his butler by working on the scenery as a practical carpenter. Among his guests and fellow actors are such Victorian worthies as the Hon. Grantley Berkeley, Hamilton Aidé, Admiral Sir William Wiseman, Colonel Scarlett, of the family later to be adopted by the childless Lady Shelley as her heirs, and J. A. Rolls, another Shelley connection, afterwards Lord Llangattock. Music is composed, playbills are printed, and gorgeous old-style melodramas (some from his own pen) are produced, with Christmas fairy tales rich in transformation scenes.

> I remember one morning [Percy Fitzgerald recalls] the host showing me his ingeniously-designed apparatus for changing the scenes, the lighting etc., all contrived in the most perfect manner.

[10] Quoted in the *Bournemouth Daily Echo*, September 19, 1925.
[11] See William Allingham, *A Diary*, ed. by H. Allingham and D. Radford (London, 1907); also Rolleston, *Talks with Lady Shelley*.

He, indeed, kept a permanent painter and property man. . . . It was always a surprise to think, and you had almost to remind yourself occasionally of the fact, that you had the great poet's son before you in this quiet, unassuming Sir Percy. He was thoroughly unaffected, and a most kindly host. . . . His acting . . . was rather jejune, and his elocution rough and stiff, often impairing the general effect. He, however, modestly enough contented himself with unobtrusive parts.[12]

Sir Percy can turn his hand to words or music, besides joining in the action together with his wife—when relics and biographers are not claiming her. Another visitor is that enterprising Captain Wingfield, who is busy introducing the new game of lawn tennis, called by him in 1873 "Sphairistike." No doubt it is played at Boscombe.

More besides shrines and theaters is being built to pain the butler. Now it is a photographic studio for the Victorian innovation of which Percy is an eager pioneer. This, too, requires backcloths of a realistic nature, so that sitters may be posed in meditation amidst the woodland glens, cascades, or colonnaded temples so gratifying to both victim and executioner. If Percy is not plagued by fine artistic notions, at least he is keen and competent in all these jobs and ready to take what offers. In 1876 what offers is the presidency of the Bournemouth Amateur Dramatic Society—a rival concern, one might guess, and perhaps a handful when the Shelleys, acquiring a London house on the Embankment, open another private theater in Chelsea. But that—and a lawsuit that it brought, to swell his troubles—are outside our present orbit. Added to all this is his passion for yachting. Like father, like son, we might have ventured at that point. But where Shelley's boating is random, unorthodox, and so amateurish that most peers other than Lord Byron (himself a bit of a vagabond) would mock at it, Sir Percy sails like a baronet and a country gentleman. Member of the Royal Yacht Squadron from 1854, a familiar figure at Cowes regattas, he cruises when he will on one of his several steam yachts (he owned a succession of ten until his death)[13] around the coasts and across to the continent of Europe.

[12] Percy Fitzgerald, *Memories of an Author* (London, 1895).
[13] See Montague Guest and W. B. Boulton, *Memorials of the Royal Yacht Squadron* (London, 1903).

This sailing gives a certain intermittency to the whole Boscombe set-up; even so, we have not yet finished with it. Here is Sir Percy as High Sherrif, as Lord Lieutenant, and, even, towards the end of his hearty career, as active tricyclist about Bournemouth, president of its Bicycle and Tricycle Club, and riding on his up-to-date three wheels to preside at an annual dinner of the Rowing and Swimming Club in his neighboring Boscombe. He is in every way a genial figure; undistinguished maybe; kind-eyed, thinly bearded, casually clothed; a man to make no enemies and to disappoint only those who expect some Heaven-sent power to reside in a poet's son. Withal "he is a gentleman," as Vanity Fair remarked in publishing its cartoon of him in 1879. What would he have made of Shelley, his "old father"? What would Percy Bysshe, who loved him in infancy, have made of him?[14] Looking from one to the other, it does appear that in one respect the son has dropped easily into the niche that evaded the younger Shelley throughout his restless life: he has the art of all-round unconventionality without committing a social crime. He is unorthodox enough to shock the butler class, but will cause no anxiety to the country house or parsonage, nor excite officious homilies in the press. Mary, as we saw, had rushed into rigidity for his up-bringing; all that Godwinian, Wollstonecraftian, and Shelleyan radicalism was to be banished from Percy Florence, who must be taught to think as others. If he does think little more than others, he is at least a man of many and curious activities—backed by the family inheritance. (He is reported to have let Field Place to a gas engineer, who may, if anyone, counteract the dampness.)

That he accepts the liability of his father's manuscripts and reputation is, in a rural baronet so diversely occupied, a feature we should praise. In practice he is glad enough to hand them to his eager partner, who will see to it that of five talents another five—if not some six or seven—are made.[15] Still, the region is not without its literati. Sir

---

[14] We could do with an imaginary conversation between Percy Florence, aged sixty, and Percy Bysshe just under thirty, meeting on the deck of a small schooner.

[15] R. Glynn Grylls, who was able to see the Journal and other unpublished manuscripts that passed to Lord Abinger on Lady Shelley's death, has given, largely from these, an over-all picture of the Boscombe period in her *Mary Shelley* (London, 1938). This decided me to cut down the product of my own researches, made at Bournemouth and Boscombe, of the Shelleys'

Henry Taylor, a dramatist of forgotten repute and a man of standing, lives there with wife and daughter. This family, and the Boscombe couple, are the chosen intimates of a livelier voyager—one in whom, as in Shelley, immortality is mingled with the seeds of an early death. Robert Louis Stevenson is to settle, briefly enough before his South Sea venture, in a house named Skerryvore (after his grandfather's lighthouse), through which the unworldly writer floats with a reluctance, even an inability, to acquire possessions, and where he is constantly laid up through ill health. Whether for these factors or his poet's nature, we are told that Lady Shelley took the greatest fancy to Louis, "and, discovering in him a close likeness to her renowned father-in-law, she forthwith claimed him as her son."[16] "One of my boys," she called him, recalling how, later, after a premonitory illness, he had told her of his vision of a dual self, good and evil—the origin of *Dr. Jekyll and Mr. Hyde*.[17]

Everyone, including Henry James, who came to visit him, loved Stevenson; and R. L. S. found that Sir Percy's "genial, kindly nature, in which shrewdness and simplicity were most attractively blended, endeared him" to all. He was one of Percy's photographic victims— "I send you two photographs," he wrote to W. H. Low on "Jan SomethingorOther-th, 1886,[18] they are both done by Sir Percy Shelley, the poet's son, which may interest. The sitting down one is, I think, the best; but if they choose that, see that the little reflected light on

---

life there; the more so as it is of very secondary importance to my principal theme. Local papers and periodicals of the time yield several accounts of the activities at Boscombe Manor, noting gala theatrical performances, yachting trips, the laying down, under Shelleyan auspices, of the first pile of Boscombe's pier, and giving an inaccurate report, at once contradicted by Sir Percy, that the "Poet's" estates in Horsham (which the poet never owned) were up for auction.

Certain quotations and information that I have used here may be found also in *The Shelley Legend*, a composite work by Robert Metcalf Smith and others (New York, 1945). Where acknowledgments are not made, it is because my facts were already gathered from the original sources before this book appeared; I have thought it unnecessary to detail these coincidental repetitions because *The Shelley Legend*, being marred by much spurious matter, is a book without a future. Besides being shown up by several scholars, it has been repudiated even by one or two who were misled into collaborating. Newman I. White described it as "a dose of the same medicine as *The Real Shelley* [by J. C. Jeaffreson; see next chapter] with more violent ingredients added."

[16] See Graham Balfour, *The Life of Robert Louis Stevenson* (London and New York, 1901).

[17] Rolleston, *Talks with Lady Shelley*.

[18] R. L. S. was notoriously shaky over dates—at least at the beginning of the year. In 1892, Henry James acknowledged a letter from the South Seas as "January—not 1891, my poor time-deluded islander."

the nose does not give me a turn-up; that would be tragic." He developed this in terms of "the old controversy about Shelley's nose,"[19] since his own hooked nose was capable of suggesting a turn-up in Sir Percy's photograph. "I have a look of him; all his sisters had noses like mine; Sir Percy has a marked hook" . . . and this traditional turn-up may have been an accident of presentation. But R. L. S. had not read, or not remembered, Shelley's own remark to Peacock when describing John Gisborne's Slawkenbergian organ: "I, you know, have a little turn-up nose." It was Hogg, apart from the altogether egregious Gisborne, who had the hook.

Perhaps Louis was equally inexact in his other comparisons: "I seem but a Shelley with less oil, and no genius; though I have had the fortune to live longer and (partly) to grow up. He was growing up. There is a manlier note in the last days . . ." but Stevenson, after hinting this now prevalent theory about Shelley's perpetual adolescence, could not surmount the Emilia Viviani episode, allowing it to grow to monstrous dimensions of imbecility, and so warp his judgment.[20]

A Boscombe occasion that fell flat was when the writer W. H. Mallock—expecting Heaven knows what outbreak of transmitted genius—introduced Byron's grandson, Lord Wentworth, to Shelley's son. No sparks were struck, and the talk was on a trivial level.[21] Another lukewarm acquaintance of Sir Percy Shelley's was the late Wilfrid Meynell, who remarked pensively to me that there was "something unsatisfactory about him." His habit of referring to the poet as "me old father" did not appeal to Meynell. Was it, perhaps, a mild form of protest on the baronet's part against the ritual going on in his wife's sanctum? Percy does appear, in some respects, to be the grandson who might have been anticipated from Sir Timothy if no freak of genius had disturbed the line.

Stevenson (whom Meynell knew at the Savile Club and introduced to the Taylor family) has referred to Shelley's sisters. Two of them, Hellen and Margaret, were still living at this period, and frequent visitors, it would seem, to Boscombe. Before his dismissal Hogg

19 A controversy that had just been renewed by James Cordy Jeaffreson in *The Real Shelley* (London, 1885, 2 vols.). See page 219 below.

20 See *the Letters of Robert Louis Stevenson*, ed. by Sidney Colvin (London and New York, 1911).

21 See W. H. Mallock, *Memoirs of Life and Literature* (London, 1920).

had managed to see them; and we have a picture from a later author, the Irish poet William Allingham who—following Wordsworthian principles—held a custom post at Lymington, in the county, from which it was easy enough to visit the Shelley monument at Christchurch Priory and walk on to Boscombe. He dined with the family, sitting between *"two sisters of Percy Bysshe Shelley"* (the date was October 29, 1864). He found Shelley's favorite, Hellen, "lively and chatty . . . tall, very slender, and must have been graceful and handsome in her youth. I saw, or fancied, a likeness to Shelley. She was sumptuous in light purple silk, which became her. She looked about fifty-six, but must be much more." She was sixty-five. "Her sister, who seemed rather younger, was much less lively." Hellen, he found, had no interest in such "modern" poets as Tennyson and Browning, and "her recollections of Leigh Hunt were not of a friendly sort." Allingham goes on to sketch his host, with a compromise on the nose question:

> Sir Percy Florence Shelley is a rather short, fair and fattish man of forty-five. The nose, which is like his mother's, projects when seen in profile, but the front face is roundish and smooth, with small eyes and a bald forehead over which the pale light brown hair is partly drawn. His voice is very quiet but in a high key (the only point reminding one of his father), his words few and whole manner placid, and even apathetic. He likes yachting and private theatricals, cares little or nothing for poetry or literature. He has a thinly-humorous, lounging, self-possessed, quietly contemptuous manner of comment and narration. When I mentioned Tennyson's poetry, Sir Percy said fellows had bored him a good deal with it at one time. He never read any of it of his own accord—saw no sense in it.[22]

No poetry for Sir Percy then; only theatrical doggerel. Yet here he can burlesque his father's cloudland when it pleases him. Take this stanza from his Christmas production of *A Fairy Tale*:

> *I soar above the clouds, I cleave the air*
> *   Just skimming near the tree-tops in my flight;*
> *I penetrate the rocky caverns where*
> *   O'er silent shadows reigns eternal night.*
> *   A king in fairyland, I work my will*
> *   On earth, in air, on men for good and ill.*

22 W. Allingham, *A Diary.*

CHAPTER XII

Pre-Raphaelites in Pursuit

◄{ 1 }►

APART FROM VISITS to Boscombe, William Allingham was to champion Shelley père against some growlers. There was Browning, for instance, who seems never to have forgiven himself for that juvenile and repudiated *Pauline*. Now he was speaking of Shelley with disparagement, especially his conduct to Harriet, while Allingham was in doubt almost how much weight to give to Browning's utterances. Or there was Emerson who "once told me he could see nothing in Shelley's poetry, beyond some pretty verses in 'The Skylark' and 'The Cloud.' "[1] Nor could one stop Carlyle from his bullying censure: "Shelley had not the least poetic faculty. I never could read anything he wrote. It was all a shriek merely." William Bell Scott, that poet of the sphinx-moths and sketcher of Shelley's bust and Cestius' pyramid, was likewise buffeted by a Carlyle "vituperative and scarifying, treating Shelley as a dog whose life ought to have been beaten out of him." Scott thought it a hatred of the man, not of the poet, and Allingham, in whose heaven Shelley was a star, forbore to argue.

But he does lead us, by his friendship, towards certain members of a new and significant Victorian sect. The Pre-Raphaelite Brotherhood, chiefly remembered now for its attitude to painting, really presented a more general outlook than crayon or canvas can convey alone. Even the king of them, Dante Gabriel Rossetti, pours out his soul in poetry no less than in painting, while his brother William Michael, making a laborious link with an unwilling Boscombe, first through Garnett, then through the chosen biographer, Edward Dowden, is to be not only the literary spokesman of the Brotherhood but an arduous, eager worker on the texts and ideas of Shelley. This

---

[1] We may note the coincidence of east and west here; for years these two particular lyrics were the only specimens of Shelley known and translated in China and Japan. See Chapter XV.

strange new fowl is born, as it were, with Shelley's wings on it. Its members, in revolt against the art conventions of the period, are steeped, almost inevitably for their creed and aspirations, in the notion of Shelley—not perhaps in any definable theory so much as in the entire sense and meaning of this poet who will not be dismissed, in retrospect, among the popular versemakers of the Romantic period. Scott, Moore, Campbell, Byron himself, once so beloved, are to the impatient innovators as outmoded as the pictures of Haydon, Frith, or Stubbs. It is of small significance here that Pre-Raphaelite art—with Holman Hunt's portrayals of Christian myth, Burne Jones's gilded angels, D. G. Rossetti's emotionally presented images of his own and William Morris's fair wives—now leaves us with no keener reaction than a marble curiosity. In its halcyon days it burns with ardor, no less than the poetic and sociological zest of Morris. It leads up to the firmer, more widespread, harder-headed cult of Fabianism. And Shelley is in that too. We may, in truth, see it as ironical or most meaningful that in twenty years these Pre-Raphaelite innovators are themselves discarded on the score of narrow formalism and a too restricting code. The spirit of Shelley simply marches through them, attaching itself to whatever mind or movement leads the vanguard.

For the moment, then, here are the Pre-Raphaelites agog with enthusiasm and collectively certain that they lead the cultural world. Allingham, not of the Brotherhood but on the edge of it (and recalling Leigh Hunt as "a tallish young old man" in 1847), has, in 1860, used several short Shelley poems in a collection of lyrics,[2] remarking—and this is evidently a new line with admirers—that "hardly any great poet, certainly no modern one, has been so *inaccurately printed* as Shelley. Helps to the very necessary revision are in existence, and ought quickly to be used."

Some years later we find Dante Gabriel Rossetti telling Allingham of how in his boyhood he had delighted in Byron, until "someone" told him of an even greater poet of the Byronian epoch, Shelley. He read little of Byron after that. About 1855, Richard Garnett met Rossetti's brother, William Michael, and found in Shelley a common bond. "There seems," he remarked to W. M. R., "to be in Shelley,

---

[2] *Nightingale Valley, a collection including a great number of the choicest Lyrics and short Poems in the English Language.* Edited by Giraldus (1860).

more than in other poets, something which binds his sympathisers closely together." We have already seen William Bell Scott introducing himself to G. H. Lewes on this footing. The next link is forged when this same Scott presents W. M. Rossetti with a copy of Mary Shelley's edition of the poems containing penciled notes. It sets William Michael examining the text of Shelley and publishing some notes on emendations. These are seen by Moxon, owner of the copyright, whose chief representative, J. Bertrand Payne, makes him an offer to edit the text. Writing to Allingham in 1868 of the proposal, he exclaims: "Is it not a glorious chance, this *Shelley* editing and biographizing? Willingly would I not only be doing it for pay, but do it for nothing, or pay to do it." Eight years have deflected Allingham a little; sending his congratulations, he observes, "I love Shelley no less; but from the critical study of his poetry I have drifted away."

Now it is curious that Rossetti—for all that Garnett is so friendly—cannot get himself invited to Boscombe at this period. The Hogg disaster has possibly made them cautious. Acutely aware that, lacking their sanction, he is missing something, he plans his prefatory memoir with only oblique aid—that is, what Allingham can glean for him during his own visits. Allingham is by no means blinded, and states baldly that they are *against outspokenness*. Sounded as to revision or correction of the text, they appear "cautious in giving away opinion," but might, he guesses, be induced to allow an examination of the manuscripts. (Shelley is perilously near to being a closed shop.) Rossetti, all for emendation, decides to consult that near Pre-Raphaelite Swinburne, who is all for sticking to the text, except that he would like to see the original *Laon and Cythna* restored in place of the edited *Revolt of Islam*.[3] Worse remains for W. M. R.: his project of a memoir, reaching Boscombe ears, is looked upon as poaching. Allingham's position, as friend of both, is delicate. In his half-role of secret agent he can extract no new material, though he gleans scraps of information to pass on. At the same time, with Payne the publisher, he is assembling a row of gossip fragments—from Jane Hogg, from Mathilde Blind, a "wild Shelley enthusiast" with a Teutonic accent,

---

[3] Even these latter-day Shelleyans find themselves strangely entangled in matters of sex. Allingham writes warningly to W. M. R.: "Shelley's sexual feeling was always and inseparably mingled up with intellectual and moral enthusiasm. I most strongly counsel you to avoid guesses in the dark." (See *Rossetti Papers, 1862–1870*, a compilation by W. M. Rossetti [London, 1903].)

from a Miss Rumble connected with the Gisbornes. They are about Hogg's later volumes, Harriet's drowning, Elizabeth Hitchener, Sophia Stacey . . . and a New Englander in Florence called Silsbee, who is hot on the trail of notebooks owned by Claire.[4] To Rossetti it must all seem bafflingly confusing, yet the ultimate reward, or *douceur,* for his importunity is that he receives from Garnett, as Boscombe's representative, a transcript of unpublished scraps and a manuscript book with some passages from *Charles I.*[5] He wins through, and publishing text and memoir in 1870, reaps both compliments and abuse for emendations. He is at last to visit the relics in 1885, and to find Sir Percy, three years later, bearing "no resemblance to his father. . . . He was more than commonly thin[6] with a very ruddy or pink complexion and noticeably blue eyes."

❧ II ❧

Even so, this meeting was in London; for in the matter of biography, at least, W. M. R. was kicking against the pricks. Boscombe had chosen, and approached through Sir Henry Taylor, its own biographer in the person of Edward Dowden of Dublin, who was to have all the private material placed at his command. Dowden showed no less excitement than Rossetti at the task assigned. He was already a true fanatic, hunting down manuscripts or unique editions of the worshiped poet. They seemed to fall into his lap, until "I think," he wrote to a friend, "I must have sold my soul, in some wicked sleep, to the Devil for the possession of rare Shelley treasures in this life, engaging to keep company for all eternity with Shelley when Satan's time to fetch me came." Not to one but numbers of correspondents he repeated this idea that Satanism or some occult power was guiding him to Shelley. His peak day was July 8, 1883, when he wrote to his friend Dr. Ingram: "To-day I got an invitation which I am better

---

[4] Scandal tells how Silsbee, failing to secure the manuscripts he wanted, "borrowed" them without returning; a case of theft glossed over.

[5] Garnett writes on February 5, 1869, promising information and help to Rossetti: "A true admirer of Shelley ought to be above all petty jealousy, and I assure you that your undertaking his biography will give me nothing but pleasure." W. M. R. found it politic to assure Garnett in his turn that his was only a prefatory memoir. (*Rossetti Papers.*)

[6] Allingham had found Sir Percy "fattish" in 1864; apparently two dozen years or so of strenuous hobbies had worn him down.

pleased with than if I were offered a Bishopric. . . . It is the demon's wish that Shelley should have a biographer who mingles sense with madness, and therefore I suppose he picked out me."[7] Before the month ended, he was sitting in his nest of documents at Boscombe Manor, and, writing with the same warm glow to Garnett, he put forth a sort of solemn vow and dedication such as a hermit might utter on approaching the biography of a saint:

> I will undertake this task with a sense of great responsibility, and a serious joy in it. . . . I will give myself up wholly . . . to Shelley until the work is done.

By the previous year Lady Shelley had already put together her manuscript letters and other papers in the three-volume *Shelley and Mary,* twelve copies only being privately printed, with a ban on publication until thirty years after her death.[8] The *Edinburgh Review,* whose critic must have been within the circle, declared, "It is impossible to read these details of Shelley's life without arriving at the conviction that monstrous injustice was done to him by the public opinion of his country and the world." These volumes were now to be consulted by the Boscombe biographers. We use the plural because Mary's life had also to be written. Garnett had recommended a great friend, Mrs. Julian Marshall, for the purpose. This lady remains wrapped in some obscurity, and not even her Christian name is given. Her main interest is said to have been music, for apart from this interlude she conducted the first amateur orchestra and wrote a life of Handel.[9] The vexed question of the hour was whether Mrs. Marshall might use the *Shelley and Mary* volumes "without detriment to the more important Life of Shelley." Her volume ought not to precede this; but, wrote the anxious Dowden, "if she goes to work now I cannot hope to keep up with her." It was arranged that he should win the competition; Dowden published in 1886, Mrs. Marshall three years later.

---

[7] *Letters of Edward Dowden and His Correspondents,* ed. by E. D. and A. M. Dowden (London, 1914).

[8] See R. Glynn Grylls, *Mary Shelley,* preface, for allocation of the volumes. She traces ten, of which four are in America. Mr. Bradford Booth wrote locating the two remaining copies in California, one being a presentation copy from Lady Shelley to James Anthony Froude, the historian, who was always her backer in the Shelley crusade.

[9] The information is from Mrs. Marshall's daughter to R. Glynn Grylls, who has kindly passed it on to me.

For Shelley's biographer—the first of a new era where profession-
alism takes the place of memory—the gilt was off the gingerbread
long before he ended; anxiety had replaced his serious joy. Dowden
might vow himself wholly to Shelley and yet keep a just balance on
the question of Harriet. Lady Shelley had been worsted by her first
biographer, endured the Peacock fight, and learned her lesson. She
scrutinized Dowden and refused his treatment of the separation. Harriet must be shown up as unfaithful; it was the same old controversy
again. Sir Percy's more placid view seems to have settled it: if the
Shelley heirs lent their imprimature to the volumes, Dowden would
be left some measure of independence—he could not be blamed for
all that happened there. For something like half a century Dowden's
work was to be judged as the "definitive" biography of Shelley. It
embodied the authentic documents, improved in some sense the
perspective, enriched the general picture, and was written with a
measure of Irish warmth. Naturally, coming from Boscombe, there
was sentiment in its sympathy. If Lady Shelley had embedded her
own myths in the heart of it, this was not to be generally conceded
at the time. We shall not examine it further here; it was, and is, a
highly readable narrative, whether complete or in the condensed,
one-volume form that followed later.

So the books come out, the critics comment, the enthusiasts seek
ever more information. Swinburne has written his commentary on
the text of Shelley,[10] and Rossetti (working in the contrary way to
Dowden) has expanded his one-volume edition into three in 1878
and revised the memoir—sometimes inaccurately. Harry Buxton Forman—a new editorial name, to be scrawled emphatically across all
these years—has brought out his edition, in four volumes, of the
Poetical Works. But he is to have Boscombe sanction, dedicate his
work to Percy Florence, and, attending again to textual inaccuracy,
find himself usually in opposition to Rossetti and in that respect frequently (to borrow from *Swellfoot the Tyrant*)

> *Only undoing that which has been done,*

and not even

> *. . . so as it may seem we but confirm it.*

[10] *Notes on the Text of Shelley* (1869); reprinted in *Essays and Studies* (1875).

As for the public, it could pay its money and take its choice of readings. In 1880, going on to edit the *Prose Works,* he was able to print for the first time the essay *On the Devil and Devils* from a proof at Boscombe that had been set up for Mary's 1840 *Works.* Discretion withdrew it then before publication; after this further forty years Shelley's spirited diabolic argument is allowed a hearing. The hunt is on by now for everyone who knew the poet, for every place that knew him, for all the survivors—Claire Clairmont, Trelawny, Jane, the "widow" of Hogg. There are idylls, there are scandals, there is chatter unending. The sculptor Thomas Woolner of the Brotherhood prowls Great Marlow, telling W. M. Rossetti how an old gentleman once met Shelley with his hat bedecked by ivy . . . that he was always reading large books and walking in a large wood. But Woolner can find out no more about "the Divine." That gentle versifier Aubrey de Vere—described by D. G. Rossetti as "surely one of the wateriest of the well-meaning"—has his own Shelleyan ecstacies, recalling how he lay floating in a boat on the lake at the foot of his lawn all night in a half-wakeful rapture "entangled in weeds" or "captured by a woody bay." "It was all Shelley's fault. His was a sleepless spirit— the worse for him, and probably for his poetry."[11]

Garnett, Dowden, and W. M. Rossetti (who tours England lecturing on Shelley, but has no monopoly) fire off letters to one another during these years of literary detection. They exchange their notions, their discoveries (such as the stupendous news that poor Jane was *never* married to Hogg); they squeeze out biographical details, they rejoice in relics and re-echoes. Because everything relative to the poet, however distant or conjectural, has value now, they preserve this triangular correspondence for the world at large to see fanaticism on its leathern wing.[12] And, indeed, theirs is an odd performance. These votaries eat, breathe, dream, and drink their Shelley, smoke him in their pipes, and fill their pens with him. They convey the illusion of having no life apart from this literary sleuthing, this turning over of the clods of secrecy to see what seeds may be caught growing there and what shivering little earthworms wriggle away.

It would be misleading to suggest that textual and biographical

[11] *Recollections of Aubrey de Vere* (1897).

[12] *Letters about Shelley,* by R. Garnett, E. Dowden, and W. M. Rossetti (London, 1917). How much scantier must our twentieth-century records be, when the telephone absorbs so much of the discussion!

criticism fills the field in the late Victorian era. Never, till now, has the poet been so much studied for his philosophy and "metaphysics." Long essays on his aesthetic aspect, his cosmogony, his radicalism, his deism (vegetarianism is to follow in time), taking the place of the crude atheistical baitings, are published in those solid literary journals that in our mid-twentieth century have bowed to the subversive tide by ceasing publication or turning to discussion of practical politics. Subscribers to the literary quarterlies and monthlies were prepared to approach them with at least the respect we now give to bound volumes. In the subjects of the essays is no frivolity, no uncertainty; the treatment is critical, analytical, explanatory; it is constructive, up to a point, and frequently prejudiced; as heavy for the most part as rich plum cake. Whether or not the Shelley of *Prometheus* and of *Oedipus Tyrannus* would have felt himself at home here is a question best avoided. The creative-argumentative Shelley of the *Defence of Poetry* would not be out of place; nor, in the more radical reviews, the author of the so long unpublished *Philosophical View of Reform*. One might—academically—set out to tabulate these longer essays, not forgetting the book reviews that stretch out into articles with profuse quotations from the text. Let us leave them, rather, as a proof and symptom that we are dealing with a literary figure of solid reputation. It has to be faced that Shelley is a Worthy; the elevation into dignity has brought with it that veil which covers the "great writer" from the eager eyes of youth. He is put in the past, a subject to be studied. For those who might—discovering him as Tennyson and Browning did—have idled with him in a pine forest, he is *work*. While Browning is putting out his now so hackneyed verses:

Ah, did you once see Shelley plain?

we have to think of a later generation not born to see Shelley, any more than Milton, Pope, or Spenser, without first boring through the deterrent varnish of an Old Master. Nothing, perhaps, more incongruous and ironical could happen than that "the author of some infidel poetry" should become a "standard poet."

⊰{ III }⊱

There was another side to professional appraisal: Shelley had new detracters. A downright philistine or naughty boy of the eighties was to flutter the innocent and shock the faithful, just as he hoped and intended. John Cordy Jeaffreson was one of the first of the image-breaking biographers. We should say now that he set out to debunk. He had already tried his hand with *The Real Lord Byron,* when in 1885 he came to Byron's friend. He was not without shrewdness and had looked round on the contemporary situation, weighing it up in his shifted but functioning scales. He found the romantic (i.e., spurious) Shelley being built up by three forces: first, the poet's family making a fanciful figure through their pious devotion; secondly, the enthusiasts who imagined the poet's character to resemble his genius in grandeur; thirdly, the Socialists who would have Free Contract recognized as a kind of marriage, and thank the poet for it.

Now, up to a point *The Real Shelley* might be salutary in preventing the clear vision from being "sicklied o'er." If Jeaffreson had been as honest as he was gimlet-eyed, a Shelley remarkably like the man who was drowned with Williams could have come back to us. But the biographer had neither that genius nor that aim. In his book he is as petty as a middle-aged spinster quarreling with her housemaid. All his argument is spite and triviality. For example, he rightly blames the angelic portrait for its share in the softening process; but what is his rejoinder? That "the original of the lovely picture had a notably unsymmetrical face, and a little turn-up nose." (Hence R. L. S. and his theories the following year.) Also, he asserts, this gentleman of "high ancestral dignity" is forever "telling fibs." (For Jeaffreson no hallucinations—*fibs.*) Since he cannot on any showing display a gluttonous man and a winebibber, he minimizes the virtue of frugality and says Shelley was a heavy laudanum drinker. In his character he was deceitful towards himself, a disloyal son, a bad husband to his first wife and not faultless to his second, a bad friend to at least one person. If this, as one suspects, is Godwin, it should have clogged the current; but there is no damming up Jeaffreson as he plunges forward, *knowing* he is right. The only account he will admit at all is Hogg's. (Because the family has condemned it. Messrs. Jefferson and Jeaffreson: reputation breakers. But Hogg at least was genial where

Jeaffreson is a pinched east wind.) The book is, throughout, a detailed review of statements about Shelley. It is enough to say that all of them are dynamited to his satisfaction except those which harm or have been generally discountenanced. The *Athenaeum* reviewer on May 30, 1885, declared that the whole purport of the book "page after page, is to strip Shelley, and exhibit him to the astonished hero-worshipper as a very sorry manikin." The *Graphic,* while allowing that he had corrected a few errors, saw him in the part, "which he seems to perform congenially, of *advocatus diaboli.*" It was left to the *Pictorial World* to give Jeaffreson what he wanted: "The book is full of highly-spiced details and racy anecdotes; it is designedly sensational from title-page to colophon: it reads like a romance."

In one sense Jeaffreson and his book could be ignored: it was a popular performance, with no serious criticism in it. This was to come, too; this was to be remembered and quoted and linked most damagingly with the Curran portrait long after J. C. Jeaffreson's growls were mute. Matthew Arnold is a name to conjure with. It is remarkable—it is almost cool presumption—that he has worded the best-known fallacy on Shelley without ever devoting an essay to the poet in question. His most sustained polemics were to be in a mere review. Though less explosive, he is hardly less irresponsible than Carlyle, parading a similar spleen and bigoted judgment. Arnold was writing a preface to an edition of Byron when he took his opportunity to glance around the Romantics. "I cannot think that Shelley's poetry, except by snatches and fragments, has the value of the good work of Wordsworth and Byron. . . . All the personal charm of Shelley cannot hinder us from at last discovering in his poetry the incurable want, in general, of a sound subject-matter, and the incurable fault, in consequence, of insubstantiality." Claiming pre-eminence among the poets of the century for Wordsworth and Byron, he then makes the fatal pronouncement:

> I for my part can never even think of equalling with them any
> other of their contemporaries;—either Coleridge, poet and philoso-
> pher wrecked in a mist of opium; or Shelley, *beautiful and
> ineffectual angel, beating in the void his luminous wings in vain.*[13]

He did not italicize the phrase, but the public did. For too long it

[13] Preface to *Poetry of Byron*, chosen and arranged by Matthew Arnold (1881).

has stood before Shelley's portals as a motto in verdigris. Arnold attacked again, still obliquely, in his "General Introduction" to *Ward's English Poets*. *English* poets, but our critic, contrariwise, focuses disproportionately on Burns. Shelley, still rankling in his system, is brought in to face the Scotsman:

> For the votary misled by a personal estimate of Shelley, as so many of us have been, are, and will be,—of that beautiful spirit building his many-coloured haze of words and images
> > *"Pinnacled dim in the intense inane"*—
> no contrast can be wholesomer than the contact with Burns at his archest and soundest.

The comparison is about as reasonable as a choice between the merits of shoes and ships. For all that, Matthew Arnold's criticism grew and spread.

Unlike the squabbling Jeaffreson he had put his finger on a real weakness in Shelley—the only creator who (unless Arnold mixed his metaphors unintentionally) could think to "build a haze." (Tennyson in 1869 rejected *The Revolt of Islam* as being "all mountain tops and glories.") Now we find other writers with the same ideas in poorer minds not fearing to express them. Coventry Patmore (himself the poet of *The Angel in the House!*) remarks:

> I have been reading Shelley again, after never having looked at him for thirty years. My young impression of him is quite unchanged. Most of his poems—even his most celebrated, as "Prometheus Bound" [sic]—is all unsubstantial splendour, like the transformation scene of a pantomime or the silvered globes hung up in gin palaces. He is least unreal when he is wicked, or representing wicked people, as in the Cenci.[14]

This may sound bold for mid-Victorianism, but he followed a growing tendency. G. H. Lewes, far back in the forties, had hailed *The Cenci* as "the greatest work of our poet."[15] Aubrey de Vere, the "watery well-meaning" who had plashed in a Shelleyan boat, now

---

[14] See *Memoirs and Correspondence of Coventry Patmore*, ed. by Basil Champneys (London, 1900).

[15] *Westminster Review*, 1841. In this he was in line with Continental preference. It was left to G. B. Shaw in the nineties to depose *The Cenci* in favor of *Queen Mab*. (See page 272 below.)

discovers in the poet "two great natural defects"; they are want of robustness and lack of reverence. There was something angelic about him, but was he "a Fallen Angel still fierce with the pride that caused that fall, or an angel in duress struggling with sad limitations?"

This fashion in judgment irritated Swinburne, whose nature was more attuned to sympathy. In an essay on "Wordsworth and Byron"[16] he urged "the Wordsworthians from Sir Henry Taylor to Mr. Matthew Arnold . . . to break themselves of . . . the habit of girding and gibing at Shelley as a morbid and delirious visionary . . . a nervous, unmanly, unnatural, unreal, unwholesome sort of poet." Swinburne was apparently unaware of Sir Henry's connection with Boscombe. The staunch old dramatist, then eighty-four, wrote protestingly that he would never gird and gibe at Shelley, though he had called him "purely and pre-eminently a visionary." Or there was Ruskin, who had missed the poet's quality more deplorably and with typical arrogance, remarking in a letter to Browning that "one might write Shelley by Shrewsbury clock." He proceeded to do so, smugly, in this manner:

> *It was a little Lawny islet*
> *By anemone and vilet*
> *Like mosaic-paven.*
> *There sat a gentleman—flushed and shy—*
> *And a girl with a corkscrew curl in her eye.*
> *On the grass, between—was a large eel-pie—*
> *And a ham-bone—cleanly shaven,*
> *And the gentleman asked—in accents*
> *mild—*
> *"Was it quite enough soaked before it was*
> *biled?"*
> *And the lady replied—as she pulled a vilet*
> *Off the little Lawny islet—*
> *"Didn't I tell you—Jane would spile it?"*[17]

[16] *Miscellanies* (1886). In 1875, Swinburne had written: "I would not pit his name against the sacred name of Milton. . . . it is enough that the country may count among her sons two of the greatest among those great poets who have been prophets and evangelists of personal, national, social, and spiritual freedom; but it is equally certain that of all forms or kinds of poetry the two highest are the lyric and the dramatic, and that as clearly as the first place in the one rank is held amongst us by Shakespeare, the first place in the other is held and will never be resigned by Shelley."

[17] No. 262 in Sotheby's catalogue, Charles Fairfax Murray sale, February 6, 1920.

(As Shelley was no true member of the Cockney School, this bit of cleverness would have been better fathered on Leigh Hunt or Keats.) Later Ruskin wrote that he had "wasted much good time over the 'Sensitive Plant' and 'Epipsychidion,' and I took a good deal of harm from him, in trying to write lines like 'prickly and pulpous and blistered and blue.' The perseverance with which I tried to wade through the 'Revolt of Islam' and find out (I never did, and don't know to this day) who revolted against whom or what, was creditable to me, and the 'Prometheus' really made me understand something of Aeschyllus. . . . With Shelley I loved the blue sky and blue eyes, but never in the least confused the heavens with my own poor little Psychidion."[18]

◄ IV ►

Oddly enough, the topmost pinnacle of the inanity school is reached with a writer who was not censuring at all, but applauding with all the dizzy-bright imagery of his own poetic furniture. Francis Thompson, a self-consciously inspired scapegrace who was to die in a condition bordering on delirium tremens, wrote his essay on Shelley in 1889. It was ecstatic, sentimental, hyperbolical, but contrived in all sincerity. Thompson, in any case, was writing in that late Victorian period when a hybrid known as prose-poetry or poetic prose was beginning to gain favor. Shelley's *Defence of Poetry* might have shown him how a Romantic poet writes prose. But neither those who now praised nor those who condemned Shelley's imponderability appear to have put their minds to his prose writings or to the satiric or satanic political poetry (to mention one branch alone that is not composed of sunbeams). The only way to savor Francis Thompson is to let him perform a little. This central passage displays his matter and manner:

> Coming to Shelley's poetry we peep over the wild mask of revolutionary metaphysics, and we see the winsome face of the child. Perhaps none of his poems is more purely and typically Shelleian than *The Cloud,* and it is interesting to note how essentially it springs from the faculty of make-believe. The same thing is conspicuous, though less purely conspicuous, throughout his singing;

[18] *Praeterita* (1886).

it is the child's faculty of make-believe raised to the *n*th power. He is still at play, save only that his play is such as manhood stops to watch, and his playthings are those which the gods give their children. The universe is his box of toys. He dabbles his fingers in the day-fall. He is gold-dusty with tumbling amidst the stars. He makes bright mischief with the moon. The meteors nuzzle their noses in his hand. He teases into growling the kennelled thunder, and laughs at the shaking of its fiery chain. He dances in and out of the gates of heaven: its floor is littered with his broken fancies. He runs wild over the fields of ether. He chases the rolling world, He gets between the feet of the horses of the sun. He stands in the lap of patient Nature, and twines her loosened tresses after a hundred wilful fashions, to see how she will look nicest in his song.

This it was which, in spite of his essentially modern character as a singer, qualified Shelley to be the poet of *Prometheus Unbound,* for it made him, in the truest sense of the word, a mythological poet. This childlike quality assimilated him to the childlike peoples among whom mythologies have their rise.

The essay was rejected by the *Dublin Review* and thrown aside. Its acceptance—by the same paper—after Thompson's death takes us away into the twentieth century. There it flames meteorically for a moment, sending the *Review* into a second edition in 1908 and being reissued separately—a model, for the time, of inspired literary criticism; now ash. (It is only a leap and a generation from here to André Maurois' *Ariel,* but we must stay the flight.)

There had been in 1872—well before Matthew Arnold—another such act of adoration, by the enthusiastic Mathilde Blind.[19] She was introducing Shelley in the Tauchnitz edition of *British Authors* for the continent of Europe—itself a Shelleyan landmark:

If we would in an embodiment of flesh and blood seek for that haunting aspiration which lurks more or less dimly in the minds of all of us; if we would seek for a being in whom the spiritual tendencies completely triumphed over the more material parts of nature; in one word if we would seek the purely human stripped

19 W. M. Rossetti told Mrs. Gilchrist that Mathilde was the daughter of an eminent German revolutionary and exile of 1848, and her brother had died in an effort to assassinate Bismarck. (*Letters* of W. M. R. concerning Whitman, Blake and Shelley, to Anne Gilchrist and her son Herbert Gilchrist, ed. by Clarence Golides and Paull Franklin Baum (Durham, N.C., 1934).

of all its grosser adjuncts and see as in a mirror how little less than angelic it is given man to be, let us turn with glad eyes and adoring hearts to Percy Bysshe Shelley.[20]

So much for the intense inane. But we are still entangled with the moralists. They bring us back, first, to Matthew Arnold who has now, in 1886, read his Dowden and burst out, in his review of it, into righteous disgust over Shelley's behavior. "What a set!"—another aphorism that has been heard, even in our own day, approvingly echoed by elderly professors in university towns. "What a set! What a world! is the exclamation that breaks from us as we come to an end of this history of the occurrences of Shelley's private life; I used the French word *bête* for a letter of Shelley's; for the world in which we find him I can only use another French word, *sâle.*" Again: "Let no one suppose that a want of humour and a self-delusion such as Shelley's have no effect upon a man's poetry. The man Shelley, in very truth, is not entirely sane, and Shelley's poetry is not entirely sane either." Should we not add—nor is Arnold's criticism, if sanity requires consistency, for he repeats his "beautiful angel" phrase from the Byron essay, and it is hard indeed to reconcile the two attacks.

To continue: It would hardly matter how the righteous Mrs. Oliphant clicked her tongue over lax behavior if she had kept her strictures for a personal essay. But it is grim to open a *Literary History of England*[21] and find there a pained discussion about foolish girls, romantically desolate widows, feelings and impulses warped into a displacement of good and evil by those who know not "the restraints of nature good and chaste." America was to take the field in 1892 when Mark Twain, having only just read his Dowden, came out with banners and trumpets. "In Defense of Harriet Shelley" makes gorgeous reading, for its wit and sarcasm, for the downright approach by a masterful mind to a subject that was fresh to it. Besides, it spares us much inquiry by stating, about the separation, that "the book's verdict is accepted in the girls' colleges of America and its view taught in their literary classes." This represents success for Lady Shelley: the Boscombe biography has become an American textbook.

[20] Quoted by Edmund Blunden in "The Fame of Shelley," in *Keats, Shelley, and Rome,* compiled by Neville Rogers (London, 1949).

[21] *The Literary History of England in the End of the Eighteenth and Beginning of the Nineteenth Century* (London, 1882, 3 vols.). Shelley is discussed in Vol. III.

Twain was irritated from the outset by the style of it: a "literary cakewalk.... All the pages, all the paragraphs, walk by sedately, elegantly, not to say mincingly, in their Sunday-best. . . . It is rare to find even a chance sentence that has forgotten to dress." As for its views and reasoning: "sometimes when a mastadon walks across the field of vision it takes it for a rat; at other times it does not see it at all." He then settles like a vulture on the Harriet episode, tearing Shelley to pieces, as "the slave of a degrading love drunk with his passion." Harriet's letters of the time were not then known. It was a point of advantage to the New World that he could plead her silence against everyone's talk. And, novelist as he is, before he is done he has made of the episode a first-class melodrama with a villain deserter and a sweet, wronged heroine, appealing to the mother-heart of the world. Gorgeous reading, to be sure, yet unprogressive; one partisan has merely fought another one—nothing new.

❧ v ❧

This, to be sure, has outleaped our time by more than a decade; that is, if we want to hear—as the Pre-Raphaelite huntsmen certainly did— the final rumblings of an old, undaunted, often carping and self-adulatory voice. Trelawny (abandoned by the beautiful former Lady Goring when he introduced a "Miss B." into the house) has kept up a melancholy correspondence with Claire Clairmont, chewing over the past. Mary he hates, for her "frivolity and hankering after frivolous society." He is convinced now of rascality in the Pisan circle. "All the men connected with Shelley, excepting only Hogg and the Smiths, were rascals. They used the poor Poet as their purse. Godwin, Peacock, Medwin, Hunt and many others. A base crew; I had antipathy to them all, and they knew it." His antipathy to Mary in particular has grown and ripened. By the time he publishes his *Records of Shelley, Byron, and the Author,* in 1878, he has become so bitterly vindictive towards her that Boscombe urgently needs Mrs. Julian Marshall's musical strains to restore the peace. "Mrs. Shelley," he writes, "was possessed of the green-eyed monster, jealousy . . . that was an insurmountable impediment to confidential intercourse with her husband." Again: "She was moping and miserable when alone, and yearning for society. Her capacity can be judged by the novels she wrote after Shelley's death, more than ordinarily commonplace and conventional. Whilst overshadowed by Shelley's greatness her faculties expanded; but when she had lost him they shrank into their essential littleness. . . . She had no faith in his views, and she grieved that he was so stubborn and inflexible." All this is poured out in a special appendix. It is his latest design in monuments to the dead.

But the old pirate, with his own spasmodic taste for high society, has become something of a shrine. While he leaves his Brompton home to settle near Worthing, the pilgrims are after him. Millais has painted his portrait as the old sea-dog in his *North West Passage* (on condition, it is reported, that the Millais family patronize a firm of Turkish baths in which the old tyrant has an interest). W. M. Rossetti, noting how his mouth is drawn aside permanently by a pistol shot in the Greek war, ignores the less materially warped features, and has offered his friendship and transacted the business affairs of the republished *Records*. Trelawny, who has approved Rossetti's edition of the Poems by damning all previous writers (i.e., the "base crew") as incompetent, grumbles to him further about Mary, and maliciously declares that Claire Clairmont (with whom he is still in correspondence) after turning Catholic has gone mad and is in an asylum. Rossetti, having himself visited Claire, discounts this privately; but one day he is thrilled to be shown a piece of Shelley's jawbone. We shall be noting more about this type of relic: it is a long time since we watched the pirate stowing away his unburned fragments from the funeral pyre. But he loses nothing. On another of his literary pursuers, Sidney Colvin, he tries out a personal relic, "showing us the scar where he had burnt his hand in plucking the poet's heart out of the ashes."[22] A scar indeed, of nearly sixty years' standing! Or should we say his humor is not dead? He appears to have shown it also to Rossetti, who thereupon addresses a sonnet to him.

Trelawny's hand, which held 'st the sacred heart . . .

Perhaps Rossetti doubts; his muse is somewhat rough in manner and matter:

[22] Sidney Colvin, *Memories and Notes* (London, 1921).

> *... Trelawny's hand, did then the outward burn*
> *As once the inward? O cor cordium*
> *Which wast a spirit of love, and now a clot [sic],*
> *What other other flame was wont to come*
> *Lambent from thee to fainter hearts, and turn—*
> *Red like thy death-pyre's heat—their lukewarmth*
> *hot!*

For years the old relic has been complaining to Claire that life is over; yet, looked after now by a so-called niece, Miss Emma Taylor, he lives in galvanic snatches. Colvin finds a shrunken old body with every sign of decrepitude, until suddenly "he would rise, almost bound up in his chair, with his eyes fastened on yours like a vice, and in tones of incredible power would roar what he had to say into your face."[23] He is eighty-eight when he gives up the struggle, dying on March 13, 1881. And he is well served by the obituary writers; by Swinburne and other poets whose verses picture him rejoining Shelley; more practically by the poet Rossetti who arranges his cremation; and most faithfully of all by the devoted Emma Taylor who carries the ashes to Rome.

In the Protestant Cemetery there is only, as he had planned, a coverlet to be lifted. It turns out not to be so easy, for there are also regulations to be faced. When the English lady arrives in October with her walnut box of ashes, she is asked for official documents, and having none, is told the ashes cannot be received. The director of the cemetery calls on the Ministry of the Interior, who says that Miss Taylor, having introduced a body into Italy without the regular documents, must now pay a fine equal to ten times the normal tax of 306 lire. (Some echo of the box-and-baby story seems creeping in to balance the queer account.) In the end it is Shelley's spirit that eases the deadlock. "I too am a great admirer of Shelley," smiles the official, whose name is Casanova. Miss Emma Taylor is let off with the single tax; formalities are concluded, and Trelawny's ashes laid beside Shelley's in the Protestant Cemetery, where over a year previously Joseph Severn has been placed next to Keats.[24] The gesture is spoiled by this palaver though, just as it had previously been with Shelley. The Pirate, anticipating his imminent death, had done all he could to avoid that

[23] *Ibid.*
[24] See Nelson Gay, in *Bulletin* of the Keats-Shelley Memorial, Rome, Vol. II (1913).

type of muddle by writing in 1880 to the cemetery director to have the grave prepared. The old man who had worked so strenuously on this burial spot ought to have been allowed a dignified entry. But Italian officials seemed bent on the ridiculous wherever the English, and their children, figured. Shelley had two epithets for Italy; besides the "Paradise of Exiles," it was "the retreat of Pariahs."[25] The Italians, when they knew whom they were dealing with, showed help and generosity beyond all obligations; but there is always the fellow who knows nothing, and to him the other term may have seemed the right one.

By this time another Italian burial had taken place—in Florence for Claire Clairmont. She had spent her last years until her death in 1879 as a Roman Catholic in a Florentine convent. In 1873, Rossetti, at Trelawny's request, had called to see some autograph documents Claire was offering to sell. He had difficulty in being received, but eventually found "a slender and pallid old lady . . . with dark and still expressive eyes," and a confirmed invalid, even apart from a recent fall. He did not get the documents, any more than, by fair means, did the American Silsbee, who is said to have employed dishonest ones. As to the latter, the most vivid account of what might have happened in such circumstances can be read in *The Aspern Papers* (1888), where Henry James embroiders brilliantly on these basic facts, with his tiresome journalist defeated by old Miss Bordereau and her rigid niece. The Aspern papers were destroyed beyond recalling and so provided James with his desired full close. But Claire's manuscripts are later to be heard of in the possession of H. Buxton Forman.

Claire, in old age, was not electrifying. The spurious, more than suspect narrative given of her last years and "revelations" by William Graham is hardly worth examining now.[26] The man was too plainly an opportunist, bent on fluttering the press and posing as a Jeaffreson. It is idle gossip about all the poetic relationships, dished out as disclosures from an old lady with luxuriant locks, a "witchlike charm," and "sad poetic face." At her feet sits a handsome youth of twenty, described Byronically. Sickening stuff. He is not even right about Claire's burial place. Last of these lone survivors, least melan-

---

[25] Letter to Medwin, Florence, January 17, 1820.
[26] *Last Links with Byron, Shelley, and Keats* (London, 1898).

choly because most satisfied in domestication, sits Jane Williams, long
called Hogg, pursued, as the rest, in her last decade by the neo-
Shelleyan biographers. Rossetti notes her "upright carriage and com-
plaisant manner," and the dark hair that is not her own. She has little
to tell them. All that is too long past to be resuscitated, and meanwhile the grave of a loyal companion is awaiting Jane, though when
she is placed in it, in 1884, surviving relatives avoid mentioning the
word "wife." More honorable posthumous awards had been made as
long as eight years previously when Ianthe Esdaile, leaving three children, had died so much younger. The *Daily Bristol Times and Mirror*
for June 19, 1876, contains this announcement:

> *Esdaile.* June 16, at 14 West Mall, Clifton, Eliza Ianthe, only
> daughter of Percy Bysshe Shelley, and beloved wife of E. J. Esdaile
> Esq. of Cothelstone, Taunton, aged 63.

So the family has acknowledged Shelley, and not, it would seem,
without some pride. Today the words "Daughter of the Poet Shelley"
are on her tombstone in Cothelstone churchyard; though an observer
in the present century was to suspect it had been added later, noting
above it a blank insertion in place of a strip of marble cut away.[27]

◆{ VI }◆

Of all the figures capering through these later pages, there is one
we could wish Shelley to have met. Edward Lear, nonsense writer,
landscape painter, almost incessant traveler in ancient lands, has the
freedom of mind and genial eccentricity that might have made—and
almost did—a poet. Lear (though he gave Queen Victoria drawing
lessons) would, born thirty years earlier, undoubtedly have been collected by the Shelley of the Pisan circle, to the enrichment of them
both. He could sketch his own self, laughably, in illustrations, or
plump it down exact in a quatrain:

> *How pleasant to know Mr. Lear!*
> *Who has written such volumes of stuff!*
> *Some think him ill-tempered and queer,*
> *But a few think him pleasant enough.*

[27] Wilfrid H. Woollen, in *Notes & Queries*, March 17, 1923.

How pleasantly might the Dong with the Luminous Nose, the spherical body and the runcible hat have taken the place of John Gisborne with his Slawkengergian organ! It is no use regretting; but Lear did know the survivors and followers. On the fringe of the Pre-Raphaelite Brotherhood, friend of the Tennysons and Holman Hunt, he knew his Shelley myths, loved his poetry, and had made drawings in 1861 of the beach at Viareggio where Trelawny had burned the bodies. Two years later than this sketch, Sir Percy and Lady Shelley on one of their cruises had met Lear at Corfu after visiting the Grave in Rome. "The people whose acquaintance has most delighted me," he wrote to Lady Waldegrave, "are the Shelleys—who are here in a yott. Think of my music to 'O world, O life, O time!'—Shelley's words—being put down in notes by Shelley's own son!" ... "Lady S.," he wrote to another friend on the same occasion, "is out and out and out a stunner of a delightful woman."[28] In 1880, Lear, on his last visit to England from Italy, made a copy of one of his Viareggio drawings for Hellen and Elizabeth. "They are both extremely clever," he wrote in his diary, "and would be delighted at any drawing or music connected with their brother's memory, so I am to make a drawing of the Viareggio coast, and am to have a letter to the two ladies at Chertsey, where they have taken a house."[29]

This Shelleyan *manqué* died alone and depressed at San Remo in 1888. Matthew Arnold, who had given birth to so much out of so little, died in the same year. The next year, in December, Browning died. It appears to be a decade heavy with departure: Sir Percy Florence himself, falling short of the longevity Sir Timothy had passed on to those two daughters, died at the age of seventy on December 6, a bare week before Browning. *The Times,* recalling his recent activity as a tricyclist, said in its obituary, "He had been in bad health for some years, but the fact was not generally known, as his indisposition had not confined him to the house." He was buried on December 10 in the grave where Mary and her parents lay already in St. Peter's Churchyard, Bournemouth. There were many mourners and a host of floral tributes.[30] According to one—and the most likely

---

[28] *Letters of Edward Lear,* ed. by Lady Strachey (London, 1907).

[29] *Edward Lear, Landscape Painter and Nonsense Poet,* by Angus Davidson (London, 1938).

[30] "The burial service yesterday was conducted by Rev. F. St. John, vicar of Kempsford and Canon of Gloucester [a brother-in-law of Lady Shelley], and the Rev. H. W. Yeatman,

—theory, the much-traveled heart of P. B. Shelley was buried with him. Of his death Robert Louis Stevenson wrote to Lady Taylor from Samoa on January 20, 1890:

> The news has reached me in the shape of a newspaper cutting, I have no particulars. He had a sweet original nature; I think I like him better than ever I should have liked his father; I am sorry he was always a little afraid of me; if I had had more chance, he would have liked me too, we had so much in common, and I valued so much his fine soul, as honest as a dog's, and the romance of him, which was like a dog's too, and like a poet's at the same time. If he had not been Shelley's son, people would have thought more of him; and yet he was the better of the two, bar verses.[31]

Later he wrote to Henry James of a project to visit "poor Lady Shelley"—meaning to comfort a lonely widow who would have no further yachting, no more theatricals at Boscombe Manor, and who looked upon R. L. S. jealously as, in a sense, her son. And yet she was unlikely to be prostrated by her bereavement; we saw in what spirit she had married Percy Florence. It was not Percy Bysshe who was now dead.

✦{ VII }✦

When Shelley was living at Marlow, George Frederick Furnivall, a

vicar of St. Bartholomew's, Sydenham, and Hon. Canon of Rochester. The chief mourners were Lady Shelley, Mr. Shelley of Avington, Hants (the heir to the title of the late baronet); Mrs. Leopold Scarlett, Mr. Lawrence Scarlett, Mr. Esdaile, of Cothelstone; the Rev. Wm. Esdaile, Rector of Sandford Orcas, Somerset; Col. Shelley, Captain Ernest Shelley, Dr. Richard Garnett, D. C. L. (of the British Museum), Rear-Admiral H. Craven St. John, and Mr. W. H. Wittall. The coffin was conveyed from Boscombe Manor on an open funeral car and arrived at the lych gate of the church, shortly after 11 o'clock. It was an oak coffin, panelled and polished, with raised lid, brass furniture, and a plate bearing the inscription: 'Percy Florence Shelley, third baronet, born Nov. 12, 1819, died Dec. 5, 1889.' . . . The archway over the entrance to the grave, which was approached by the incline, was lined with moss and violets, while the coffin was covered with about 20 floral wreaths and crosses. One design was in the form of an anchor (probably in memory of the late Sir Percy's connection with yachting) worked in grey lichen, with the initials 'P. F. S.' in white hyacinths, the whole entwined with white corded rope. . . .

"The bell of St. Peter's was tolled for a short time prior to the funeral, and at Boscombe many of the tradesmen drew their blinds and put up shutters during the hour of burial." (*Bournemouth Observer & Visitor's List*, December 11, 1889.)

[31] In May, 1889, Stevenson, in Waikiki, had dedicated *The Master of Ballantrae* to Sir Percy and Lady Shelley. Mrs. R. L. Stevenson, in her preface to *Island Nights Entertainments* (1921 edition), describes the Shelleys' Boscombe activities.

Robert Louis Stevenson

From a photograph by Sir Percy Florence Shelley, 1885

surgeon at Egham, attended Mary at the birth of her second child, Clara. Their relationship was on a friendly footing—if Shelley sometimes forgot his bills for a while—and it was said that Furnivall would frequently ride the seventeen miles to visit him at Marlow. Or Shelley would walk from Windsor to Runnymede to sit on the surgeon's counter for a chat. His son, Dr. F. J. Furnivall, developed literary interests as patron rather than producer. Wits had been known to call him a "Society" man, for in the space of twenty years he had founded the Early English Text Society, the Ballad Society, the Chaucer Society, the New Shakespeare Society, the Browning Society (this in 1881, with its living lion to grace it), and the Wyclif Society. It was suggested he should found a Shelley Society. "By Jove, I will," he is said to have exclaimed, as a reason struck him (if so assiduous a founder should need extra inducement): "By Jove, I will, he was my father's friend!"

In 1886, with a lavish use of paper, tongue, and clatter, the Shelley Society was inaugurated—early enough for Percy Florence to be impelled, in those last years of the hidden indisposition, to attend some of the meetings. Early enough for Browning to decline the presidency; he was determined not to be entrapped by Shelley again. In the epilogue we shall look briefly at this Established Church of Shelleyan devotion, where the faithful, regimented on hard chairs with notebook and pencil, could hear the preachers expound in learned convocation what had been written long ago by their prophet, alone amongst the ruins and pine woods or afloat on an azure sea. But before that, and before a final glimpsed impression of a subject now too great to be "contained," and hastening away on all sides of the picture, there is one more aspect. Concerned with neither art nor morals, it has, in the case of this particular poet, yet held an odd importance, never to lessen throughout the century—or indeed in the next one. Although reduced so soon to ash and incense, the mortal remains of Shelley have enticed with a peculiar magnetism. The treasures of time, as the author of *Urn Burial* wrote in his echo of cosmic thunder —"the treasures of time lie high, in urns, coynes, and monuments. . . ." The tomb, the relic, the memorial marble should not chain Prometheus; and yet, beside his deepest immortality, this graveyard aspect marches, supplying a drum roll or a cymbal clash. Idyllic, ironic, tweaked into humor or debased to pettiness, it keeps recurring.

243

No account of Shelley's posthumous adventures is complete without it. Those who prefer a Francis Thompson phantom "tumbling amidst the stars" can skip; but with the unflinching residue

Let's talk of graves, of worms and epitaphs

for a chapter, and assemble this curious infra-red or X-ray portrait that falls outside the province of both critic and biographer proper, but suits here with our historical reflections.

CHAPTER XIII

Sepulchral Progress

C orpses are dead in the tomb—" sang Shelley; and this is
true of the average case of the defunct. His own was somewhat different. In one way and another Shelley was buried
five times: once under the sea, once under the sand, once
by fire, and twice under the earth. Or it is even six times, if we count
a sojourn of several months in a wine cellar. And for all that he is
as rich in relics as any saint, for a surprising number of his fragments remain uninterred.

These burials have been for the most part noted in the course of
our narrative. Here we may recapitulate them from a worm's-eye
viewpoint. More than a week after the drowning (1) the bodies were
washed up on the beach near Viareggio; and here the Italian sanitary
authorities stepped in: the strict quarantine laws of Italy dictated
that anything cast up from the sea must be burned, for fear of its
bringing in the plague. As this required preparation, the two bodies
were buried temporarily in the sand (2), where they lay for some
three weeks and were near to being lost. The world in general cared
as little about Shelley's obsequies as it did about his work. But of
the cremation (3) so spectacularly staged by Trelawny on the beach
of Viareggio it was to hear enough. A few points may be added: the
body was burned in an iron brazier made by one Nella the Blacksmith,
and although it had decayed no further, frankincense was used, not
for its ritual significance but on hygienic grounds. More wine, Trelawny says, was poured on it than ever Shelley drank in his lifetime.
When the business became too much for Byron's nerves, he swam off
to his schooner and back—about three miles—and brought on an
attack of fever. Afterwards he wrote to Tom Moore, "You can have
no idea what an extraordinary effect such a funeral pile has, on a
desolate shore, with mountains in the background and the sea before,

and the singular appearance the salt and frankincense gave to the flame. . . ."

We saw how the ashes, forbidden burial in the Old Cemetery at Rome, lay for some months in John Freeborn's wine cellar (4) and how little William's grave revealed a full-sized skeleton. On January 21, 1823, Shelley was buried (5) with a certain honor but without distinction in the New Cemetery, until Trelawny dug his two graves near the pyramid of Caius Cestius in February (6). Here he planted cypresses—six in his letter to Mary, but, increasing like Falstaff's rogues in buckram, eight in the *Recollections*. On Shelley's tomb he placed a plain flat stone, engraved with Leigh Hunt's motto, *Cor Cordium,* that was to mislead so many pious visitors. (We shall see in time how much confusion these two have to answer for: the one for tearing out the heart and the other for choosing the motto.) Under it Trelawny added his own choice from *The Tempest*:

> *Nothing of him that doth fade*
> *But doth suffer a sea change*
> *Into something rich and strange.*

Shelley was ashes and could hardly, in this respect, be transmuted further. But as we hope to have shown, it was the world's conception of Shelley that was to change. And since mankind, however progressive, likes material idols, the grave, as his name and fame increased, became an object of pilgrimage. It was so convenient; almost everyone who traveled went to Rome, and when in Rome it was a pleasant respite from Catholicism and classicism (how many realized what an earnest classical scholar Shelley had been?) to visit the "atheist's" tomb. Besides, there was Keats within a stone's throw—two English poets, and a cemetery as fair as a garden, that had made Shelley himself write, "It might make one in love with death, to think that one should be buried in so sweet a place."

Modern visitors may find themselves rather wanly searching for the loveliness of the once "romantic and lonely cemetery." Sightseers and custodians are undodgeable; the graves with their massive heterogeneous stone monuments are sewn as thick as dragons' teeth in the huddled enclosure, and the trees that find their way between them to the upper air serve only to cut out the sunshine from a spot that should have been forever bathed in it. Now it is as dim and dusty as a small-town recreation ground. Shelley is up against an outer wall, Keats is up against an outer hedge, and the pyramid is, and always has been, despite the cunning of draughtsmen, at an oblique angle, hard to incorporate in a view of either. But the early tourists purred contentment; the cemetery must have been—*was*—beautiful. Those who traveled were the intelligent and discriminating, who wrote their letters, kept their journals, made their sketches and their verses. The place became a breeding ground for journalism, rhyme, and correspondence. Inspiration was caught and concentrated there like sunbeams in a glass house; and in time it was to become a sort of pious hobby to plant flowers there or to gather them. We shall take a look at some of these Italian visits in the nineteenth century without pretending to exhaust the matter.

❈{ II }❈

Early mourners were some of that "base crew" who had known Shelley and could hope to add a postscript to their memoirs. Here, for instance, is Tom Medwin, ready to cash in when the time was ripe. He had had a friend, or correspondent, at the Roman funeral, who followed the proceedings with a suitable emotion, being at last blinded by his tears "that fell fast and silently on the poet's grave." Medwin himself seems to have been content with a visit to the house at Lerici and later to Field Place. All this was laid up carefully, to be trimmed into his *Life*.

Another opportunist in this line of business was the future biographer T. J. Hogg. On those travels of 1825–26 that he was writing up for the *London Magazine* and retailing to Jane Williams, he walked, in a Roman December, "to pay a visit to a sad spot." He had heard, in England, "that it was an odious and unworthy place," but found it "the most interesting corner of the most interesting city in the world. . . . I stood there," he goes on in his letter to Jane, "a long time, alone, with tears in my eyes, and with my hat in my hand; some daisies were flowering there, and the cypresses, wch had been planted, were growing so straight and well, that they will, in time, serve to conceal and to point out the spot."[1] Like Medwin's, the typical sen-

[1] Norman, *After Shelley.*

tentious journalist's account, though tautened by the twist of personal contact. Shelley's less designing friends, Leigh Hunt and Peacock, recalling his living memory in their writing, appear to have left his tomb alone.

It is those who have never known the poet in his lifetime who can painlessly contemplate his resting place, meditating in a verdant bower on the deaths of poets. One of these gentlemen—anonymous—looked round in 1832. He had been there sixteen years previously when, as he writes, "a look of tranquillity and repose not to be described hung over every object." For this lover of the natural it had already gone downhill by Shelley's time; an English colony was buried there, walls had been built, and Christian order marred the unplanned beauty of its wilderness. Yet our recorder is an orthodox moralist: when he arrives at Shelley's tomb, walking between lines of aloes, rose trees, and rosemary hedges, he remarks, "This unfortunate man of genius was bitterly sensible before he died of the mischievous tendency of some of the opinions he had maintained, which drew upon him so much indignation, reproach and contumely; for he confessed with tears that he well knew he had been always in the wrong."

Three years later, in 1835, a young American, N. P. Willis, published an account of his visit to the Protestant burial ground. ". . . The sun lies warm and soft upon its banks, and the grass and wild-flowers are there the earliest and tallest of the Campagna. . . . With a cloudless sky and the most delicious air ever breathed, we sat down upon the marble slab laid over the ashes of poor Shelley"—a little less than deference, surely—"and read his own lament over Keats, who sleeps just below, at the foot of the hill."[2] He describes the grave as occupying, with one other nameless one—he did not know that it was also tenantless!—a small nook "made by the projections of a mouldering wall-tower, and crowded with ivy and shrubs, and a peculiarly fragrant yellow flower, which perfumes the air around for several feet." Another ten years, and another English visitor, J. T. Headley, writes a patronizing but well-meaning report of Shelley under the chapter heading "Ruins and Epitaphs in Rome": "With all his scepticism, he was a kind-hearted man. His Italian teacher was mine at Genoa, and he told me that Shelley was a nobler man than either Byron or Hunt."[3]

It would be pleasant to quote a noble tribute from Charles Dickens, who spent some time in Rome in 1846. He is disappointingly negligent. Returning by night from a day's excursion in the Campagna he has only this to say:

> From one part of the city, looking out beyond the walls, a squat and stunted pyramid (the burial place of Caius Cestius) makes an opaque triangle in the moonlight. But to an English traveler it serves to mark the grave of Shelley too, whose ashes lie in a little garden near it.[4]

He has not even spared the time for a visit; hence this note from hearsay of a little garden, and the absurd implication that moonlight is a permanent feature of the scene.

Mary herself, as we saw, had visited the place with Percy in 1843: "the bourne of a pious pilgrimage; the treasures of my youth lie buried here." No more. We saw, too, how her globe-trotting had irritated Browning—Browning who, say what he might and fight as he would, was ever attached to Shelley. He and Elizabeth Barrett, now his wife, visited the cemetery in January of 1854, but it was a doomed visit, colored by sudden personal stresses. Two children of their friend W. W. Story had become ill. The boy, in convulsions, died that evening; the girl, Edith, sent down to the artist Page on the floor below, was soon joined in her symptoms by Page's youngest daughter, Emma, and the Story's nurse was ill of the same fever. "Now you will understand," Elizabeth wrote, "what ghastly flakes of death have changed the sense of Rome to me. The first day by a death-bed, the first drive—out to the cemetery, where poor little Joe is laid close to Shelley's heart (*Cor Cordium,* says the epitaph) and where the mother insisted on going when she and I went out in the carriage together. . . . I can't look on the earth-side of death; I flinch from corpses and graves, and never meet a common funeral without a sort of horror." In the spring of 1860, George Eliot made a less hampered approach to the grave in the general course of sightseeing, but her remarks are undistinguished.

[2] N. P. Willis, *Pencillings by the Way* (London, 1835, 3 vols.).

[3] *Letters from Italy* (1845).

[4] *Pictures from Italy* (1846).

We move on to a pastoral period of what may be termed Grave Horti-
culture—demonstrating that poets burned or buried provide excellent
soil for flowers, besides food for meditation. Keats had talked of
daisies; Shelley in one of his lyrics says, *"Pansies let my flowers be."*
They turned out to be almost exclusively violets. A story attaches
to their blossoming: In 1863, Lady Shelley, having heard that the
grave was in a neglected state, went off to Rome, towing Sir Percy with
her, to improve it. Instead of facing the expected wilderness, she had
a surprise. On their arrival they had "found it in perfect order and
looking lovely, with roses and violets blooming round it. We were
told by the *custode* that it had only just been done by the order of a
young gentleman who had visited it with two ladies. We tried in
every way to find out who had done this work of love, but in vain."
It was twelve years before she did find out, for the *custode* could only
tell her of "a certain young Englishman, whose name I have forgotten." The young Englishman was in fact a future if minor poet
laureate, Alfred Austin.

Austin made the common mistake of believing Shelley's heart was
there, and looking on the grave in April 1863 wrote a poem to that
effect, beginning:

> *Beneath this marble, mute of praise,*
> *Is hushed the heart of One*
> *Who, whilst it beat, had eagle's gaze*
> *To stare upon the sun.*
>   *Equal in flight*
>   *To any height,*
> *He lies where they that crawl but come,*
> *Sleeping most sound,—Cor Cordium.*

Shelley, he said, had sung too early to be heard by a drowsy world:

> *But when the Day shall come whose dawn*
> *He early did forbode,*
> *When men by Knowledge shall be drawn,*
> *Not driven by the goad,*
>   *This spot apart,*
>   *Where sleeps his heart,*
> *Deaf to all clamour, wrong, or rage,*
> *Shall be their choicest pilgrimage.*[5]

Searching, then, for the magic words *cor cordium,* he found, as he reported years later, that "they were scarcely to be deciphered"; for Shelley worship, in later years carried almost to excess, had not yet become the fashion. "The tomb was lichen-covered and grass-invaded; and scandalized at the sight, I wrote an anonymous regretful letter to some English daily paper. . . . . Weeks passed on. I went again to the grave, and, as I had first found it, such it still remained. Not without some hesitation I had it reverently cleaned and relieved of the weeds that trespassed on it; and then, carrying my temerity still further, I planted pansies and violets round it and before leaving Rome some months later, left with the *custode* of the Cemetery a trifling sum for keeping the spot neat and flower-girt."[6] When Lady Shelley did find out, she wrote to Austin in the words quoted above, adding, "We have one more wish now—to clasp your hand and thank you face to face." The meeting took place, not at the graveside, but at dinner in a friend's house.

Austin had fairly started the game up. At once it became fashionable for the intelligentsia to go violet hunting on Shelley's tomb. Coventry Patmore was one of the first of the tomb robbers. In the spring of 1864, he wrote from Rome to Richard Garnett: "I went to the Protestant Burial Ground to see if I could find some violets for you on the graves of Shelley and Keats. I have got one from Shelley's and three from Keats's. It was a little too late. A week before, I was told, the two graves were a mass of violets."[7] The sculptor Thomas Woolner, whom we saw talking at Marlow to an old, old man, tried his luck, too, and related to William Allingham, "Though I did not write I bore you in mind and when I went to visit the grave of Shelley I gathered a violet from it to send you; but now the poor shrivelled little thing seems a mockery and makes me almost ashamed to send it."[8]

There came, too, the innocent Mrs. Houston, after visiting the family at Field Place. That *ménage* was long since broken up, but Shelley's two sisters were now living in Berkshire. This lady, instead of picking a violet or two, had the larger idea of digging up whole plants. She dug them up, as she says, with reverence, and carefully

[5] *Interludes* (1872).
[6] *Autobiography* (1911).
[7] Basil Champneys, *Memoirs and Correspondence of Coventry Patmore* (London, 1900).
[8] Amy Woolner, *Thomas Woolner, R. A., Sculptor and Poet* (London, 1917).

took them home to be presented to Hellen and Margaret. When the plants arrived, the unromantic Hellen summoned the family gardener. "You know what a poet is, don't you, Challis?" she asked. And, Challis apparently giving a satisfactory answer, went on, "Well, these were brought from a poet's grave, a long way off, so you must find a place for them somewhere, and take care that they don't come to grief."[9] And they are said to have flourished well enough on the Berkshire estate, weathering the partial frost of Hellen's reception. So much for Mrs. Houston, who possibly tinted her memoirs as she wished.

In 1872, Walter Crane—in whom "free thought" had been induced, to a point, by reading Shelley—came to make drawings of the tomb. The next year he drew Keats's. It was congenial: "Working in that restful garden, beneath the murmur of the cypresses, one might almost feel the spirits of the poets still haunted the place, and could understand the feeling expressed by Shelley." Alas, he too fell into the ever ready trap: "While drawing at Shelley's grave my thought shaped themselves in the following sonnet:

Cor Cordium

Tread softly, here the heart of Shelley lies:
 His grave a garden, 'neath the cypress wood
 Stirred with the tongues his spirit understood,
And spake in deathless song that vivifies
Men's souls made heavy with the world's sad cries,
 Still when the darkness hides the dragon brood
 Of evil, and while yet innocent blood
Is shed, and Truth and Falsehood change their dyes.

Thy voice is heard above this silent tomb,
 And shall be heard until the end of days
 While Freedom lives, and whatsoever things
Are good and lovely—still thy spirit sings;
 And by thy grave to-day fresh violets bloom,
 But on thy head imperishable bays."[10]

Likewise in the trap is Augustus J. C. Hare in his guidebook peregrination of the cemetery: "Amid the forests of tombs we may

[9] Houstoun, *A Woman's memories of World-known Men.*
[10] *An Artist's Reminiscences* (New York, 1907).

notice that which contains the heart of Shelley (his body having been burnt upon the shore at Lerici [*sic*], where it was thrown up by the sea)."[11] Hare, as a guide, is—otherwise—conscientious and gives historic facts about the Caius Cestius pyramid. But a different idea of this monument's significance was getting around. Thomas Hardy —an ardent Shelleyan, by the way, throughout his life—was to give it perfect utterance. Before him, W. St. Clair Baddeley had a similar thought:

The Pyramid of C. Cestius

Grey leader of yon dark-processioned trees,—
  Gaunt silver pyramid, there standest thou,
Herald of fore-known scenes and memories!
  Before thee as our shrine we pilgrims bow:
Not that in thee the tombs we honour, lie,
  But an enduring sign—dost stand between,
Those violet-bordered camps, and solemnly
  By wandering worshippers thou art far-seen.
High land mark of all poets! Cenotaph
  Of Caius Cestius; none who views but greets
In thee, if not for self, on friend's behalf,
  A pledge between our Shelley and dear Keats.
Hear, guess, and keep this mystery's wide intent;
  "THEY were before, yet since, their monument."[12]

Two years later, in 1887, came Hardy, perhaps the most distinguished of the cemetery pilgrims; a skeptic concerning the forgotten feats of Cestius, until

                          in death all silently
      He does a finer thing,

    In beckoning pilgrim feet
    With marble finger high
To where, by shadowy wall and history-haunted street,
    Those matchless singers lie. . . .

    —Say, then, he lived and died
    That stones which bear his name

[11] *Walks in Rome* (1876).
[12] *Dramatic and Narrative Poems* (1885).

253

Should mark through Time, where two immortal Shades abide;
It is an ample fame.

The pilgrimage is not without its light relief: among the artists,
poets, and literary gardeners there came a novelist, masterly in the
presenting of incident. This is what Wilkie Collins wrote to a friend
in 1886:

> Oh, I wanted you so at Rome—in the Protestant Cemetery—
> don't start! No ghosts—only a cat. I went to show my friend Pigott
> the grave of the illustrious Shelley. Approaching the resting-place
> of the divine poet in a bright sunlight, the finest black Tom you
> ever saw discovered at an incredible distance that a catanthropist
> had entered the cemetery—rushed up at a gallop, with his tail at
> right angles to his spine—turned over on his back with his four
> paws in the air, and said in the language of cats: "Shelley be hanged!
> Come and tickle me!" I stopped and tickled him. We were both
> profoundly affected.[13]

The English visitors and the local cats had no exclusive rights here.
Gabriele D'Annunzio, in *Il Piacere* (1889), sent his characters walking through the silent cemetery, where,

> between the low myrtle bushes they reached the graves of Shelley
> and Trelawny. The jessamine climbing over the ancient ruin was
> in flower but of the violets only thick growing leaves remained.
> From here the cypress-tips were level with the eye-line and they
> glowed still brighter in the sun now sinking behind Monte
> Testaccio. Aloft, towards the Aventine swam a violet cloud rimmed
> with burning gold.[14]

Most skillful of the artists who placed Shelley and Cestius in one field
of vision was undoubtedly William Bell Scott. He has pyramid,
cypresses, and a side-long angle on the tomb felicitously knit together
in a drawing that has been endlessly reproduced.

[13] *Memoirs of Half a Century*, ed. by K. C. Lehmann (1908).
[14] Translated by Neville Rogers in *Keats, Shelley, and Rome*.

Something of the cold haunting of mortality spread, not unnaturally, from the Roman tomb to Lerici; Lerici, the little seashore town waiting, forever desolate, like that of Keats's Grecian urn, for the poet who would never return to it.

> Strange and special the effect, in Italy, of the empty places (and there are many) that we stand and wonder in to-day for the sake of the vanished, the English poets; the irresistible reconstruction, to the all but baffled vision, of irrecoverable presences and aspects, the conscious, shining, mocking void, sad somehow with excess of serenity. There is positively no great difference between the impression of the Lerici of Shelley, that of the Ravenna of Byron, that of the painted chamber of Keats by the Spanish Steps in Rome.[15]

Cousin Medwin had hurried to Lerici, to contemplate "the solitary villa ... which was about to waken in me so many bitter recollections," and where he found "a deaf, unfeeling old wretch" who told him "with a savage unconcern" of the desolation she had either seen or heard about. He was soon enough after the event to scratch about for firsthand information. Hogg, on his Grand Tour, was or hoped to be the sentimental traveler when, "turning the corner by an old olive, I saw beneath my feet the fatal, but lovely bay, & all the beautiful neighbourhood, at sunset." Having experienced "a certain utmost sensation of grief," he continued his journey from Spezia in the moonlight morning, and "felt a kind of pleasure in quitting these scenes for ever." Like the tomb, the Casa Magni—Shelley's "white house with arches"—has been under observation. It was noted when it seemed half derelict, when a third story was built on by a new occupant, and when, some fifty years ago, a coastal motor road with a sea wall was constructed to bring the hum of regular traffic to that lonely spot.[16] When Sir Percy and Lady Shelley called at Lerici, the latter—whom Mathilde Blind was to remember from Boscombe as an earnest spiritualist—lay unsleeping in the poet's bedroom hoping to see his ghost; but she was unrewarded.[17] She and Sir Percy thought of buy-

[15] Henry James, *William Wetmore Story and His Friends* (Boston, 1903).

[16] For some impressions by the present writer, see "Shelley's Last Residence," *Keats-Shelley Journal*, Vol. II (New York, January, 1953).

[17] It was left to the mid-twentieth century to see, or believe it was seeing, Shelley's ghost.

ing the house; but the landlord, knowing it was Shelley's son who wanted it, put the price up, and went into a frenzy when negotiations broke down. Here they met an old sailor who referred to Shelley as *"mio bimbo"* and—kissing Percy Florence's feet on learning his identity—declared of the poet, "He was fair, he was beautiful, he was like Jesus Christ. I carried him in my arms through the water—yes, he was like Jesus Christ." This new myth Lady Shelley related, and her hearer wrote down.[18]

But for the perfect sentimental pilgrimage why should we not go back to so beautiful a master of perception and evoked nostalgia as Henry James, whose passage on "the empty places" has been quoted above? James visited the spot in 1877. From his comments on Lerici and Shelley we may steal a passage or two to gild these too funereal pages:

> The house he occupied is strangly shabby, and as sad as you may choose to find it. It stands directly upon the beach, with scarred and battered walls, and a loggia of several arches opening upon a little terrace with a rugged parapet, which, when the wind blows, must be drenched with the salt spray. The place is very lonely—all over-wearied with sun and breeze and brine—very close to nature, as it was Shelley's passion to be. I can fancy a great lyric poet sitting on the terrace, of a warm evening, far from England, in the early years of the century.... It is a place where an English-speaking traveler may very honestly be sentimental and feel moved, himself, to lyric utterance. But I must content myself with saying in halting prose that I remember few episodes of Italian travel more sympathetic,

An Italian newspaper in May, 1952, reported that this phantom, having already apparently been seen many times, had appeared again at the Casa Magni. The report says: "A few days ago Mr. Ratti during a night of strong sirocco wind, woke up suddenly and saw that a long white evanescent form was slowly entering the door. This phantom took definite shape as a tall human being (it is known that Shelley was slender and very tall) and approached the bed and leaned on it.

"Mr. Ratti yelled and the white form, still very slowly, straightened itself up and went out of the door." When Mr. Ratti roused his wife, she revealed that a year before, on a night of sirocco, "she too had had a visit of the same phantom, which had awakened her."

The story is quoted in the *Keats-Shelley Journal* cited above, together with a reference to my own article on the Casa Magni, visited a year previous to the Ratti affair. Let me state that I am making no personal claims about the ghost of Shelley, and subscribing to no new myths at this eleventh hour. I am not a clairvoyant subject. At the same time it is hardly necessary to be a clod. I did see a light that was not as other lights, and I wrote down what I saw because it was part of the temper and atmosphere of the scene. A suspension of disbelief is as far as I am prepared to go in the matter.

[18] Rolleston, *Talks with Lady Shelley.*

as they have it here, than that perfect autumn afternoon; the half-hour's station on the little battered terrace of the villa; the climb to the singularly picturesque old castle that hangs above Lerici; the meditative lounge, in the fading light, on the vine-decked platform that looked out towards the sunset and the darkening mountains, and, far below, upon the quiet sea, beyond which the pale-faced villa stared up at the brightening moon.[19]

He has wrapped scene and associations into a typical Jamesian awareness, molding and shaping it to a whole that Shelley himself might approve, for all that he was happier in a boat than on the terrace.

One pilgrim to Shelley's Italian haunts was free enough of sentiment to try practical research. In the early seventies, Trelawny's daughter Laetitia Call sent home a story of another old sailor who, dying at Spezia, claimed in his last confession to be one of the crew of a felucca that ran down the *Don Juan* thinking Lord Byron and his money were aboard her. W. M. Rossetti sent an extract of this to the *Times* in December, 1875; the *Athenaeum,* commenting, urged an inquiry by the British Consular Service; Trelawny argued in favor of the theory in the *Times,* as the year was ending. An Italian naval captain, inquiring in Spezia, submitted that the dying sailor was a fable invented by some of the local boatmen for credulous tourists. The excitement died, not without evoking a poetic outburst of nine stanzas from the violet planter Alfred Austin. Here is the first of them:

> *What! And it was so! Thou wert then*
> *Death-stricken from behind,*
> *O heart of hearts! and they were men,*
> *That rent thee from mankind!*
> *Greedy hatred chasing love,*
> *As a hawk pursues a dove,*
> *Till the soft feathers float upon the care-*
> *less wind.*[20]

Viareggio, too, had its investigation when in 1890 the Italian author Guido Biagi assembled a number of old men who thought they could remember, as children, being present at the cremation, and heard their evidence.[21]

---

[19] *Portraits of Places* (1884).
[20] Reprinted in *Soliloquies in Song* (1882).
[21] *Gli Ultimi Giorni di P. B. Shelley* (Florence, 1892).

To return to the Roman cemetery: all this time, except for the plant-
ing and uprooting of violets, there had been no alteration to the furniture of Shelley's tomb. Still the flat stone and the repeatedly misinterpreted *Cor Cordium*. But, by 1891, Lady Shelley had decided—
characteristically—to erect a monument, and had commissioned the
sculptor Onslow Ford for it. His design was hugeously of Victoria's
era. The white body of Shelley lay in nude perfection as it might have
been, but was not, cast up after drowning; supporting it, a bronze
base decorated with the Muse of Poetry—a female form. Lady Shelley's excuse for this hyperbole was that she must frustrate the Italians
who had threatened to erect a worse and more enormous one. She
had reckoned without the "dead hand" of E. J. Trelawny, raised in
the person of his alert daughter, Mrs. Laetitia Call. She claimed now
that the ground and tomb were the property of her father; he had
paid for it—a very small sum, was Lady Shelley's feline comment—
and his original stone was not to be altered or defaced. A plan to
erect a bust from Marianne Hunt's model of 1836 had long ago been
talked of, for Mrs. Call could quote a letter from her father to Rossetti,
back in 1879:

> I should resist every innovation. If you have an opportunity tell
> Garnett this. The sticking up a good bust would be absurd: but one
> modelled from Mrs. Hunt's would be only fit for a scarecrow.[22]

So here we have Trelawny's personal assessment of Marianne's controversial product. We can hardly suppose that Lady Shelley was
backing that project; now she had the Ford creation—an embodiment
in bronze and marble of the Boscombe dream. This Call claim was
a setback. Both disputants applied to Lord Dufferin, the British am-
bassador, to find out in whom the property of the graves was vested.
Sir Rennell Rodd wrote tactfully from the Embassy, suggesting to
Lady Shelley that the monument involved too much alteration of a
consecrated spot. (In fact, it would have straddled the grave of Trelawny, too, so that measurements alone precluded it.) Lady Shelley
agreed to place her monument somewhere else, if given a guarantee

[22] Quoted by R. Glynn Grylls in *Trelawny*.

258

that no alteration would be made in the present tomb. This suited Laetitia, and an agreement was drawn up between the two expressing their common aim to keep the graves unchanged.

For the second time, then, Lady Shelley found herself with a grandiose monument left on her hands. She made what—in view of the conservative tradition of Oxford colleges—must be considered a bold move: in December, 1891, she wrote to the college that had sent down the poet for obstinacy and contumely eighty years before.

> Boscombe Manor, December 1, 1891
>
> To the Master and Fellows of University College, Oxford.
>
> Gentlemen,
>
> I desire to offer for the acceptance of the College, a monument of Percy Bysshe Shelley the Poet, once a member of your College.
>
> It is a beautiful work in marble and bronze by Onslow Ford.
>
> I must require, as a condition, that it be placed in a suitable position and light, towards the expense of which I will contribute £500, the remainder of the sum may, it is hoped, be raised by the Poet's admirers.
>
> The place was one in which he must have passed many happy hours, and the circumstances under which he left the College, are hardly worth considering now.
>
> I remain, Gentlemen,
>
> Your obedient servant,
>
> Jane Shelley.[23]

The Fellows met at once; on December 5 the Master (Dr. Bright) wrote back that they "expressed a strong desire to accept as soon as possible the gift you are offering, and warm gratitude to you for choosing the college as a home for the Memorial." Certain conditions as to money grants and alteration of the site remained to be sanctioned, but she was assured that this implied no coldness; "the College will do all that it feels justified in doing to secure a proper resting place within its walls for the beautiful work of art which you are offering to it."[24]

[23] From correspondence kindly lent me by the Master of University College.

[24] It is not clear to me whether or not the Fellows knew they were being offered a reject. If so, this would seem to increase their magnanimity.

The following year a cast of the "work of art" was exhibited in the congenial setting of the Royal Academy. And on June 14, 1893, the Memorial was opened in the presence of numerous heads of colleges, the Bishop of Southwark, and Ianthe's son.[25] It was Lady Shelley's moment. Handing the gold key of the chamber to the Master, she declared that for over forty years she had striven to give the world a just impression of Shelley's character. She had lived in the companionship of his noble-minded wife and his son and had known most of his friends, none of whom now survived. Shelley and Mary, she urged, were not regardless of the duties of life, though men of genius could not be reduced to rule. If they erred sometimes, they were not to be deprived of the love and admiration of their countrymen. The Master, in his reply, showed Oxford advancing with the world by its acceptance not only of a modern work of art, but of the great poet who "was prophetic in all directions of what was to come to the world." The gift was the symbol of the rubbing out of old ill-wills. He was not blaming his predecessor for an action that had to be taken. The very greatness of the man had laid him open to it; his hatred of the false and oppressive, the gloomy and sad, had made him a rebel. But (and Dr. Bright sums up much that has been traced here gradually) the rebel of eighty years ago was the hero of the present century [*sic*] and for eighty years they had been learning to share his admirations and his hatreds.[26]

It is tempting to picture the phantom of Shelley tiptoeing in among these worthies, listening, half in satisfaction, half in a wistful irony, to their admirable sentiments, and sighing a little that it should have taken eighty years for his old college to catch up with him. Now he is housed, Napoleon-like, in this ornate sarcophagus surmounted by a dome or cupola. Not a fragment of his body lies under it; and who can wish that his restless spirit should submit and chain itself to that Promethean rock? Considered now, it is the perfect memorial to the Boscombe era, the translation and apotheosis of Lady Shelley's shrine.

[25] The *Times* of June 15, 1893, gives the following list: Lady Shelley, Bishop of Southwark, Master of University (Dr. Bright), Master of Balliol (Prof. Jowett), Sir William Markley, Warden of All Souls, President of Magdalen, Warden of Merton, Rector of Exeter, Mr. Arthur Sidgwick, Mr. Onslow Ford, Canon St. John, Dr. Garnett, Mr. William Esdaile (grandson of the poet), Mr. Hamilton Aidé, Mr. Champneys (who designed the chamber in which the memorial is placed), and Mr. H. M. Burge.

[26] The *Times*, as above.

But Shelley's Italian admirers did erect a monument, not at Rome, but at Viareggio. By the efforts of Cesar Riccione, a local lawyer, an executive committee was formed, with himself as president, to raise funds by public subscription. In October, 1894, on an inclement Sunday, the Paolino Square was thronged for the unveiling of a bust by Urbano Lucchesi. "The eyes are gazing meditatively across the sea," writes a reporter,[27] "and a pen just laid down appears from under the folds of the cloak." The Casa Magni, too, was to have its memorial plaque in Carrara marble, with a legend by Ceccardo Roccatagliata. A translation reads, "From this portico, on which there played the shadow of an ancient ilex, in July, 1822, Mary Godwin and Jane Williams awaited with tearful anxiety Percy Bysshe Shelley who, sailing from Leghorn on fragile craft, had landed by unforeseen fortune amid the silences of the Elysian Isles.

> *O blessed shores,*
> *Where love, liberty, dreams*
> *Have no chains."*[28]

The road through the Protestant Cemetery, threatened in 1888, was never made, but at San Terenzo the regular buses linking La Spezia with Lerici go roaring past Shelley's "lonely house, close by the sea-side,"[29] where once the storm waves, unimpeded, would come rolling in and lashing up to the arches. For time may work two ways. Shelley, who sat among the Caesars' antique ruins to compose *Prometheus,* pictured the wreck of Ozymandius in the sands of a bare desert, or foresaw, on the tempest-shaken beach,

> *One white skull and seven dry bones,*
> *On the margin of the stones*
> *Where a few gray rushes stand,*
> *Boundaries of the sea and land . . .*

Today, where the "empty places" become peopled by an insistent and ever-growing population, there is barely room to isolate the memorial

[27] From the *Bournemouth Observer*, October 3, 1894.
[28] *O benedette spiagge*
  Que l'amore, la libertà, i sogni
  Non hanno catene.
[29] Letter to Horace Smith, May, 1822.

of a poet from the encroaching pressure of highways, tombstones, and commercialized transport. With this in mind we should be thankful for the monstrous pimple in the precincts of an Oxford college carved out from the rooms and corridors of the living, until some future reform sweeps it away.

In the New Protestant Cemetery, then, Shelley remained under Trelawny's plain white marble. Alfred Austin, poet laureate in a meager hour and in no sense an immortal, could not forever trim the grave; and Lady Shelley was herself to die in 1899, leaving heirs by adoption only. On the brink of the new century, peering forward, we may see some slatternly neglect and shabbiness creeping in again. Wars produce their own sad graves and monuments; while they drain treasuries, public and personal, Old Unquenchables must bide awhile in the weeds and thickets. In 1948 one of our modern poets made the pilgrimage and versified his impressions. That they are woefully different from those glowing words of earlier visitors has led to some reproof for flippancy. On the contrary, rather, at a time when the graves had lapsed to a pre-Austin seediness in the crowded plot, an honest recorder had dreamed of a shrine and found a shrubbery. So, in *An Italian Visit,* C. Day Lewis writes:

> *Here is one corner of a foreign field*
> *That is for ever garden suburb. See,*
> *In their detached and smug-lawned residences,*
> *Behind a gauze of dusty shrubs, the English*
> *Indulge their life-long taste for privacy.*
> *Garish Campagna knocks at' the back door,*
> *Rome calls* en grande tenue: *but "not at home"*
> *Murmur these tombs, and "far from home they died,*
> *The eccentric couple you have come to visit—*
> *One spitting blood, an outsider and a failure,*
> *One sailing a boat, his mind on higher things."*
> *Somewhere close to the pyramid a loud-speaker*
> *Blared jazz while we lingered at Keats' shabby mound,*
> *But the air was drowned by the ghost of the nightingale;*
> *The ground was swimming with anemone tears*
> *Where Shelley lay.*

It is not the mind, but the place, that is out of tune. Never again (unless by its removal to some lonelier, less time-ridden locality) will Shelley's tomb be free of jostling neighbors and overshadowing trees. But there can be trimness, reverence, and flowers still; and in this matter the new associated body that links Shelley and Keats in its protection takes the place of lone philanthropists.[30]

❧{ VI }❧

One white skull and seven dry bones . . .

There is another odd discussion about Shelley's burial: how much of him—still in physical terms of bones and organs—has escaped interment? Tracking his friends and worshipers through this nineteenth century, one comes across so many references to saintly relics that he would seem to have been fairly broken up and dispersed before cremation, leaving a mere nucleus to endure the flames. Trelawny is, of course, responsible as officiator. There was nothing to stop him from snatching relics. Equally, there is no means of checking his veracity when he declares some chip or shaving to be a fragment of his lamented friend. He appears never to have been challenged; the honored recipients have been only too eager to accept in faith what the eye could not disprove or ratify. Let us, in any case, take a glance at these wandering relics, without, again, the least claim to completeness.

First and most important is of course the heart—"My heart which, in its time, has had so much rubbing that it ought to be hard by this time," Shelley had written to Elizabeth Hitchener in 1812. It may be reasonably accepted that Trelawny did extract this organ, unburned, from the funeral pyre. We have seen something of its further adventures: how Mary and Leigh Hunt squabbled for possession, with Jane Williams as peacemaker, and Byron—who disapproved of relics—cynically observing, "What does Hunt want with the heart?

---

[30] In 1950 the two graves were put in order by means of a fund raised by British subscribers to the Keats-Shelley Memorial Association; while American funds were used to restore the condition of the cemetery where they lie. As one who was bitterly disappointed by their appearance early in 1949, I welcome the reassurance, but am still heretic enough to long to see Shelley transferred to a less populated and more richly classic position, near, say, the Via Appia Antica, where Imperial Romans have their mausoleums and the long-abandoned Claudian aqueduct staggers its broken arches across the plain.

He'll only put it in a glass case and make sonnets on it." Of Jane, who had *her* husband's ashes in an urn, he mocked that she would one day forget what the receptacle contained, and make tea in it. Yet Byron himself, it appears, wanted Shelley's skull. What would he have done with his souvenir? Trelawny remembered that he had used one as a drinking vessel. Byron was not allowed the skull, or such section of it as the pirate is supposed to have put by.

The heart, then, travels to England with Mary and is generally quiescent until her death in 1851, when we have that tale of Lady Shelley's about finding a folded page from Adonais containing ashes and dust, the remnants of the heart. It has dwindled considerably, but its posthumous career is not over. Controversy begins again. Where is this heart? Where was it? We have seen how numbers of visitors were deluded by Hunt's *Cor Cordium* into thinking that the heart, and perhaps only the heart, was buried in the Roman grave. That theory—unless Trelawny made an anatomical error—may be dismissed. Beginning then from the Adonais ash of 1851, Lady Shelley says, first, that she left it as she found it; then, that it was in her Boscombe shrine. All those who visited this were shown some object that was fabled to contain the heart. Yet there was a period when it seems to have had an active existence. One story says it was enclosed in a silver case. Again, it was kept in a cushion or muff and carried by Lady Shelley when she traveled. Thus it was taken to Shelley House in Chelsea, and, when the house was burgled, cushion and contents were thrown on the floor.[31] (The housebreakers were evidently not relic thieves.) All this may be apocryphal, or it may be true. It is a dreary and knockabout sort of after-life for the auricles and ventricles of a Romantic poet. But those who hang around the affairs of famous men could never keep their paws off the subject, and their minds were busy guessing all the time. Even some who should have been reasonably certain—Trelawny and Lady Shelley—had a public argument when Trelawny stated in the *Records* that the heart had been given to Sir Percy Florence by Leigh Hunt. This seems to have been sheer perversity on the pirate's part; likewise, his repetition of a tale that Shelley's other ashes had been taken from Rome by stealth and were now in Lady Shelley's possession.

After the death of these "responsible" persons, *Where is the heart*

[31] Ingpen, *Shelley in England*.

buried? becomes almost a parlor game. From the *Times Literary Supplement* to the *Christchurch Parish Review* the question is debated. It was buried in St. Peter's Churchyard, Bournemouth, with Sir Percy, one (and the most plausible) declares. Another—claiming Lady Shelley's authority—says it was sent by Sir Percy to be buried in Rome when Mary died. (This would rule out cushions, muffs, shrines, and the urn that rises at one point in the story.) Yet another of these cardiac authorities states that the relic was given by Sir Percy to "Boscombe Church"—an unidentifiable building—to be placed in a case and embedded in the wall, where it remains. One more report— or "statement"—coming from a relative of Lady Shelley's, says that her brother Canon St. John (i.e., brother-in-law), after trying for years to persuade her to give it "decent burial," at last had his way and interred it in the grave of Mary Wollstonecraft. (He might have said Mary Shelley and so avoided the implication that hearts are due to mothers-in-law, but in fact the two Marys, as we saw, were now in the same grave.) In 1923 an Indian correspondent in *Notes and Queries* summed up the whole puzzle and asked for enlightenment. He appears to have had no answer.

But long before that a more sinister note had crept into the argument: the existence and identity of the heart had been challenged. In the 1840's the Rector of Bushey, Herts, had found at Viareggio another of those sailors who claimed to know something. This one had been present when Shelley's remains were dug up from the sand. He said, "We found only the bones of the said body, the flesh having been consumed by lime."[32] In that case there was no heart at all, and who could say what this long-preserved and worshiped bit of ash might represent? One man believed he knew. In 1885, Mr. A. S. Bicknell communicated to the *Athenaeum* his scientific doubts of the unburned heart. The organ, he wrote, which longest resists the action of fire is not the heart which, small and hollow, is easily consumed; it is that moist and solid mass, the liver. This repels intense heat (and intense romanticism), depositing an ash of pure carbon which can suffer no further change. In Shelley's case its saturation by salt water would render it still more incombustible. Mr. Bicknell was convinced that neither Byron, Leigh Hunt, nor Trelawny knew

---

[32] This was long before Trelawny's statement in the *Records* that the remains of the body were entire, only the legs and wrists having separated at the joints.

enough anatomy to distinguish the one organ from the other. And so we have the hypothesis of the poet's liver being reverently handed down the years.[33]

So much for the heart—or liver—though we could find more. Trelawny, as we noted at the outset, kept some further relics. First, the Hunts did not go empty-handed from the funeral. Hunt acquired a fragment of Shelley's jawbone and gave it to Marianne. On September 18, 1822, she wrote a note in her diary which makes uneasy reading: "I look at my little box and think of the lip that covered what it contains until I can bear it no longer. A lip from whence every pure and generous feeling issued daily, hourly and momentarily." (This fragment was eventually to be presented by Hunt's grandson to the Keats–Shelley Memorial House in Rome, enclosed in an opaque blue jar, with the stipulation, passed on from Hunt, that it should not be extracted.) Nor was this the only specimen. In 1872, W. M. Rossetti reported, "Trelawny has a piece of Shelley's jawbone—charred, of course—which he showed me. Oh that it were mine one day! I would imitate the priests of the bloody faith and enshrine it." He was to have his thrill when one day Trelawny gave him "a strange and precious relic, a fragment of Shelley's charred skull, which he had picked out of the funeral furnace. I put it into a very simple locket, and he, liking this arrangement, got me to bespeak a similar locket for another fragment of the skull which he retained."[34] Rossetti's piece of skull, enclosed in the locket, was left to his daughter in his will.

And one more relic—to match that final suggestion about the liver. The pirate chose to pick out, too, a piece of kidney from the burning, and to show it to the poet's physician, Vaccà, who expressed an opinion, on examining it, that the disease Shelley had suffered from was not nephritic. (Whether the kidney went into a test tube or a casket must depend on the doctor's relative enthusiasm for science and poetry.)

There may be—probably have been—more of these small remnants; there are certainly numerous of those nineteenth-century favor-

[33] Guido Biagi, in a new edition of *Gli Ultimi Giorni de P. B. Shelley* (Florence, 1922), sums up the correspondence in the *Times Literary Supplement* during 1920 and concludes that the heart is now buried with Sir Percy in St. Peter's Churchyard, Bournemouth. (See Wilfrid H. Woollen, in *Notes & Queries*, May 19, 1923.)

[34] *Some Reminiscenes.*

ites, "locks of hair."[35] But at this point it becomes excusable to say, with Browning in his *Memorabilia*, "Well, I forget the rest." A footnote to this Browning tale deserves a mention although it spills over into the new century: in May, 1913, when the property of Browning's son "Pen" was sold by auction in London, the Browning relics included "a small weightless object, carefully wrapped and labelled. It was a flower plucked from Shelley's grave." But in the same sale the Marianne Hunt bust of Shelley went "for a song" to Wilfrid Meynell, having been described as "Bust of the Poet's Uncle"![36] This one persisting copy of the bust has at last become a memorial after further adventures. Sold to Dr. Rosenbach of New York, it returned to England to be presented by Mr. Marshall Field of Chicago in 1939 to the school where Shelley had been plentifully unhappy—Eton College. Only one reinstatement of the rebel remains outstanding. It is soon to be made, for plans are advanced to install memorial plaques to Shelley and Keats in the Poets' Corner of Westminster Abbey.[37] The site secured is just over the Shakespeare monument. Honorable amends can hardly be carried further.

[35] Everything connected with T. J. Wise is suspect, but in this case perhaps hardly more so than the other scraps. His Ashley Library included a volume under Mary Shelley's name, with three small glass-covered cases inserted in the binding. They were said to contain "locks of the hair of Shelley and Mary, and the Ashes of Shelley including a fragment of the skull." (Wilfred Partington, in the *Bookman's Journal*, December, 1924, where the binding is reproduced.)

[36] Information given me by Sir Shane Leslie who had it from Meynell, and who was instrumental in bringing the bust home to England from America.

[37] See Fifth and Sixth Annual Reports, Keats-Shelley Memorial Association (British Committee), 1951, 1952.

CHAPTER XIV

Expansion as Epilogue

❦ 1 ❧

THE DATE: Wednesday, March 10, 1886. The place: University College, London. The Speaker: the Reverend Stopford Brooke (substituting at short notice for W. M. Rossetti). The audience: some one hundred members gathered with their friends at the inaugural meeting of the new Society. "Shelley," declares the speaker, "is one of the most striking instances in our time of the way in which an artist, ignored or abused in his own day, rises from the grave into which the critics have trampled him, and, when their noxious names have perished, lives as a power in the hearts of men." Mr. Brooke,[1] we are told, "was listened to throughout with deep attention, and was enthusiastically applauded at the conclusion of his lecture." No doubt the listeners were keyed up to spontaneous recognition. But we have, as it were, lived longer and are looking on this enterprise in the guise of at least comparative immortals. How often have we not heard something similar: the summing up, the simplified resurgence, the confidence that a poet once universally vilified is now universally enshrined? The Shelley Society in its moment seemed a culmination. Now it has gone by with other protuberances on the moving landscape, leaving, in the material way, a pile of print and paper, some in facsimile of a familiar hand, much of it of real benefit as reproducing Shelley's lesser-known works. We shall not examine it in detail; the blue paper-covered notebooks, when available, still bulge with particulars of its officers, its lectures, its discussions, publications, and stage productions. It is to be found disclaiming with likable honesty any intention to last (like the sturdier type of mausoleum) forever; by ten years it expects to have done its duty. And it does hang on—by the figurative eyebrows—for approximately that time.

---

[1] Stopford Brooke was the father of Maud Rolleston, whose *Talks with Lady Shelley* has been frequently quoted here.

Possibly its right location is in the previous chapter, with the monuments. It is adorned with good-sized names. Richard Garnett keeps clear, having, as he states, no confidence in the promoters, and recommends Sir Percy Florence to do no more than join for the sake of Shelley's memory, but to accept no post on the committee.[2] He could hardly know that it was serving as an ample practice-ground for one man's roguery, in the making of facsimiles by Major Byron's more artistic follower, T. J. Wise.[3] That is undreamed of even by his innocent colleagues, whose ambitions are realized when in May, 1886, they stage *The Cenci,* with Alma Murray in the part of Beatrice.[4] The performance was strictly noncommercial, since no licence could be granted for such incestuous stuff. A good part of the press was sympathetic; Oxford University was not: the suggestion that the Oxford Union Society should expend a guinea on a subscription to the Shelley Society was strongly opposed by Lord Robert Cecil and other guardians of undergraduate morals on the grounds that the performance of *The Cenci* was an overwhelming proof of the Society's degrading tendencies. So the upright young Oxonians refused their patronage by a majority of over forty. (It was, as we saw, their seniors who were soon to accept Lady Shelley's monument.) Yet *The Cenci* sent up the membership of the Shelley Society, for one had to join in order to see the play.

We refrain from criticism of all these matters, merely noting facts and oddities. Thus, in October, a performance of *Hellas* (something more, perhaps, than Shelley ever hoped for) seems to have been notable for the atrocity of the musical score by an "old-fashioned" composer[5] and by the number of distinguished figures who sent regrets for absence. These included the Prince of Wales, Tennyson,

---

[2] From a letter of Richard Garnett to Lady Shelley, December 14, 1888, in the Abinger Collection. No doubt this suggestion matched Sir Percy's inclination.

[3] See Wilfred Partington, *Forging Ahead: The True Story of the Upward Progress of Thomas James Wise, Prince of Book Collectors, Bibliographer Extraordinary and Otherwise* (New York, 1939).

[4] It was performed on Friday, May 7, at the Grand Theater, Croydon, with Hermann Vezin as Count Cenci. Browning, Meredith, and the Shelleys were present. The play was widely and variously reviewed, even the Paris *Figaro* noticing it in its *Supplément Littéraire,* and the *New York World* heading its report "a Remarkable Performance." Browning wrote to Alma Murray on the following day, praising the "admirable impersonation" by that "Poetic Actress without a rival." (Shelley Society Notebook, 1886.)

[5] Dr. W. C. Sellé, who set the choruses to music. This was generally condemned, even by the committee, and copies of the score were sold off cheap to members. In every way a sell!

Matthew Arnold, Meredith, Gladstone, Swinburne, Prince Lucien Bonaparte, and Sir Percy and Lady Shelley.[6] Among those who did attend were Oscar Wilde, Browning, H. Rider Haggard, and Mrs. Eliza Lynn Lynton.

Branches, complete with honorary secretaries, are suddenly reporting progress—like the Seven Churches of Asia—in the Society's Notebook. Or sometimes Hon. Secretaries with a very bare branch; such as the professor in charge at Cambridge, Massachusetts, where "the dispersion of people which takes place here in the summer has prevented my obtaining any new members for the Society." New York lags also, but as far afield as Melbourne, Australia, "a healthy and vigorous branch" rides out the criticism of stuffy theologians. For all this, "Why a Shelley Society?" is continually being asked. It is not sufficient, after all, that Stopford Brooke should say, "It is our humor" (not, be it noted, meaning humor in the sense of fun); not enough, either, that the founder's father should be Shelley's friend. As to this, the inaugural meeting has heard a word or two. Here was the visiting poet from Marlow taking only a dish of milk and a piece of bread as he sat on the counter of his surgeon, Mr. Furnivall, who really preferred Pope. The phrase, "By Jove I will; he was my father's friend," reaches the quick ears of Andrew Lang, who unluckily discovers blank verse in it. He uses it as the opening of a verse still blanker that records the initial session in over seventy lines, of which we give some samples:

> *"Why do not you a new communion found—*
> *" 'Shelley Society' might be the name—*
> *"Where men might worry over Shelley's bones?"*
> *"By Jove, I will! he was my father's friend,"*
> *Said Furnival; and lo, the thing was done!*
>
> . . .
>
> *"A thoughtful and most temperate address"*
> *Was Stopford Brooke's, who, as we learn with grief*
> *From the reporter of this merry fit,*
> *"Knocked Mr. Matthew Arnold out of time."*

[6] As this is nearly two years before Garnett's cautionary letter, it suggests that the Shelley heirs were already thinking along his lines. Lady Shelley no doubt felt a sense of rivalry; she was anxious to remain the one official propagator of the poet's name and works.

The dish-of-milk anecdote limps in, and a guess at the poet's "pious socialism";

> *Then these weird figures went their several ways,*
> *All the Society of Shelleyites . . .*[7]

But members *were* told that another reason for the founding was to debate and discuss the by-no-means accepted and established ideas of Shelley himself.

Punch, that organ of Tory respectability, for which radical poets and plays on incest were equally fair game, had its own "humor," and its doubts "as to the *raison d'être* of that apparently quite unnecessary body." *Punch* was resigned, augustly, to believing that "from time to time some such eruptions of dilettantism as that of which the Shelley Society is an average specimen, are inevitable, and that whenever they occur, there will be a temporary upheaval of nobodies." After damning the *Cenci* performance in hard prose, it proceeded to burlesque it in stanzas that we shall quote, excusably, as being less accessible than Browning's original inspiration:

Atrabilia

> *And did you once see SHELLEY'S play?*
> *And did you really sit it through?*
> *Nor at the Tenth Act sneak away?—*
> *How strange it seems and new!*
>
> *There are plays a many, mostly decent,*
> *You'd feel no sense of nausea after;*
> *I can't help wondering you were present—*
> *My wonder moves your laughter?*
>
> *I stopped at a book-stall in the City;*
> *The name of the street I clean forget;*
> *But the spot itself—the more's the pity—*
> *Lives in my brain-pan yet.*
>
> *For there I picked up, just to charm a*
> *Minute away in mental quest,*
> *A morbid drama, a nasty drama!*
> *Well—I prefer the rest.*

[7] Published in the *Saturday Review,* March 13, 1886.

Glancing through the first Shelley Society Notebook, we may pick out sundry items: Dr. Furnivall protests that it is not Matthew Arnold, but "that respectable person Mr. J. Cordy Jeaffreson" whom he has called "a Philistine of the Philistines." Henry S. Salt is writing a Shelley Primer. The Hon. Secretary thanks T. J. Wise for his help with the seating of the *Cenci* audience (a harmless, almost a pastoral, employment for the villain concerned). *The Cenci* stimulates membership, which touches on 350. The performance of *Hellas* brings a grave financial loss. (Ominous, this note). Mr. F. S. Ellis appeals to members for help in editing a concordance lexicon to Shelley's poetry. (This was a big task duly carried out, to the enrichment of Shelley bibliography.) Or we may follow the comments of George Bernard Shaw, an early member and a regular attendant who never left without enlivening the discussions. Shaw—the essential puritan—has no use for *The Cenci,* which is "simply an abomination," and "as bad a piece of work as a man of Shelley's genius could be capable of." He regards *Queen Mab* as far superior. Shelley here shows "a remarkable grasp of facts, anticipating also the modern view that sociological problems are being slowly worked out independently of the conscious interference of man." Discussing *The Revolt of Islam,* Shaw says, "A poem ought to be didactic, and ought to be in the nature of a political treatise." He is himself the perfect Fabian who cares more for Socialism than for art. His choice is Shelley the conspirator, not Shelley the poet. The latter he would readily tear for his bad verses, which get in the way of the maxims.[8]

The Notebooks, crammed as they are with the Society's practical politics, yet omit the troubles behind the scenes. For these we may go again to W. M. Rossetti.[9] Again, after all these years, the "Alpha and Omega" that Mary so complained of, is money—the want of it. The Society has issued too much literature for the subscription of one guinea to cover the cost of it. A debt to the printer accumulates, the issue of books is restricted, and membership accordingly falls off. Funds come in towards a second performance of *The Cenci.* Difficulties over theater and cast delay the production, and when all is

[8] On one of his typical postcards, Shaw, in answer to a query about his part in the discussions, warned me to beware of the reporting of the Shelley, New Shakespeare, and Browning societies, all of which was often inaccurate. He was himself one of the worst, perhaps *the* worst, of sufferers.

[9] *Some Reminiscences.*

fixed, hey presto! the money has gone—swallowed in general expenses, especially in paying the printer. Even so he remains a creditor; the Society is now "woefully impecunious," a few committee members have to meet the deficit. The decline becomes a fall; "our meetings dwindled to a mere figure-head," says Rossetti—who has paid up to the tune of £120. In gloom and ignominy the flashing inauguration staggers to its defeat. Dissolved officially in 1895, the Society is wound up and the last liabilities only settled in November, 1902.

> *Then these weird figures went their several ways,*
> *All the Society of Shelleyites.*

Lang's doggerel, penned so lightheartedly after the launching, takes on sinister shadows as this company of devotees, like the musicians in Haydn's *Farewell Symphony,* successively lay down their instruments, to leave a couple of wind-players piping plaintively of finance before they turn out the last desk light and steal thoughtfully away.

❦ 11 ❧

It should be clear now why we met the fanfares cautiously and declined to place Shelley's reputation in the hands of the Shelley Society to be safe forevermore. Indeed, human fallibility is never more evident than when judging human permanence and safety. There has been a swifter, more dramatic instance, but without the bombast, in our own time. We are with the relics again—relics of Keats and Shelley that began, in 1943, to seem gravely endangered in the Rome Museum, where, after the Badoglio armistice, the Piazza di Spagna was under German shellfire. The story is a modern classic, already much retold: how the closest treasures were removed for safekeeping to the Monte Cassino Monastery and, in the irony of its special destruction, were smuggled out boldly by the archivist, Don Mauro Inguanez, as his personal baggage in a German staff car, and returned to Rome.[10]

If relics are symbols, then this incident is symbolic of what happens to an indestructible Shelley. He will not be regulated by the plans of any coterie, sect, or association that believes it is helping

[10] See *Keats, Shelley, and Rome.*

him to immortality, or by any individual devilry that wants him cursed. For the moment he has seized our own pen as a battering ram to knock down the last barriers of chronology and destroy some grandiose mansions "built of haze." What of the centenary celebrations, for example? Horsham, birthplace of the poet, August, 1892. Attended by the epoch's literati, with a rousing address by Edmund Gosse. How the names reverberate with a creaking chime! Frederic Harrison, Roden Noel, Henry Arthur Jones, Richard le Gallienne, H. S. Salt, William Watson, Alma Murray of *Cenci* notability, William Archer, G. Bernard Shaw (to criticize), and T. J. Wise (to conceal his cloven hoof). A memorial plaque to be erected, a local museum and library to be formed. "Look on my works, ye mighty"—or prick the air bubble with G. B. Shaw. What, he asked, is this buffoonery but another genteel conspiracy to submerge a rascal in a spate of words? But then we have to prick Shaw's bubble, too; Shaw who walked out of that worshipful assembly in Sussex to attend a proletarian gathering in the East End of London, where he might establish that *Queen Mab* was still known as the Chartist's Bible, and join a community that claimed Shelley as a fellow Socialist and ignored his verse. G. B. S., strenuously confining art and poesy to humanity's nursery, is something of a Shelley without the lyre. Even those hardy influential figures Sidney and Beatrice Webb, with not an hour to spare for idle poetry and scarcely a feature molded into charm, have some traceable drops of Shelley's blood in them.

What is truth? The Horsham celebration—formal, fund-getting, stiff with personalities binding Shelley to a classic pose? The proletarian faction using him, like Richard Carlile and his earlier Chartists, as a finger-post to socialism and the emergent labor movement? The Shelley Society a burnt-out meteorite choked by its own ash. At the same time, lecturers talking on him up and down the country; writers—so many of them that to pursue them has become impractical. Newman I. White, who would never allow that matters could go beyond his ability to contain them (though he gives only two years to the Shelley Society), prints an alphabetical saga of the late Victorian commentators, from Mrs. Angeli and Arnold to G. E. Woodberry and Yeats. There are many more, especially if we bring in the verse writers.

By now the English-speaking world has no monopoly—except

Monument to Percy Bysshe Shelley in Christchurch Priory, Hampshire

Engraved by G. Stodart from the group by H. Weekes, A.R.A.

insofar as Shelley himself held, in his *Defence of Poetry,* that a translated poem was dead. The Shelley Society Notebooks show W. M. Rossetti—who stands out as a man of bone and sinew amid voluble ghosts—in correspondence with two French Shelleyans: T. Rabbé, who in 1886 sends the first installment of his three-volume *traduction française de Shelley* to be preceded by a biographical and critical study; and Gabriel Sarrazin, who has joined the Society's committee and extends its vision by news of two German scholars. One is Otto Schlapp of Strasbourg, *"qui s'est épris de Shelley d'une façon toute particulière et le révèle à ses camarades d'Université."* The other is Mme H. Druskowitz of Berlin, who has published a critical biography in 1884. Germany has translated *Prometheus, The Cenci,* and *Queen Mab (Feenkönigin");* France, *The Cenci* and *Hellas.* Italy, land of his final choice for life and of his unchosen death, has, in this epoch of its own romantics D'Annunzio and Carducci, taken Shelley uncritically to its heart. The angelic figure has been given another twist in Carducci's much publicized epithet, *"Spirito di titano entro virginee forme."*[11] More practically, several of his lyrics are translated between the sixties and the nineties, *The Cenci* (Ettore Sanfelice) and *Julian and Maddalo* (Carlo Faccioli) in 1892. A more notable interpreter, the poet Adolfo de Bosis, associates himself particularly with Shelley, presenting *La Sensitiva, I Cenci, Prometeo Liberato,* and *Inno alla Belleza Intellettuale* before the end of the century. (It will be noted how the "incestuous" full-blooded *Cenci* is picked out by all three countries as an early choice. Apart from other preference, it is easier than most to translate.) We can even find Greek renderings of *Love's Philosophy* and a part of *Adonais* in 1885; but the Athenians, appropriate though it would have been to their lifelong worshiper, have no hand in it: these academics are Oxford University men.

Our bird's-eye view of Shelley abroad at the turn of the century can give no more than a hint how well he travels; how—while his home-advocate Lady Shelley goes in 1899 to join her son and his moldered heart in the family vault at Bournemouth,[12]—Shelley on

---

[11] "A Titan's spirit in a virgin's shape." Contrast this with the German of Herwegh: "An elfin spirit in a man's body." The two could hardly be more opposite; another instance of Shelley's being all things to all men according to their preference.

[12] The *Bournemouth Observer & Visitor's List* for June 28, 1899, reported: "The late Lady Shelley, who was in her 79th year, had for some time previous to her death been a great

swift and conquering wing is flying out over Europe, having long since been caught for analysis and criticism in the United States of America.

His behavior as a time traveler—now that we have followed him through eight decades—should emerge more clearly from this eminence of the changing reign and century. Down in the heat and noise it was shadowed by arguments and rivalries—sects and individuals assessing from their own wildly differing standpoints and bending their judgment of the poet to suit with these. The significant fact is that something of Shelley can be seen from all these angles. It is positive evidence of a mental and spiritual extension along so many lines that the poet, the critic, the scientist, the classical scholar, the politician—as well as, undefeatedly, the moralist—find him on their territory. What is more, they find him there in no rigid or exclusive capacity. As a poet he can be made to answer most requirements from transcendentalism to naturalism; as a thinker he is both classicist and romantic, as a radical he is alike impassioned and hardheaded. As a scientist he is imaginative and exact. His polemic is applauded, mocked, or doubted, not without justification for each view. His very phraseology may be admired for its resource and ornament, disliked for its extravagance; and again, both approved for directness and censured for savagery. No wonder there is room—and always will be —for every sort of critic to tackle him!

So with his personality. We have seen him interpreted variously, from the noblest to the nastiest of characters. He has been judged as a man of bold action, as incompetent milksop, as most lovable, most despicable, as the most loyal of friends, the worst betrayer. The bigots condemn his atheism, the fanatics impale him on a monolith,

---

sufferer; but those who knew her most intimately could not but admire her great kindness of heart and practical sympathy for those who were in want or distress. She was always ready to help those who appealed to her, and the public of Bournemouth, particularly those resident in the Boscombe district, will ever have cause to remember the generosity and readiness with which she in recent years handed over the care of a good stretch of cliffland abutting on her estate for the benefit of the public."

On July 1, the same paper reported: "Immediately after burial of her husband, the deceased lady had her own name affixed to the stone covering the vault, but it has always been covered with a brass plate, which will now be removed, and the date of the death added." There follows a list of mourners and officiators. The funeral service was conducted in part by the Bishop of Southwark, and in part by her brother-in-law, Canon F. St. John, of Gloucester. "The coffin was placed by the side of that containing the remains of the late Sir Percy Shelley."

the perceptive find in him a deep sense of religion and world order. All things to all people—a chameleon only in the sense of changing form and color according to the lens that examines him. Of the theories, myths, and movements that have grown up around Shelley in these after-years of "progress," none has contained and bound him finally. His spirit has tended—as we noticed when discussing the Pre-Raphaelites—to attach itself to whichever mind or movement leads the vanguard. And when that movement, child of its own age, stiffens into formalism, Shelley is found to be out of it, free as the skylark for the next adventure, now that the "heavy weight of hours" and the imprisonment of the tortured flesh no longer, as in his lifetime, hold it back. It is only with the twentieth century that the "modern" schools reject him as old-fashioned. We shall return to them shortly and suggest a reason or two.

"*Let us see the truth, whatever that may be. The destiny of man can scarcely be so degraded, that he was born only to die.*" Shelley wrote that to Horace Smith nine days before his drowning. At the same time, in his boat on the treacherous waters of the Bay of Lerici, he was composing his unfinished enigmatic final lines where, under the defiant title of *The Triumph of Life,* little clue emerges beyond the terrible mortality even of great spirits such as Plato, Voltaire, Bacon, the "grim Feature" who was once Rousseau, and the world conqueror whom opportunity had carried to the peak

> *From which a thousand climbers have before*
> *Fallen, as Napoleon fell.*

Yet in the visions of a submerged Rousseau is promise; Shelley's obsession here, we suspect, is not that of his American disciple Edgar Allan Poe:

> *. . . the play is the tragedy "Man,"*
> *And its hero the Conqueror Worm.*

The proud and revolutionary spirits are defeated, not by corruption, but by an opposite force:

> *For in the battle Life and they did wage*
> *She remained conqueror.*

277

Have we a key here to the riddle and contradiction? Does not life claim "all that is mortal of great Plato" and the other transcendent spirits that in the upshot they—as Keats who "is made one with Nature"—shall be a part of vision and creation, strengthening the spirit—a spirit of love, as Shelley sees it—that cannot be quenched in a world of evils and destruction? "Then what is life? I cried." It may be that Shelley's own posthumous persistence is presenting us with an answer to the riddle and an understanding of the poem. If so, our survey of his progress after "all that is mortal" has gone down, results in something very like this triumph of life, of vision, of creative passion, and of the love that is co-existent with the universe but remains unsatisfied by earthly shapes.

❧{ III }❦

Triumph, so long after death and disappointment, might be expected to proclaim finality. But we are not dealing here with saints and martyrs; at this far end of the vista we have something other, something less solemn but of no small importance in assessing Shelley: we have now a new prospect, of the twentieth century, and the hastiest glance along it brings the cold conclusion that all positives must have their negatives, and if there is triumph, there is also, at the hands of his living examiners, depreciation. We profit only partially from the labors of our predecessors; research workers (as they now like to be labeled) of the century beyond Shelley's set to work in a way that differs in particulars, but in general behavior carries on the process much as we have seen it operating.

There is of course one main, initial difference: Shelley begins this period as a "classic" (the pride of an Oxford edition arrives in 1904). For the critics building their own reputations it is bolder and more profitable to attack—"debunk"—than to accept any favorable verdict given by the Victorians. Besides, the natural reaction of the years encourages it. *Their* line is easy; but the biographers have either to present new detail, a new outlook, or recapitulate in tabloid form. The hugest biography (in physical weight: six pounds) ever produced on a Romantic poet was Newman Ivey White's two-volume *Shelley*—encyclopedic, comprehensive, charged with annotations and appendices; nearing (but never quite achieving) the last word on the material side. Almost a Shelley Society in itself, it stands in danger of being used—at least by scholars in its country of origin—as a first-and-last textbook superseding everyone and everything. England has tended to by-pass the mountain except as an excuse for overthrowing White's American predecessor Walter Peck. For a single brain it is an awesome product; the unavoidable handicap to such a scheme is Shelley's propensity to avoid, after a trial or two, cohabitation with his monuments. At the other pole, Edmund Blunden's so-called "popular" biography is the work of a poet and illuminates a congenial spirit. The correspondence of Sir Timothy with his two solicitors was combed by Roger Ingpen for numbers of odd, corroborative details that give the family frictions from Sir Timothy's side. *Shelley in England,* freely drawn on in this chronicle, was thrown out in clumsy format in the year 1917, and half swamped at the outset by the novel element of a first world war, but it provided pickings for all subsequent pens.

Mary's fortunes were again the more spectacular; from being the successful playwright, she was to be adopted by the youngest art (or entertainment) form, by having her *Frankenstein* filmed for the general picture-goer. (The public even learned, through this means, that the man, and not the monster, was called Frankenstein—a mistake that those who used the symbol, having never read the novel, had made invariably.) Mary, after Mrs. Julian Marshall's Boscombe product, was to have her several recorders, English and American, and to see some indiscretions of the heart torn from their context to be boldly flaunted. She, with Leigh Hunt, Peacock, and her father Godwin, earn their biographies through their own distinction. Edward Williams lives for us through his journal, now, after Garnett's ragged effort, published in a complete text. But a new line is open to the twentieth-century student: that is, to biographize the biographers, or trace out the complete lives of Shelley's friends. These careers, begun (bar the Pirate's) in decent, variant obscurity and ending usually like a clock run down, have all a central portion where their destinies touch Shelley's; so we are given recurrence and repetition of some part of the Shelleyan story, each time with a different figure posed in the foreground. It is noticeable, too, that these flanking personalities are, like Brutus and his fellow conspirators, honorable men (or women). There is no debunking, no attacking. Three separate portraits of Trelawny allow the Pirate all his dash and enterprise; we have the history of Claire Clairmont, and the brief life of Allegra. (In all these Byron hovers, a hooded hawk, in the middle distance. If anything remains yet to be grappled with wholly, it is the mutual influence, aesthetic and personal, of these two poets.)

Surviving the full disclosure of his falsifications, T. J. Hogg comes into prominence with his romantic novel *Prince Alexy Haimatoff* (decked with alluring pictures), his letters to Jane Williams, and a biographical study worthy in length and honor of a cabinet minister or a judge. Hogg, who was expelled with Shelley, tried Harriet's virtue, flirted with Mary, cohabited with Jane, and distorted his friend's portrait in a manner all his own, has taken the stage as an honorable Athenian—or very nearly, but that no degree of worship and devotion will conceal the lathes and wires that bind him to his greater, nor the contortions behind his posture as an upright man. When all is said, he has his virtues, and there is a funny side to his rogueries.

Other figures of the Pisan circle struggle towards a moment's prominence: Dr. Polidori—no fine character, but the uncle of W. M. Rossetti—kept a diary;[13] so too did the Gisbornes. Count Taaffe, the Irishman, is found to have a background, not so unromantic;[14] the full story of Emilia (who was really Teresa) Viviani is given in Italian by a member of the family.[15] The unpublished diary of Captain Daniel Roberts, who both built and refloated the *Don Juan*, lies restively in the Keats-Shelley Museum at Piazza di Spagna, Rome, and may be expected to appear in print. Mrs. Mason is liable to come under the microscope; Elizabeth Hitchener, the Brown Demon, has excited some inquiries; Harriet Westbrook is under a close scrutiny and the mystery of her death comes up again. Take Shelley away from all these persons and their record makers: What remains? The traditional quandary—Socrates missing from the Athenian Grove, *Hamlet* without the Prince of Denmark, or, astronomically, the solar system cheated of its sun. "We degenerated apace" . . . Trelawny said it;

---

[13] *The Diary of Dr. John William Polidori, 1816*, edited and elucidated by William Michael Rossetti (London, 1911).

[14] See C. L. Cline, *Byron, Shelley, and Their Pisan Circle*.

[15] Enrica Viviani della Robbia, *Vita di una Donna (L'Emily di Shelley)* (Florence, 1936).

under all his posturings he felt something, and occasionally the truth
slipped out.

⚜ IV ⚜

Coming back, then, from these planetary epicycles, we find Shelley
somewhat as he has been throughout the nineteenth century—subject
of much study and more argument; used, especially in American
university circles, to provide a lively core for philosophical theses—
even, we may put it, as the selected guinea pig in an inquiry (to take
one example) on the treatment of Plato by Romantic poets. Bio-
graphically a new myth has arisen, based, to be sure, on an incident
well known last century as "the Hoppner scandal." Led by the
Boscombe school, biographers did not easily desert their Harriet
pickings for this doubtful prey. The Shelleys' disclaimer of a revenge-
ful libel was allowed to stand, and the incident was often cited merely
for duplicity on Byron's part. Unfortunately for its state of suspended
animation, Newman I. White in 1936 pursued the hunt to the State
Archives of Naples, where birth, baptismal, and death registrations
made of the hypothetical infant a first-class mystery. The hoary
Hoppner scandal, under its new name of Elena Adelaide Shelley (as
the child was registered) attracts the chatter of the century, with
lively speculation concerning Claire as mother, Shelley as father, the
altering of birth dates or of death place, the ignorance or connivance
of Mary, the chances-of-an-adoption theory, a surviving infant, and
an unknown woman who has followed Shelley to Naples and there
died. Fresh young inquirers thrash around it and about, supposing,
speculating, giving evidence for this and doubts for that solution, till
they turn away baffled, content to seal off their loose ends with the
balm of some genial philosophy from Shelley's verse.[16]

For the moment, this Elena Adelaide mystery—unless some
further document comes out—is as incapable of settlement as the old
Harriet problem. Its eruption is unfortunate, since it has given the
twentieth century a new excuse for focusing on Shelley's sexual
aspect. Naturally, White and his successors may retaliate: "Let us see
the truth, whatever that may be." What truths are these that the

[16] See especially Ivan Roe, *Shelley: The Last Phase* (London, 1953).

scholars are always looking for? How much, in the long run, do these personalia count? Up to a point, by all means let us have them, to help in interpreting our Romantic poets. The affair of Annette Vallon did shed a light on Wordsworth. We should not overlook how Coleridge's first love, Mary Evans, was supplanted by that pantisocratic domestic square dance arranged by Southey with the Fricker sisters. Hazlitt, poor fellow, gave away his own obsession with the landlady's daughter. His friends were all ashamed of him, but we have *Liber Amoris* as our heritage. Again, the friction between Meredith and Peacock's daughter must be noted, as begetting the sonnet cycle *Modern Love*. The letters of Keats to Fanny Brawne, that caused an outcry, had to be before us: so much of the dying poet's diseased psychology was in them.

And so with Shelley. Apart from Mary, we have always had to scrutinize Harriet Westbrook, watch Jane Williams, remember Cornelia Turner and Emilia Viviani. The research student who shall prove that Shelley the man and poet was affected, even transiently, by this matter of Elena Adelaide, born in Naples and dying there aged fifteen months—or possibly not dying—will again have justified this type of inquiry. We admit it with reluctance, after our journey through the shoals of the nineteenth century. We laugh—and we have to emulate. Here is a symbol or example of that triumph of life which is also the despair of hope that Shelley the poet may ever be judged for his vision in all purity. The nineteenth century is too near to us, and, thanks to the processes we have been watching here, it will never recede except by the poet's submergence. We can read Shelley's ancestor Sir Philip Sidney for his verse alone; the biographical line is broken, the circumstances are remote. But these Romantics, though they came before mechanization, large-scale industry, and atomic science had changed the surface of our conscious experience, are like ourselves. Their minds are essentially our minds, and, whatever extravagance they might use in verse, their everyday language expresses nothing alien or distant. One has only to read through Shelley's Italian letters to be struck by that.

The nineteenth-century critics of pure literature went beyond their scope to carp at Shelley's morality. Those of the twentieth, anxious to throw overboard all that was once termed philosophy, find (as we shall be seeing soon) that they cannot reject his ideas and approve his poetry. They, too, are biased arbiters, in a quandary because their own limitations prompt them to reject too much. A new generation will make new adjustments, but it seems unlikely that we shall ever acquire enough detachment to arrive at a final unchanging estimate of Shelley's position. His survival, then, may be a triumph with bitterness in it, but it is undoubtedly and, it would seem, unalterably, life.

To return from this digression, it became impossible for the twentieth century to have done with the old talk either. When Leslie Hotson found and published *The Lost Letters to Harriet* in 1930, the "world"—at least of England and America—was shaken. The discovery was so sensational that it sounded like one more literary fake. In fact, the thing was too bold for the fakers; neither T. J. Wise nor Major Byron would have dared to fabricate it. They worked on cautious lines. The location of these wanted letters in a remote department of Chancery was either the start of a romantic fiction or, what in solemn truth it was, a "find." For Lady Shelley and her Boscombe school it was lucky enough that they were hidden. They have been read and discussed by an era that can more easily take the shock. They do no direct good to Shelley's character—unless it be good that they help to kill the Arnold-Curran legend and install the "blackguard" theme which is on its way to us. He says hard things of Harriet—harder than any English gentleman should be expected to put down in writing to his wife. But then—oddly, it may be—Shelley no more set out (though heir to a baronetcy) to pose as an English gentleman than as an innocent angel. He was a trapped man in desperate love and driven to extremes of speech and action. As the letters show, his behavior, quixotic and naïve in some respects, is truly and tragically human. If it is a mercy that the twentieth and not the nineteenth century saw these letters, that is because, among more doubtful traits of progress, we have to some degree exchanged an ethical righteousness for the science of psychology. (This too, as we shall see, can be a danger.) But in England a tough core of Victorianism survived through the Edwardian to the Georgian epoch. And in America the breath of scandal, even conveyed by so dignified a medium as the *Atlantic Monthly* (which published the *Lost Letters*), proved soon enough that interpretive studies of the poet and thinker took a relatively low place in the public's favor as compared with food for gossip.

France, which we saw translating and interpreting Shelley with close sympathy, comes into the international picture as providing another landslide. From that country, notable for its academic studies of the English romantics, had come Professor A. Koszul's remarkable *La Jeunesse de Shelley* (1910)—a biographical study that stands out, for the discriminating, beyond the barriers of time and territory. But what the greater world scoops up, re-reads and recommends, is not *La Jeunesse,* a work of scholarship, but André Maurois' *Ariel, La Vie de Shelley,* a commercial tale. In *Ariel,* with its phenomenally wide diffusion and translation, we have the third companion to the Curran portrait and the Arnold angel. Maurois, in writing a biography of that phantom, has proved deplorably that, no matter what truth the critics may be after, the general fiction-reading, film-going, television-watching public craves a story. So, too, it may be argued, did the Elizabethan playgoer, and picked out the story element in Shakespeare. That did no harm: the poetry was spoken, whether or not the audience cared to hear it. But from *Ariel* the real poet is absent. There exist now countless thousands in America, in England, and in Germany (maybe France knows better) who on hearing the name of Shelley will eagerly refer to *Ariel* and believe they have it all. (Some, no doubt, think Maurois has invented him.) Nothing quite comparable has happened to any other poet—the almost occult materialization of a following phantom, born of the portrait, the epithet, and the book. All that is wanting is a theme song or "Shelley Symphony" on the lines of the *Warsaw Concerto* or the *Rhapsody in Blue.*

This may yet follow—for Shelley does trail some odd appendages. In America several young male and female students, one is credibly informed, believe themselves to be reincarnations. Another of these *revenants* may or may not be Elinor Wylie, whose curious poetic fiction, *The Orphan Angel,* portrayed the poet rescued from drowning by an American brig, and enjoying divers picaresque adventures in the New World. A lady medium has claimed to be in contact with the spirit of Shelley and published some vague messages. They are less cunning than some of Major Byron's bygone but still dangerous products. A more material and satisfying tribute to the poet's memory is the "Hotel Shelley e delle Palme" at Lerici, where those who clatter past the Casa Magni in touristical coaches pull in for a substantial lunch. On its restaurant walls they may see modern frescoes that include a weak Shelleyan figure posed—perhaps in reminiscence of

Joseph Severn's poet amongst the ruins a century earlier—in a romantic setting of the local bay.

None of this harlequinade need disturb us greatly; but when serious-minded interpreters begin rearranging the known counters into the shape of a new myth, it is time to wonder a little. As we write, the latest theory, built on no firmer basis than a browsing speculation, concerns Mary and Hogg. A very young Mary, as we know, wrote some naively affectionate letters to Jefferson, whom, in accordance with a "share-out" principle, she was trying to love while Claire walked out with Shelley. We are to suppose now, says the new mythologist, that Hogg then seduced the unmarried Mary, who had a child by him; that Shelley was not told until the Italian months of 1818 when there was serious trouble between him and Mary, as reflected in his poetry and in her prose;[17] that, finally, the fruit of this union was none other than little William, who was to die in 1819 leaving Shelley, no less than Mary, inconsolable:

> *Where art thou, my gentle child?*
> *Let me think thy spirit feeds,*
> *With its life intense and mild,*
> *The love of living leaves and weeds*
> *Among these tombs and ruins wild;—*
> *Let me think that through low seeds*
> *Of sweet flowers and sunny grass*
> *Into their hues and scents may pass*
> *A portion—*

A portion . . . Shelley ceases, almost to resume the broken image two years later, moved by the same pure elegaic spirit for another too early buried among those tombs and ruins:

> *He is a portion of the loveliness*
> *Which once he made more lovely—*

And—for those who distrust poetic sublimation—the day after William's death he had written to Peacock, "It seems to me as if,

[17] Elizabeth Nitchie, in her *Mary Shelley, Author of "Frankenstein,"* examines the unpublished story "Mathilda" for its autobiographical evidence of Mary's rift with Shelley. She does not suggest a cause.

hunted by calamity as I have been, that I should never recover any cheerfulness again." Is it possible to twist this pure emotion and make Shelley's grief over the son for whose safety he left England a complex, tainted matter? Is there any hint that he was mourning with embittered sorrow the loss of one who had never been his own?

There comes a point where critics and interpreters tie themselves into the knots of their own patterns, even with the best of motives. They would tie their readers, too. It becomes urgent, sometimes, to break free of all this clever apocrypha and return, as far as may be, to the poet himself.

❈ v ❈

The question for this century must be how far the poet can be read for pleasure or provide any deep satisfaction to the spirit that pervades the age. To this we can give no final or even hasty answer, only attempt to grope for certain directives. There has been, in both Europe and America, reaction against all romanticism, with a phase, especially after the first world war, of revolt from the expression of natural beauty, in favor of a dry attempt at "realism," or a still more exclusive effort at "*sur*realism." Painting reduced its subject to a matter of lines and cubes and angles; music fled from the melodic line and the rich harmony to a cacophonous arrangement of pure sounds. Poetry became a pattern of sparse words supercharged with an impacted meaning. The intellectuals practicing this austerity could not for long impose it, but they did disseminate a spirit of opposition to all that seemed lush, extravagant, obscure, and overloaded. This fault can readily be found in Shelley's longer works—especially when skimmed hastily as one reads a news sheet. To the general reader in both England and America, Shelley's cosmic imagery has made some of his urgent, revolutionary subjects seem remote and almost suffocated by their trappings. It goes deeper than a passing fashion. As we have seen, the public never took to Shelley as popular reading. If the poet was only in advance of his age, we should be walking with him now without a stumble. It is certain enough that in his longer works there is a barrier—not so impassable as Blake's, but calling for patient penetration and not invariably rewarding. He is by far the most "difficult" of the Romantics. Byron wrote racy novels in verse; Keats is unreadable only where the flowers grow lush and sickly with overcrowding and decay; Wordsworth (unlike Dryden's estimate of Shadwell) in his worst moods deviates into sense on a highly intelligible plane of dullness; and nothing in Coleridge, whose poetry is nearly all creative, is one-tenth so hard to grasp as Shelley at his densest—Shelley when he appears set to "build a haze."

So, while the arid postwar phase passed over, it did leave a new freedom to reject what honesty could not swallow, and refrain from kissing the toe of every sanctified priest. Then, too, the very fact that Shelley had become a university study and school textbook was enough to scare the ever suspicious pupil, who rarely if ever reads for relaxation what has been handed out to him as a task.[18] The anthologist, however, has found plentiful material in the shorter lyrics; so, too, has the song writer, and, we may add, the translator. If the Continent still puts Byron first in popularity, Shelley is a regular study in French, German, and Italian universities; nor have two wars prevented the appearance of critical studies in Germany, besides translations.[19] Italy has her own more personal interest in her visitant, surviving a reaction that swept him away for a period with D'Annunzio and all he stood for; with Carducci's Titan in a virgin's shape. After the second world war a new, more critical, soberly based appreciation begins to draw Shelley out of the shadows again. The Keats-Shelley Memorial House in Rome is in itself a center of study. A new Italian translation appeared in 1947, and a notable critical work in 1951.[20] His fame began to penetrate farther east. Already in the eighties and nineties Chinese translations of *To a Skylark* had been made, and some passages from the preface to *Alastor* translated into Japanese. For some time the *Skylark* and *The Cloud* continued as the

18 The latest policy in planning English school editions of poets is to avoid giving any editorial lead that may bias the pupil either way. An excellent course in theory, but doubtful of success in practice. Even advanced classes may find difficulty in forming their own judgment, with the result that the middleman, or local teacher, will be driven to impose his own. And this may prove less balanced than the editor's.

19 My friend Fritz Schneider writes: "Our most gifted translators, Stefan George, Rainer Maria Rilke, do not seem to have attempted to translate Shelley. I can't think why." The answer may well lie in that same antipathy to romanticism that has characterized the twentieth-century intellectuals in England.

20 A translation of selected works with introduction by Roberto Ascoli, 1947. *P. B. Shelley*, by Elio Chinol (1951).

only poems presented to Japan, though fragments (not too accurate) of the life of Shelley and even Harriet chatter were beginning to seep through. From a general background of "Romantic poets" he was detached into individuality in the new century, and it is notable that twenty-nine poems were translated into Japanese in 1906.[21] Today all students of English literature study Shelley, who has his own authorities and collectors, outstanding amongst whom is Professor Takeshi Saito of Tokyo University.

But indeed, study of Shelley on the continent of Europe would repay the fortunate holder of a traveling scholarship. A big gulf will almost certainly be found between the attentions of the student and of the general book-borrowing public. The latter will often be content with the anthologized pieces—those unfortunately destined masterstrokes that are lifted from one anthology to another, together with any chance misreadings, without consulting the original source. Even in England the reader who besieges the libraries for the latest in fiction, travel, or biography, leaves the "classics" in his own tongue on the shelves, unless they are newly re-edited in attractive format. This is a penalty Shelley, with all Romantic and early or Mid-Victorian poets, pays for his official recognition. The best-seller and the work designed for posterity have rarely synchronized, and could only do so in an ideal state of culture hardly desirable in a working world. There is no real necessity for the factory hand or motor mechanic to be spouting Wordsworth, Shelley, or Coleridge, perhaps at the expense of his own job. In the long run, as we have seen in the course of this survey, it is the professional critics, the creative writers, and the universities— backed by enlightened publishers—who will mold and modify a reputation. Under the first we include, besides critical books, the higher journalism; and the last implies all students, scholars, and academics—present-day substitutes for monastic brotherhoods—who preserve the text besides interpreting it.

The creative writers are more slippery fish who judge in their own manner, perverse and individual, often letting impulse and prejudice be their guide. Where they are too egregious, they defeat their estimate: all Carlyle's splenetic rumblings have rolled harmlessly off Shelley, leaving no more than amusement at their overemphasis.

[21] I am indebted for these notes to a typescript thesis on "Shelley in Japan," by Shogoro Ogita. A shortened version of it was published in *Notes & Queries* (1951).

Some admire, like Browning, because their own consciousness is involved in the impact, and turn away for complex personal reasons. Some are plainly jealous; some guided by their own creative principles, little as these may apply in tune or time to the work they judge. The most perfect assessor is—or ought to be, for Matthew Arnold broke down on this rule—the creative artist who is also by profession a critic or analyst. We need only think of Coleridge on Shakespeare and be sorry that he did not know Shelley personally instead of swallowing scandal from the waspish Southey. A Coleridge living in our present era could, at this distance, have interpreted Shelley with imaginative sympathy free from bias.

We have no Coleridge. It is hard, in fact, to pick on any outstanding figures whose creative powers and critical acumen can stand up to the minds of that less turbid age. Our nearest to Coleridge is undoubtedly I. A. Richards, though he writes no poetry for publication and leans more heavily—as befits our epoch—towards the scientific approach. Richards, who is held to lead a "school of criticism," keeps his disciples guessing for the most part. He is nearly always a few moves ahead of them and, when they have crystalized his teaching into dogma, is found (very much like Shelley himself with the early radicals, Chartists, or Pre-Raphaelites) to have slipped out of it and preserved his independence. He is the one critic who can assess alike by contemporary and by ultimate valuations.[22]

Richards apart, the writers of most intellect and personality too often reject balance as a factor lowering to their sensation value. Thus we had Aldous Huxley, in the days of his irridescent semimaturity, shuffling responsibility on to one of his fictitious characters for what he might have liked to say himself—as a rebel from tutorage—of Shelley: "a mixture of fairy and white slug." Then we have T. S. Eliot, who accepts his own responsibility for both verse and criticism, but is no more disposed than Arnold was to check up on his personal bias. A glance at Eliot's attack on Shelley, and its sequel, will provide one strand at least of Shelleyan argument in the present age. In a lecture

22 Richards notes that interpretive skill in criticism, recovered at the time of the Romantics, was maintained throughout the nineteenth century. "Then came a sudden decline in performance. Twentieth-century criticism has been marked not so much by any enlightening reaction against the biased preference of the nineteenth century, as by the betrayal of general inability to read anything with safety on the part of most of those who have anything to say." *Coleridge on Imagination* (2nd. ed., London, 1950).

published as "The Use of Poetry and the Use of Criticism," in 1933, Eliot rejects Shelley as an adolescent. It is by no means a new theory among critics. "If I die tomorrow," Shelley himself had said when the shadow was on him, "I have lived to be older than my father." Those are his words, so memorable to Mary. They would dispose of the "perpetual adolescent" theory, but that the holders of it are incapable of believing that he knew—in the brain and on the pulses—what he was saying; knew it beyond doubt or hesitation, as a mature mind knows. Here, however, is Eliot's opinion:

"The ideas of Shelley seem to me always to be ideas of adolescence —as there is every reason why they should be. And an enthusiasm for Shelley seems to me also to be an affair of adolescence: for most of us, Shelley has marked an intense period before maturity, but for how many does Shelley remain the companion of age? . . . I find his ideas repellent—" and Eliot complains that he cannot separate Shelley from his ideas and beliefs or read the poetry without remembering the man. The man to him is "humorless, pedantic, self-centered, and sometimes almost a blackguard." Is it possible, he asks, to ignore the ideas and yet admire the poetry? Not, he decides, "for a reader of well-developed mind" for whom a "childish and feeble doctrine" may set up an almost complete check. Shelley, he declares, borrowed shabby ideas and muddled them up with his own intuitions.

Here, we may say, is the view of a twentieth-century "naughty-boy" Jeaffreson, equally bald and unmatured, but with a saving clause (if it is one), for he allows Shelley, with D. H. Lawrence, to "belong with the numbers of the great heretics of all times." Because Eliot is our contemporary and has been claimed as the father of modern verse, we stop to listen, and to look round for a contemporary answer. He is answered, three years later, by Herbert Read's essay, "In Defence of Shelley." The defense is as strange a one as ever a critic brought forward, and would have caused far greater horror to the Boscombe school than Eliot's carping. A poet who can only be defended in this fashion seems lost indeed. Read's approach is psychoanalytical—a term that has already passed the heyday of its fashion. The argument has been so ably summarized by an anonymous journalist reviewing Read that we can do no better than quote his exposition:

Certainly [Read says] Shelley was immature; moreover he was an unconscious and self-absorbed homosexual, who had fantasies about incest, and recurrent guilty delusions of persecution; he was incapable of taking a permanent interest in other people, or an objective view of the world; he lived in a universe of projections; and that is why he is such a good poet of his kind. Shelley's psychosis is . . . the ground of his special gifts—his generality, his rapidity, his unifying sweep. . . . "In the case of the incompletely adapted individual, his essential subjectivity will demand a more generalized kind of unity, in which there is no separation of the individual from the world at large." Thus when we know in one sense "the worst" about Shelley, we are in a position to appreciate the best.[23]

It is as well to know the worst, of course. Shelley suggested that the answer to his not being a great poet might be "guilty—death." The new suggestion is "innocent, but (psychoanalytically) insane." A "mad Shelley" we have had since his Eton days. It is ironical that we travel through so long a vista of analysis to reach as a peak of twentieth-century criticism an apparatus for dissecting the sick souls of poets! In Read's jargon of subjectivity and projections there is not even a clear argument. Whence and what is the guilt that causes "delusions of persecution"? How could a man whose friendships were undying be incapable of retaining an interest in people? (Do these theorists never read the letters?) As for the homosexual gibe, it leaves one suspecting a printer's error or slip of the pen—perhaps for *egocentric*. If we are to take it, for a moment, seriously, all the evidence refutes the bare suggestion. (There was, of course, Charles Kingsley, who gave us Beatrice Cenci as a Shelley in petticoats.) Who, then, are the women who attached themselves to a spirit never free of feminine webs? Do we look on them as factors in his universe of projections? Are these passionate survivors, lone and aging in their chilly world, only shadows? Shelley knew well enough that one must always be in love with something and plant one's visions in a human form. Where the flesh ends and the vision begins is a wonder that only mathematical minds would wish destroyed. If Shelley magnified, for a while, the women he loved, so too do less articulate worshipers; and it did not, in his case, preclude a physical urge. The fantasies here are of his

[23] The *Times Literary Supplement*, March 13, 1953, in an article on Read's *The True Voice of Feeling*, which contains the republished essay.

critic's making; the historian notes them only for their novelty. In all these years we had not yet had a homosexual, psychosis-ridden Shelley. Probably we shall not again have this phenomenon. The fashion for psychoses and the stress on homosexuality will decline and be outvoted by some newer jargon.

Attached to, or preceding, the Eliot outlook, there have been, in America, such critics as Paul Elmer More and Irving Babbitt, labeled the New Humanists, leading a revolt from Shelley that has not surprisingly been joined by F. R. Leavis and other products of a century suspicious of romantic richness. For their own guidance they have adopted a type of "poetic utterance" suitable for an age of ugliness, and are eager to dismiss all poetry whose language and aspirations are too lavish to be contained in it. Imagination has become "escapism." Frederick Pottle, in an illuminating essay on this modern attempt to denigrate Shelley, concludes that although liable to set the tone for years to come, it is wanting in final validity, truth, and candor.[4] "The New Critics," he affirms, "show a remarkable want of delicacy of touch in handling Shelley, and they too often misread the poems they condemn." I. A. Richards, also, finds "our Neo-Classic age . . . showing a fascinating versatility in travesty. And the poets of the 'Romantic' period provide for it what Shakespeare, Milton, and Donne were to the early eighteenth-century grammarians and emendators—effigies to be shot at because what they represent is no longer understood."[25]

Here, then, we have nothing new except the moment, and the particular arguments that make up the attack. To show Shelley's fame as being steadily on the increase until this modern clique reversed the tendency is to ignore the details of our longer view. Jeaffresons and Kingsleys had their followers; today we may honor Matthew Arnold as a critic but reject his dictum in this special case. Besides— returning to our new dictators—it means much that T. S. Eliot, in 1950, admitted to deriving "a new and more sympathetic appreciation of Shelley" from a book by an Italian philosopher.[26] This, in addition to showing that Eliot is not hidebound, raises a wider issue. The nine-

[24] "The Case of Shelley," in *PMLA*, Vol. LXVII, No. 5 (September, 1952).

[25] *Coleridge on Imagination*. Also quoted by Pottle, but I found it too apt to leave it out on that account.

[26] Pottle, "The Case of Shelley," in *PMLA*, Vol. LXVII, No. 5 (September, 1952), footnote. Attention is also drawn here to Eliot's "Talk on Dante" (1951), where *The Triumph of Life* is spoken of as "one of the supreme tributes to Dante in English, for it testifies to what Dante has done, both for the style and for the soul of a great English poet."

teenth-century Romantics who had flocked to Shelley had fallen away
in later years because their own conceptions had been immature. But
our younger critics of the atomic age may be hastily rejecting Shelley
for his indigestible factors, and come in their maturity to an estimate
based on calm discrimination. Because a poet has immortality in him,
he is not of necessity inviolate; nor can an epoch discount its own
experience. It can only, in the end, transcend the details of it. As
children of our age we have to admit that much of Shelley is not ours
"on the pulses," whether we call that his fault or our own. We cannot
plunge about in transcendentalism with comfort—perhaps because
practical science has captured so much from ethereal speculation. For
the first time mankind—complete with passports, baggage, and travel
tickets—may live for long hours in the upper air, above the clouds and
in them. We may write our own poetry on the wonder of it,[27] but we
are mentally uneasy in Shelley's fancied empyrean with its azure
gleams. So many stage effects are altered for us, since our eyes beheld
and our bodies felt their impact. "The magic car moves on" now gives
us the wrong image while we cling to our century; it is the image of
lumbering slowness, where Shelley was all speed. This is what
development ("progress" is not the word for it) has done for us; aery
conceptions become entangled with material notions, and the comic
or absurd shoots up where none was sewn. Shelley is not the only
sufferer; we all recall the unhappy line in *Kubla Khan*:

> *As if this earth in fast thick pants were breathing.*

In Coleridge's day it was meteorological and marvelous; now it suggests shrunken nether garments. Even Shakespeare is not secure: "The
isle is full of noises, Sounds, and sweet airs . . ." It has lost its magic
when we think of radios and loud speakers parked among the trees.

[27] See, for example, C. Day Lewis, *An Italian Visit* (New York, Harper and Brothers,
1953). The author describes in verse his flight to Rome:

> . . .
> *The clouds redouble, as nearer we climb,*
> *Their toppling fantasy. We skirt the fringe of icebergs,*
> *Diver under eiderdowns, disport with snowmen*
> *On fields of melting snow dinted by the wind's feet.*
> *Gleefully brush past atom-bomb cauliflowers,*
> *Frozen fluffs of spray from naval gunfire.*

It is not so far from Shelley, but every metaphor is securely earthbound. This makes it easier
for the present age.

The unknown has receded; to some degree we have become kings with no more worlds to conquer.

Yet this is to bind ourselves to the confines of our moment (like the watchers of television sitting in their fixed chairs). These period misadventures will never be enough to kill a poet. When Shelley awaited a verdict of posterity, he implied a posterity that could rise above the tumult and the shouting, alike of his and its own immediate age. He did not demand hysterical adulation, but he hoped for vision. In this study we have not been determining his final status; that may be undefinable, except by a process of mathematical ratios and averages, yielding a mean (if not a meaningless) result. What we do claim to have pictured is his immortality, not in the sense of godhead or impregnability, but on the grounds of staying power. We have seen enough, in 130 years, to know that he outrides exclusive movements, temporal sects, and the kind of interpretation that displays the critic chasing his own tail. Returning from this many-colored clamor to search for the white radiance of eternity, we may submit that Shelley, at the peak of his mature production, does touch a truth beyond their argument—beyond the busy shuffling threat of the changing years. Whatever he may undergo from perceptive critics, he is safe against all that has been and that will be argued by those whose thoughts remain "senseless and shapeless," shorn of harmony:

> *Man, one harmonious soul of many a soul.*
> *Whose nature is its own divine control,*
> *Where all things flow to all, as rivers to the sea;*
> *Familiar acts are beautiful through love;*
> *Labour, and pain, and grief, in life's green grove*
> *Sport like tame beasts, none knew how gentle they could be!*

> *His will, with all mean passions, bad delights,*
> *And selfish cares, its trembling satellites,*
> *A spirit ill to guide, but mighty to obey,*
> *Is as a tempest-winged ship, whose helm*
> *Love rules, through waves which dare not overwhelm,*
> *Forcing life's wildest shores to own its sovereign sway.*

Expansion as Epilogue

All things confess his strength. Through the cold mass
Of marble and of colour his dreams pass;
Bright threads whence mothers weave the robes their children wear;
Language is a perpetual Orphic song
Which rules with Daedal harmony a throng
Of thoughts and forms, which else senseless and shapeless were.

Index

303